SPITFIRES, THUNDERBOLTS, AND WARM BEER

SPITFIRES, THUNDERBOLTS, AND WARM BEER

An American Fighter Pilot over Europe

Philip D. Caine

POTOMAC BOOKS, INC.
Washington, D.C.

First Warriors edition published in 2005

Library of Congress Cataloging-in-Publication Data

Caine, Philip D., 1933—
      Spitfires, Thunderbolts, and warm beer: an American fighter pilot over
Europe/Philip D. Caine.
         p.   cm.
      ISBN 0-02-881115-1
   1. Gover, LeRoy.   2. United States. Army Air Forces—Biography.   3. Great
Britain—Royal Air Force—Biography.   4. World War, 1939–1945—Aerial
operations, American.   5. World War, 1939–1945—Aerial operations, British.
6. World war, 1939–1945—Campaigns—Europe.   7. Fighter pilots—United
States—Biography.   I. Title.
D790.C255   1995
940.54'4973—dc20   94-32706
                                                                          CIP

ISBN 1-57488-844-7 (paperback)

Potomac Books, Inc.
22841 Quicksilver Dr.
Dulles, VA 20166

10   9   8   7   6   5   4   3   2   1

Printed in Canada

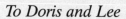

To Doris and Lee

CONTENTS

PREFACE

I FIRST MET LEROY GOVER ON SEPTEMBER 10, 1987, WHEN I interviewed him in connection with the research I was doing for my book *American Pilots in the RAF* (Brassey's, 1993). I sought him out because Major General Chesley Peterson, the leader of the American Eagle Squadrons, had told me that Lee was one of the best combat leaders he had ever known and would answer my questions and tell his stories without any exaggeration or attempt to make himself a hero. On the occasion of our first visit, I was struck by Lee's quiet and engaging personality, his forthright comments about his place in World War II, his sense of history in having kept a daily diary, and that of his mother in saving all the letters he wrote home. I put the idea of writing a book about this quiet air leader's experiences in World War II in the back of my mind.

Because he is such a modest individual, Lee was initially reluctant to have his story told. But we were able to convince him that it was people like himself who were responsible for our victory in World War II and that his story would tell others of the challenges and life of a fighter pilot in that war. Since I began work on this book I have been in almost weekly contact with Lee, and he has read the entire volume many times. Because of this, I am confident that it is accurate, unlike many books that are written to glorify the accomplishments of the subject.

This, then, is the story of LeRoy Gover, an American fighter pilot in England during the first nearly two and a half years of World War II. I have been fortunate to have access to Lee's diary, which has an entry for almost every day from November 3, 1941, the day he began his journey to England to fly for the Royal Air Force, through March 12, 1944, the day he arrived back in San Carlos, California. I have reproduced his diary entries just as he wrote them. In addition, I have used his flying log books, the letters he wrote to his parents and sisters during his time in Europe, a number of accounts of incidents that he wrote after the war, and my notes from many hours of personal interviews. The quotations of Lee in the narrative are from these sources.

This book was written primarily with the help of only two people, Lee Gover and my wife, Doris. They read and reread the drafts, made valuable suggestions, and ensured that it all made good sense.

Lee had a number of his friends read the manuscript, and, although I don't know them, they have my thanks. I also appreciate the insights I gained from Lee's sisters, Juanita and Betty. As always, the facilities of the Air Force Academy library were made available to me, and I appreciate that. Finally, a special word about the role of my wife, Doris. She willingly accompanied me on all of my interview trips and spent countless hours patiently taking notes to back up my tape recordings. Time and again, she asked the critical question that I either hadn't thought of or forgot and that made the interview a success. And I really think that it was her charm that won Lee's approval of my writing the book. She read every draft, made the tough comments, and provided the encouragement and patience that are essential to the success of any book.

Monument, Colorado
May 1994

INTRODUCTION

ON JUNE 22, 1940, NEWSPAPER HEADLINES AROUND THE WORLD blared that France had surrendered to the German onslaught. Europe, it seemed, was on the verge of complete domination by Hitler. England stood alone as the obstacle to the fulfillment of the Führer's misguided dream. Hitler evidently hoped that England would see the futility in her position and come to terms. But Britain's dynamic Prime Minister, Winston Churchill, had other ideas. He eloquently told the Germans and the world: ". . . we shall fight on the beaches, we shall fight on the landing grounds, we shall fight in the fields and in the streets, we shall fight in the hills; we shall never surrender."

Less than a month later, on July 16, 1940, Hitler issued orders for Operation Sea Lion, the invasion of England. To succeed, Germany had to control the air over the Channel. Standing alone to face the German onslaught of over 2,500 aircraft were the fewer than 1,500 planes of the RAF. The result was the Battle of Britain. On August 13, 1940, "Eagle Day," the Luftwaffe launched the attack that was intended to drive the fighters of the RAF from the skies. Almost every day, for nearly three months, waves of German aircraft attacked targets ranging from airfields and radar installations to ports and the populace of London. And every day the Hurricanes and Spitfires of the Royal Air Force took to the skies to oppose the superior German force. In the end, Hitler had to postpone his invasion of England—as it turned out, forever. With his usual style, Churchill echoed the mood of all of England in saying: "The gratitude of every home in our island, in our Empire and indeed in the world, goes out to the British airmen. Never in the field of human conflict was so much owed by so many to so few."

Stopping Hitler took a terrible toll on the RAF. Over 400 fighter pilots were killed and another 350 wounded—more than half of the force. Since no one knew just what the Luftwaffe's situation was or when the onslaught might resume, England was in desperate straits for pilots. And while the various members of the Commonwealth were furnishing all they could, the shortage remained. The one major untapped source was the neutral United States. How to get American pilots into the RAF pipeline was a problem which, fortunately, had been addressed even before the war began.

In 1939, a Canadian war hero and air power visionary, Air Marshal Billy Bishop, took upon himself the task of finding a way to provide American pilots for both the British and Canadian forces in the event of another war. In September of that year, Bishop contacted a fellow World War I flier and well-known American aviation artist, Clayton Knight, and asked him to devise a system that might enable American pilots to become members of the British forces. Knight responded by formulating a plan that was implemented in the spring of 1940, as Hitler invaded Belgium, Denmark, Norway, Holland and Luxembourg.

The Battle of Britain was daily news throughout the United States, and the pilots of the RAF were everyone's heroes. Clayton Knight's plan was to capitalize on this spirit by making the opportunity to fly for the RAF known around airports and flying circles throughout the United States. He then took a suite of rooms, under the name of the Clayton Knight Committee, in the best hotel in each of several cities that were hubs of private flying—Los Angeles, Oakland, Chicago, Dallas, New York and others. These offices were manned by very attractive receptionists and at least one flying veteran of World War I. Interested pilots were encouraged to present themselves at one of these facilities, and if they were qualified, they would be trained and sent to Canada or England to fly. Using this system, Knight was able to recruit over 6,700 pilots between April 1940 and October 1942. Most of these pilots remained in Canada as flight instructors, but a significant number went on to fly with almost every squadron in the RAF.

One of these young American fliers was LeRoy Gover from San Carlos, California, who joined the RAF, through the Clayton Knight Committee, in May 1941. He served first in a British fighter squadron, then in one of the American Eagle Squadrons and subsequently he transferred to the U.S. Army Air Forces. Lee was one of the hundreds of young American men who saw their duty early and decided to serve in the skies over Europe before the United States entered World War II. While he was decorated for heroism, he set no records in the number of enemy aircraft shot down. He simply did his duty every day, in whatever manner he was assigned, and did it well. This is the story of a highly decorated World War II combat pilot who typifies the fighting spirit and devotion to duty that is the hallmark of the American fighting man. It is the LeRoy Govers who won World War II and still stand ready, every day, to defend the freedom for which our nation stands.

Northwestern Europe

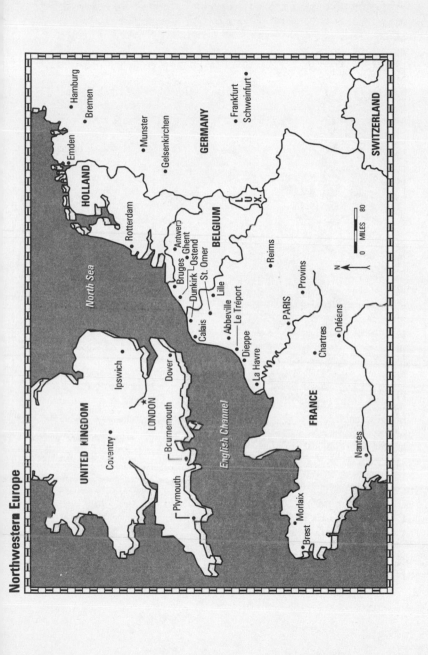

The United Kingdom

N

0 MILES 80

North Sea

Glasgow • Edinburgh

Belfast •

IRELAND

Irish Sea

Dublin •

• York

Liverpool
• Manchester

Birmingham •

Coventry •

Llantwitt-Major

Martlesham Heath

Cambridge •
• Debden

Great Sampford •

Southend-on-Sea ★ LONDON

Biggin Hill •   Dover •

Plymouth
Bolt Head

Ibsley • • Bournemouth

• Redruth

Land's End

English Channel

FRANCE

Ipswich

SPITFIRES, THUNDERBOLTS, AND WARM BEER

1. I'm Gonna Fly the Spitfire

Wᴴᴬᵀ ᴀ ʙᴇᴀᴜᴛɪꜰᴜʟ ᴅᴀʏ, ᴛʜᴏᴜɢʜᴛ Pɪʟᴏᴛ Oꜰꜰɪᴄᴇʀ LᴇRᴏʏ Gover as he sat in readiness in the cockpit of his Spitfire. *The sun is finally shining and I'm warm for a change. Maybe the long-awaited spring that all the English people have been telling me about has really arrived.* He and his wingman were on cockpit alert, which meant that they had to sit in the aircraft with parachute and helmet on, seat harness hooked up, and oxygen mask fastened to the helmet, for a two-hour shift waiting for a red flare to be shot into the sky. If that happened, they were expected to be airborne within thirty seconds to intercept a German aircraft, offer protection for an English town, or simply deal with a perceived emergency. While cockpit alert could get the adrenaline flowing in a split second, it was also a time when you could get away from the war for a few minutes, especially if the warm sun of an English spring day was beating down. This seemed to be one of those occasions.

Lee's mind wandered as he watched a lazy white cloud slowly drift across the field. *I wonder if I'll be lucky enough to find another really good-looking girl at the Regent Palace on Friday night,* he thought, reminding himself that two weeks ago things had worked out well and he had ended up with a great date. That was to be expected fairly regularly, and he hoped this Friday would be no exception. "Some of those women are real lookers," he had often been told, and certainly that was

1

the case, but a Royal Air Force flight officer didn't have much money, so wining and dining were not in the cards often. I just have to keep my eyes open and. . . .

Lee's thoughts were broken by the crack of the Very pistol and the arc of a red flare across the sky. Scramble! Quickly, get it together! You have to be off the ground in thirty seconds! Flip on the ignition switch, hit the starter and listen to that big Merlin V-12 immediately catch. Thumbs up to your wingman, throttle open, a small heading change and pour the coal to it. Raise the tail, speed to 90 miles per hour, ease back and let her fly off. Gear up, flaps up and then point that beautiful ship to the clouds and climb like a homesick angel.

"Blue One, this is Kirton Control, heading one two zero, climb to Angels one five for a possible German bomber, type unknown."

The controller had such a businesslike way about her, just the facts and getting you moving in the direction of that possible enemy. Lee was not surprised about the bomber because a few minutes before the scramble he had heard what sounded like bombs exploding nearby.

"Blue One, turn left to heading zero nine zero, say altitude."

"Kirton Control, Blue Section presently at Angels one two and climbing." Time to check the oxygen flow, look over the cockpit and see that everything was in proper order. Gunsight on and wait for the glow that indicated it was working properly, because if there was a German up above, there would be no time to get set up when you made contact.

"Blue One, Kirton Control, target is at your twelve-o'clock position, two miles, altitude unknown."

Lee and his wingman searched the airspace in front of them. "Blue Section has contact, Kirton," Lee exclaimed. "A Heinkel 111. We are attacking."

Nothing else existed in the world for the two fighter pilots at that instant. Every nerve was one with their Spitfires as they were pushed deep into their seats by the terrific G forces while they maneuvered to put the German in their sights. Just a couple more seconds and he'll be in range, Lee thought as he remained glued to his gunsight. Damn, he made it to the clouds, but he'll have to come out sooner or later.

For the next ten minutes the two RAF pilots searched, but to no avail. "We are getting too far out over the Channel," Lee told his wingman. "I guess we lost him."

Lee reluctantly reported to Kirton Control, "Blue Section has lost contact."

"Roger, I no longer have your target either. You are released from my control. Do you wish a heading back to base?" came the reply.

No heading for me right now, Lee thought. I'll just stay up here for a bit and take advantage of the beautiful day. "No thanks, Kirton, Blue Section will do some practice and then get a steer if we need it."

With those words the pressure seemed to ease, the sweat stopped running and the entire system seemed to take a deep breath and relax. No German left to engage, so might as well turn off the gunsight and enjoy the blue sky.

After all, it was being in the blue sky and the exhilaration of flying that had caused Lee to go to the offices of the Clayton Knight Committee in the Lemington Hotel in Oakland on that spring day in 1941, nearly a year ago. There he had told the glamorous blond secretary who greeted him that he wanted to join the RAF and fly fighters.

Flying had always been Lee's life. In fact, he could fly an airplane before he could legally drive a car, and he soloed a biplane on his sixteenth birthday. This had been a very big moment both for Lee and for those he knew, since there weren't a great many pilots around in 1929. No one had been surprised, though, because the constant subject of Lee's conversations was flying. "I was glued to the radio when Lindbergh flew across the Atlantic, and I just seemed to go every mile with him," he told his dad. And when his uncle, a newspaperman in New York, gave Lee some photos of Lindbergh they became cherished possessions. Never one to get really excited about school, he had spent as much time as possible at the San Carlos airport doing whatever he could to get a little flying time. And it gradually added up, an hour here and another there. The pilots who flew out of airports in Northern California came to know and like the enthusiastic young man with a ready smile, hazel eyes that would sparkle at any mention of airplanes, a willingness to work and an insatiable appetite for anything to do with flying. So Lee got the jobs that led to flying time. He really didn't mind filling planes with fuel from five-gallon cans or washing and cleaning those that landed in San Carlos, "but I sure didn't like it when I was asked to clean out the cabin after someone got sick," Lee grimaced.

Unfortunately, Gover could not make a living working part-time at the airport, so, after he graduated from Sequoia Union High School in Redwood City, California, it was time to find a real job. Things were tough in 1931—tough enough that all Lee's high school friends had to work, and many graduated in the middle of the year so they could get on with a job. For Lee, that was construction. His father built houses in San Carlos, so when his dad needed help, Lee got the call and the two of them did all the work. Lee was always ready to put his five-foot-nine, 145-pound body into the job, and his ruddy complexion, which he kept all his life, testified to his love of the outdoors. "I had learned how to build a complete house by the time I was twenty-one, but in the early years of working with my dad, it seemed like a lot of my experience was in digging basements, trenches or anything else that required a shovel."

In 1935, Lee's dad gave him the plans for a building and sent him to the neighboring town of Redwood City to build it. That put Lee on his way to becoming an established builder. But construction was never his real choice.

Lee continued to haunt the airport on the weekends and bought as much flying time as he could afford. And his love of flying seemed to be reinforced at every turn. He spent hours watching the great Pan American Clippers leave San Francisco for Hawaii and the Far East; he had a ringside seat to the development of commercial aviation in the San Francisco area. "It was the golden age of flying," Gover remarked with excitement in his voice some sixty years later.

He would always remember that day in 1934 when he went to his dad and asked if he could borrow $1,600 to buy an airplane. "And what a beauty it was. It was just a plain 37-horsepower Cub, but when I got done putting wheel pants on it and a spinner on the propeller, it was a real looker," Lee remembered. He was able to earn back some of the cost by giving flying lessons or sightseeing rides around the Bay Area for $3.

"I'll never forget one experience with that little plane," Lee wrote.

I guess everyone has heard of "Wrong Way" Corrigan, the pilot who said he was going to fly nonstop from New York to San Francisco and flew to Europe instead. When he got back from Europe, he flew around the U.S. on a goodwill tour. One of his stops was at Mills Field in San Francisco. His plane was a high-wing job, and I guess it looked kind of like a Cub. Anyway, on the day he was to arrive, I flew my Cub up to San Francisco about the time he was supposed to land so I could see him. All the newspeople and photographers were there for his arrival, and when I landed and taxied up they all started taking pictures of me while the crowd gathered around my plane. They thought I was Corrigan. Since we did not have any radios on the planes, we would just waggle our wings and wait for a green light to land, so I guess the control tower operator didn't know the difference either. Anyway, I convinced them I wasn't Corrigan, and about that time he landed and took all my crowd away. At least I was famous for a moment.

Lee got serious about trying to make his living by flying in 1937 and spent two summers crop dusting in the Bakersfield area. And while the old Waco biplanes were good experience, he thought that it was boring "just doing the same thing day after day." In those days, chemical dust was used on the crops, and Lee would cough for hours after a day of breathing it. "I soon decided this was not the life for me," he wrote. But if he was not going to dust crops, he saw no way to make a living flying, so the construction business continued.

Things began to change for Gover in 1940, and he would soon find that his life was to take a very new and unplanned direction. Like everyone else, Lee was concerned about the situation in Europe.

I watched the fall of Poland, the Low Countries and France with anxious thoughts. I certainly didn't know if the United States would become involved in the war, but the passage of the Selective Service Act by Congress and England's struggle to survive during the Battle of Britain sure made me figure that I was going to war pretty soon. It seemed like that was the talk almost everywhere, especially around the airport. I think that I became aware that it was time to make a decision when my good flying friend Bill Nichols decided to join the RAF. I really wasn't sure that was the direction I should take at that time (late 1940), but when I heard that he was in the Eagle Squadron and was flying Spitfires, I started to think seriously about joining the RAF myself. I knew that I had plenty of flying experience but couldn't qualify for Army or Navy pilot training since I hadn't gone to college. And flying the Spitfire, wow! My decision was also influenced by unfortunate circumstances at my job. For over two years I had been working for a construction firm in Redwood City and had been promised 10 percent ownership in the business. That deal fell through in early 1941, so I decided that I would go up to Oakland and check out this Clayton Knight Committee that was recruiting pilots to fly for the RAF.

The requirement for acceptance into the RAF program was two hundred hours of flying, and by 1941 Lee had accumulated nearly eight hundred. On May 6, 1941, he wrote, "Passed my physical and flight test for British Refresher School—RAF—through the Clayton Knight Committee in Oakland, California." Lee had been confident about the flight test, since he had found out beforehand that the flight would be in a Waco Cabin Biplane and had paid $20 for an hour of practice in the plane. "I had no problem with the evaluation flight and so was not surprised when I was told I had passed. They then said to go back to San Carlos and wait for a date to begin training."

"The entire family was happy for Lee, and I thought his going into the RAF was really quite glamorous," his younger sister Betty remembered. "My mother was worried sick, but my dad and I had great confidence in Lee's flying ability and knew this was what he wanted to do, so we supported him."

A United Airlines passenger log dated August 10, 1941, notes that Gover flew from San Francisco to Bakersfield, California, via Fresno, on Flight 26, to begin his RAF refresher training at the Bakersfield airport. Of interest is a letter home on the back of that log noting that "the captain on this plane was the one in 'Ripley's Believe It or Not' last week, Captain Lee. He has flown more miles than any other person—over three million—and he has 33,000 hours, so I feel pretty safe." (Little did Gover know that one day he would have over 28,000 hours flying time and probably as much time flying fighters as any person alive.)

From Gover's perspective, accommodations in Bakersfield were very good.

> We live in town in a boardinghouse—big, old-fashioned place. OK, though, since it's right in town. There will be sixteen of us in the class. There are five of the kids here so far, two from New York City, one from Washington, D.C., one from Texas and one from Oklahoma.

Breakfast was provided in an old house near where they lived, while lunch was at the airfield and dinner at a cafeteria in town. Overall, the group rated the food as "not too bad."

The curriculum was intense, and that concerned Lee. Although he had more flying time than the others in his class, he had never had formal courses in most of the subjects in the curriculum, which included "meteorology, navigation, engines, and we are also learning Morse code. They take us up tomorrow for a check ride which tells whether you stay or not—OH BOY." Lee's letter home on August 14 told his folks about the program and his check.

> They sure gave me the works on the check ride, but I got by OK, so I know I'll be here for at least another week when we get another one. I made a sloppy landing yesterday and could just see myself coming home. First thing today my instructor had me make landings and I dropped them in perfect, so he said OK. They say this course is just twice as hard as the Army.

Of the thirteen students that began training in the previous class, only three were left when Gover's class began. Just one week after arriving, Lee wrote that three in his class had also been washed out.

Gover was impressed by both of the school's new aircraft, the Stearman PT-17, an open-cockpit biplane, and the North

American AT-6 "Harvard," a low-wing monoplane with a closed cockpit. While he had flown other planes of similar size and power, he had not been required to complete such an intense curriculum, nor was he used to check rides once a week. His letters home were punctuated with comments on the challenge of the program.

> They give us about ten hours dual first, then solo us, if we last (they're really strict as hell—you fly right or else). And can these boys fly . . . ! After we solo, we get another ten hours dual, ten hours solo, ten hours night and ten hours instrument in the PT-17. Then, if we make the grade, we go into the AT-6s, 600-horsepower Army advanced training ships. We just got three more of them, makes six at $40,000 apiece, six PT-17s at $15,000, and three, two-engine Cessnas at $50,000 apiece—about half a million dollars in equipment. Sure hope I get through the PT-17s, AT-6s, and then into the Cessnas, since they are on the order of little Boeings. I got fifty minutes my first flight and then was up for another 1:15 in the PT-17. They sure are swell planes—225 hp. They have sensitive altimeters, and when you make steep turns and such you can't lose or gain over twenty feet, which isn't very much in an airplane.

Gover, who was only interested in being a fighter pilot, rapidly lost his enthusiasm for the Cessnas when he found that they were only for those students picked to go to bombers.

Lee rapidly demonstrated his proficiency in the PT-17 and also a lifelong desire to be the best at everything having to do with flying. The occasion came when one of the students came back from a flight and told his classmates that he had spun the PT-17 nineteen revolutions from five thousand feet. This was all the challenge that many of them needed, and they immediately set out to beat the record. Several tried and failed—fortunately there were no accidents as a result. Gover also decided that he could beat the mark. When he got a chance, "I flew to five thousand feet, slowed it up real slow, kicked hard rudder, tight back on the stick and spun it twenty-eight times before I pulled out just barely above the ground." No one would have believed that he had done the "impossible," but Mick Lambert was his witness and Lee became the spin champion of his class. His instructor thought that was a dubious honor.

The spin caper seemed typical of the actions of the spirited young men in Gover's class. Had the scheduling officer known the students better, he would never have scheduled Gover, Mick Lambert and George Middleton to go solo at the same time. But when that combination was posted on the scheduling board, the three decided to make the most of it. The plan was soon made. "I know a great place where we can go tail chasing"—one airplane trying to get away from the other two—"and no one will ever know the difference," bragged Lambert. Both Gover and Middleton agreed that it would be fun, and any thought of the consequences was rapidly dismissed. The trio took off in their PT-17s and flew to Lambert's appointed spot, a lake about twenty miles south of the field. There they had a field day diving down and chasing away the ducks that populated the lake. Several other "daring" escapades followed, and eventually the three returned to Bakersfield. "When we got out of our planes we noticed a group of five or six men standing talking. One of the men in the group was Mr. Seaton, who ran the school. He motioned us over and I broke out in a cold sweat," wrote Gover.

One of the men in the group was Clark Gable. Mr. Gable complimented us on our flying, but then he dropped the bombshell. It seemed that the lake belonged to him and he went there duck hunting to relieve the tension of Hollywood. We feared the worst. But he just asked us not to buzz his lake anymore and then took us all downtown for a root beer float. Although we feared the worst, that was the end of it.

The biggest scare of Gover's young life came on August 25.

Herb Tansey, my instructor, decided to show me some property he wanted to buy that was located up a blind canyon. After locating the property, we found we were unable to turn or climb enough to avoid crashing into the hillside. We crashed and were both knocked out by the impact. When I came to, there was fire all over and I couldn't find Herb. I finally located him slumped over in the wreckage and pulled him out. The fire from the plane caught the brush on fire and we were in the middle of a big fire we couldn't put out. We walked for about twenty miles before we could get any help, and the fire burned hundreds of acres. Nothing ever came of the whole thing, although the airplane was totally destroyed, and we both just went on flying.

This was the only crash that Gover had in his nearly sixty-five years of active flying. Gover's parents didn't know about it, for he never mentioned it in any of his letters home.

Being away from home for the first time provided various temptations for the students in Lee's class.

There were a couple of bars downtown that we would visit on Saturday night if we couldn't find a dance. I was the only one in the class with a car, a dark blue Star Four coupe, and there would be eight or ten guys hanging all over that poor car when we went to town. Some of the guys tried to party it up and chase girls during the week, but most of us knew why we were there and that a good night's sleep was essential to flying well the next day. We were actually pretty successful with the girls, but since we only made about $18 a week we had to watch what we spent. The young ladies were impressed with guys who knew how to fly, and especially with those of us who were training to go to England and fly the Spitfire. Since I had a car, I managed to go home about every three weeks. It was a long drive, nearly 250 miles at 45 or 50 miles an hour, but I enjoyed seeing everyone at home and bringing them up to date on what I was doing.

Lee also flew home illegally on occasion, and during his time at Bakersfield he managed to give both his father and his mother a flight in the AT-6 by dressing them in the tan coveralls worn by students in flight training.

Because of his flying experience, Lee progressed much more rapidly than his classmates. On September 9, he had his first flight in the AT-6, and his excitement was obvious in his letter to his family.

Some fun scooting along at 200 miles per hour. I was the first in my class to get in the AT-6. At full throttle they develop 600 hp.

You get up to ten thousand feet in nothing flat in these things and come in to land at around 80 miles per hour. I've been flying every night also and am getting pretty good at it. It sure is a funny feeling the first few times because you can't see a single thing. You just feel your way in and when she hits you push the stick forward to hold her down—then fight it to a standstill. We use a farmer's field near Cochran that has no lights whatsoever.

The euphoria of the day was dampened when "I read in the paper that Bill Nichols was shot down today." (Nichols had been Gover's flying buddy for a number of years and had joined the RAF several months prior to Lee. He was captured and spent World War II in a German prison camp.)

Flying at night was a new experience to Lee. San Carlos, like most little airports in the thirties and forties, was not lighted, so, even though he had nearly eight hundred hours of flying, he had never flown at night. The nearest he came was late in the 1930s. "One afternoon I flew over to Oakland airport to visit a pilot friend of mine and ended up staying too long," he wrote.

I was flying a Long Wing Eagle Rock biplane. It was a very nice ship that the owner let me fly now and then for work I did for him. But it had no battery or any lights. Hell, it didn't even have a starter, so you had to wind it up with a crank to get it running. Anyway, it was turning dark when I taxied out, and the manager of the field came racing out in his car and said I couldn't take off because I had no wing lights. So I ended up spending the night in my friend's hangar.

Just nine days later, on September 18, a very proud LeRoy wrote:

Your little boy soloed the AT-6 today. Boy, I'm just one hot pilot. You're supposed to have nineteen hours dual first and no one here has ever soloed one under twelve, and I (modest little me) soloed one today after eight hours and twelve minutes. So I had to buy a quart and the boys are having a hell of a time. Just think, a couple of years ago Dad and I used to wish we could just touch Fuller's ship and now I can fly one of the damn things. [Frank Fuller was a wealthy industrialist who had a plane similar to an AT-6 at the San Francisco airport. Gover would occasionally talk with him about flying.]

Because of his achievement in the AT-6, and also being the first to solo in the PT-17, Gover finished the curriculum almost a month early and served as an instructor for students in the next class. On October 24, 1941, Lee and thirteen others graduated from the RAF Refresher School and were given time to go home and prepare for the long trip to England. (Gover was to speak often of his classmates at Bakersfield, with whom he developed a genuine closeness. Only seven of them survived the war.)

Preparation for the trip included much more than packing clothes in a small bag and saying good-bye to friends and loved ones. What Gover and the other graduates of the several Clayton Knight–sponsored flying schools in the United States were doing was technically illegal. In a desperate effort to stay out of the war in Europe, the United States had passed a Neutrality Act almost annually from 1936 through 1941. Two provisions of these acts were especially significant to Lee and his compatriots. The first specified that service in the armed forces of a foreign power without authorization and with the resultant acquisition of foreign nationality would expatriate an individual. In other words, they could lose their American citizenship. Fortunately for Gover and the hundreds of other young men who joined the Royal Air Force, the State Department made the decision in June 1940 that so long as a person did not swear allegiance to another government, he would not lose his citizenship. The other provision provided that travel through a designated war zone (the North Atlantic) or on board a belligerent ship (British) could result in a prison sentence of up to two years and/or a $10,000 fine. Fortunately for everyone involved, there were never any prosecutions under this law. Apparently the danger in traveling across the submarine-infested North Atlantic was punishment enough.

In addition, it was illegal for any person registered with Selective Service to leave his home area without telling his draft board where he was going. Travel to Canada was particularly suspect, because most draft boards knew that many Americans, especially pilots, were going to Canada as a first step in eventually getting to England. When Gover first made his decision to sign up for the RAF, he talked to his girlfriend's father, the president of the San Carlos draft board, about what he intended to do. The result was a "Permit of Local Board for Registrant to Depart from the United States," which gave Gover permission to go to Canada on a business trip for sixty days. Although a provision of the permit stated that "the granting of such permit will not result in the evasion of or interference with the execution of the Selective Service Law," the board knew that Gover was going to Canada and then to England to be a member of the RAF, so was clearly making it impossible to draft him.

I think one reason the draft board let me go was the long talks that I had with the board president about the prospect of war and my inability to get into U.S. pilot training because I lacked the required two years of college. I used to take his daughter to San Francisco on dates, and we would sit and watch the Japanese ships loaded to capacity with scrap metal sailing through the Golden Gate for Japan. I really believed that someday that metal would be used against us just as it was then being used against China. He agreed with my thoughts and understood well why I wanted so badly to fly. Once I got the permit, the rest was easy. I crossed the border with no trouble and never heard anything about it.

At 8:43 on Monday evening, November 3, 1941, another chapter in Lee's life began when he and Jay Reed, a classmate from Bakersfield, left Oakland, California, on the *Challenger*, the mainline train bound for Chicago, where they would transfer to a Canadian train. While both knew they had to go to Canada to ship out to England, the seriousness of their decision became very real when the train pulled out of Oakland. Just twenty-four hours later they arrived in Ogden, Utah, where they had a one-day layover. Lee knew a girl there, the daughter of a friend of his mother, so he called her up and found that young pilots going off to fly the Spitfire had the same magic in Ogden as they had in Bakersfield.

Helen got a friend for Jay and we took in the town. Met the girls again at 12:00 noon—took pictures—went to the show—had dinner and walked to the station—left Ogden at 8:55 p.m. Helen confided to me that they were quite the celebrities in their group by having dates with two future RAF pilots.

Lee and Jay talked for hours on the train about everything from what they might see in Chicago and Canada to the probability of getting seasick and how a bomb sounded when it exploded. And while they had no second thoughts, they were apprehensive just the same. "It really doesn't make any difference if I am seasick for the entire voyage," Lee had commented, "as long as I can fly that Spitfire as an RAF pilot officer when we get to England." Jay had agreed but was not as ready to minimize the problem of seasickness or the danger of German submarines. On Friday, November 7, they arrived in Chicago, where they

walked around town—changed trains and met Donald Young [who had trained with them at Bakersfield]. We are now on a funny little Canadian train. Changed trains in Toronto and arrived in Ottawa at 7:30 Saturday morning, where we were met by RAF representatives and checked in at the Lord Elgin Hotel.

There they met Jack Mause, another Bakersfield buddy, and the foursome that would travel to England together was complete.

The Canadian weather was good for November. There was no snow initially, and all four were much taken by the grand sights of Ottawa. Lee took a number of pictures, since he was the only one in the group with a camera.

"Just now got settled," Lee wrote his parents on November 10, two days after his arrival in Ottawa.

This is a swell town—sure pretty—snowed this morning. Was in Quebec yesterday. Never saw so many Frenchmen in my life. Food and everything up here is cheaper than there. . . . We get 10 percent more for our U.S. dollars. Had a fifty cent lunch, gave them a U.S. $5 bill and got a Canadian $5 bill back—not bad. It would sure do everyone down there a lot of good to see the people up here. Boy, they've really got a spirit. Really doing all they can to help win this war. Boys not over fifteen or sixteen in the army and air corps and the women doing the men's work makes you realize that we're not doing such a hell of a lot.

"Went to collect my salary again—we get paid every day," began Lee's diary entry for November 11, 1941. "Don Young and I went to the House of Parliament—took more pictures— House was in session and it was a great thing to see. There are lots of cute French gals in town. Jay and I went out this evening—HOOKED."

The time in Canada was enjoyable and the Lord Elgin Hotel luxurious, but Gover and his friends were soon brought back to the reality of why they were there. His folks certainly got a glimpse of that reality in his letter of November 14, from Halifax, Nova Scotia.

Arrived here last night at 8:30 p.m. and were taken to the Air Corps Barracks. Boy, we're in the army now, and that means no more hotels. We each have a bunk in one room—there must be fifty of us—so you get to know the other guys fast. Made my bed, brushed my teeth and went to sleep. Breakfast at 6:45 a.m. and went directly to the parade ground for one hour. Then had a pep talk and lunch. Have to report to the parade ground at 1:15 and after that we can leave the post. There were a bunch that left for England yesterday and another this morning. The CO [commanding officer] said we'd leave by Monday—probably before. They treat us swell here and good food, if you can get used to it. We are officers and get the best of everything, which is really a good deal. All the other fellows here are Royal Canadian Air Force [RCAF], while we four [Americans] are RAF. We wait for our uniforms until we get to London, as they are a little different from those of the RCAF. There are a lot of fellows from Australia and New Zealand here as well. Drop a line now every week and tell lots of people to write, 'cause I'll sure want to hear from you all.

Little changed for the next few days. "Got up too late for breakfast so went to the parade ground—practiced shooting with .303 rifles and I scored 99 out of 125," wrote Lee in his diary. "Jay and I sure mess their parade up"—no doubt because neither of them had had any military training, while the RCAF and other Allied officers had had several months. "Everyone is swell—they don't seem to give a damn and we don't either." The American free spirit was evident the next day as they "reported to parade at 10:00 today but had overslept and missed breakfast again. Marched us off to church—Jay, Mause and I slipped off and went downtown to eat." They were impressed by the quaintness of Halifax, and Gover again took a number of pictures of the city, the base and his friends.

But Lee and his three buddies from Bakersfield, Don Young, Jay Reed and Jack Mause, knew that the voyage lay ahead and they might as well get going. "I am starting to get tired of this waiting around," Don had remarked, and everyone agreed. Jack had speculated that they would soon forget how to fly an airplane, or at least be pretty rusty when they finally got to England. They wondered just what kind of plane they would fly first and when they would get to the Spitfire. Still another consideration was voiced by Jay when he thought about how cold it would get on the trip. "I wish someone had told us it would be this cold in Canada. The best thing we ever did was to buy those long johns today, but I'll bet that it is even colder on the ocean, and these California clothes and my light topcoat probably don't stand a chance of keeping me warm. Maybe we can get an RAF overcoat or something to keep us warm!" But the answer to that was—RAF pilots would not receive their uniforms until they got to England.

Stories of the voyage abounded in camp and not all were reassuring. The biggest concern was the German submarine "wolf packs" that roamed the North Atlantic and had already sent scores of ships to the bottom. It was the risk of being sunk that had led the United States to make travel on the North Atlantic illegal. And despite the brave face that most of the young men displayed, in every mind was a fear that the ship just might not make it and that you might be added to the toll of that terrible, cold North Atlantic. Still, all probably thought about the same as Lee when he simply said, "I signed up to fly for the RAF and I wish we would get moving." All were relieved but apprehensive when, on November 19, they "reported to roll call and were informed we were in the draft call for tomorrow. We went to a lecture, then down into

Halifax to buy a few things, had a physical checkup and packed for the voyage." On November 20, 1941, the great adventure began. The voyage lasted sixteen days, and neither Lee nor his friends would ever forget the experience.

November 20, 1940 Parade at 9:15. Put our baggage out. Marched from the depot to Pier 21 (four miles) and boarded the boat at 3:00 p.m. Assigned to room 311, berth number one. Spent the afternoon looking the boat over and playing cards. The boat is staying here tonight (I guess)—quite a day.

This is a rather casual diary entry for what was one of the biggest days of Lee's and his friends' lives. They slept little the night before as they speculated on the voyage and what lay ahead when it was completed. For each of the four it was the first trip by sea and a final dose of the reality that they were really committed and going to war. The morning of November 20 dawned overcast, but at least there was no snow. It was one of those cold days when the trees stand out stark and leafless against the gray horizon—a grayness that Lee and his friends would certainly get used to in the days to come. As the Americans, Canadians, Australians and New Zealanders formed up for the four-mile march to the ship one could almost imagine a comic opera if the purpose had not been so serious. There was a polyglot mixture of army and air force, Canadian, Australian and New Zealander, each having a different uniform. Some had overcoats while some were in their service blouses. Some carried duffel bags, some suitcases, depending on what they had. Some were lined up and ready to step out in formation, while others had no intention of staying in step for the entire four miles. And mixed in with the various uniforms were the Americans in their civilian clothes, some with overcoats and some without, many with business hats and all with a coat and tie, most appearing ill prepared for the cold voyage ahead. Their belongings were carried in whatever they had, mostly small suitcases. Off they went on the trek to the pier.

It was over two hours later when the front ranks saw the harbor and the ship that was to be their home for nearly three weeks, the *Emma Alexander*. She was 450 feet long and displaced 7,793 tons—not a very big ship, but to the lads from

Bakersfield she seemed huge. The ship did not send waves of confidence through them, however. It was obvious, as they looked up the seemingly towering sides of the craft, that she had seen better days, as indeed she had. The ship had been built in the early 1920s as a coastal cargo ship and had plied the route between San Diego and Seattle for nearly two decades. It had been purchased by the British at the start of the war and overhauled in dry dock to make it minimally acceptable to haul about one hundred troops, in addition to cargo, across the treacherous North Atlantic. Gover was on her first voyage since overhaul, and first ever on the high seas, so there may have been ample cause for concern.

As Lee wound his way around the vessel seeking room 311, bunk one, he was impressed with the complexity of an ocean-going ship. It took a couple of bumps on the head before he learned to duck for the low doors. Everything was newly painted, and both the ship and her crew had a certain air of serious purpose that instilled confidence.

Room 311 was scarcely large enough to accommodate the four bunks for its occupants. There seemed to be no room to do anything but sleep, and little enough of that—a sprawl on his bunk gave Lee the initial impression that it was going to be very cramped and uncomfortable. Nonetheless, the four room-mates rapidly learned that there was at least room to sit and talk, if two sat on each bottom bunk. There was a sense of isolation in the room, since there was no window or porthole. More than once, Gover would remark on something that happened on the vessel about which he could get no details because all the passengers were so isolated in their living areas. Still, there was a rather comfortable mess room and an area where the passengers whiled away the endless hours writing letters, reading, playing cards and maybe winning some money, or just relaxing. It was also a good place to escape the confines of your room, especially when one of your roommates was sick, as seemed to be the case more often than not. Sixty years later, Gover remarked, "I still feel seasick when I think about that voyage." While still in camp at Halifax, they had often heard that the one redeeming element of the voyage was the excellent food on the ship, if you were not seasick and could eat it. And that proved to be the case. Don Young was much impressed with the food, compared with what they had had in camp, and he always remembered it as one of the high points of the voyage.

The last activity of the busy first day aboard was a session on how to wear a life jacket and man the lifeboats, and the meaning of various signals that might be given by the horns or bells. The crew took this briefing seriously, and so did the passengers, for they knew that sometime that night or the next day, whenever they were finished loading the cargo, they would be on the high seas and the fate of the *Emma Alexander* would be their fate, too.

Early the next afternoon, they were under way, and for the next sixteen days, Gover's diary gives a vivid account of the voyage.

November 21, 1941 Breakfast at 8:00 a.m. Boat pulled out at 1:00 p.m. Tried out the machine guns, antiaircraft guns, and four-inch cannon, and it really barks. Feeling pretty seasick. It is now 10:00 p.m. The ship is completely blacked out—we are out in the open sea. Subs are reported to be near. Can't see any other boats, but there are some others in the convoy (I hope)—and so to sleep (maybe).

November 22, 1941. Boats all around us this morning when I got up. I counted forty-four. There are two destroyers zigzagging out in front looking for subs. We are heading the convoy, which I don't exactly like. Still feeling sick as hell. There is one PBY flying boat patrolling. We are supposed to join a convoy of sixty American ships tomorrow night—I sure hope so. [In November 1941, Congress authorized American merchant ships to carry lend-lease goods to England, and other recipients, escorted by American destroyers.] We are ordered to carry our life belts at all times—even when eating—and to sleep in our clothes.

November 23, 1941 About 3:00 a.m. this morning there was a terrible crash—the boat lurched over and everything crashed to the floor. We thought we were hit, and people started running down the corridors. Can't get any information—imagine we sideswiped another boat, because it's a complete blackout and forty-four ships are pretty close together. Were all here this a.m. (8:00 a.m.) and there are two PBY flying boats patrolling. We had roll call at 9:45 a.m. and all attended church at 10:20. Jay is down and out (11:15 a.m.) and I'm feeling about 50-50. —4:00 p.m. Three of the ships had engine trouble and dropped out. We now have five destroyers patrolling. —11:30 p.m. Everything is OK. Haven't seen the other convoy as yet. Got over my seasickness but now have a hell of a headache.

November 24, 1941   Got up at 8:30 a.m. Took my clothes off last night after I found the boat was loaded with live ammunition. Wouldn't make any difference whether you had your clothes on or off if a torpedo hit that stuff. There are now just thirty-seven of us (ships)—one tanker went down last night and three others just disappeared. There was a collision. —4:00 p.m. Pretty fair storm blowing and you can't see seventy-five yards on account of fog. We just had a good scare. The "On Deck and Life Boats" whistle blew. Stayed there half an hour till "All Clear" was given. It is now 1:00 a.m., and I think I'll hit the hay. We just set our watches up one hour—we're about six hundred miles at sea. It is rough and a 50-mph wind is blowing. Water is coming over the decks. I took a check on the sun today and we must be heading pretty well northeast. We must be going to Glasgow, Scotland, but one never knows. So I'll see you in the morn—I hope.

November 25, 1941   Another day—went to breakfast. The ship now stinks so bad you can't eat. Then at 9:45 a.m. to roll call and at 10:30 a.m. "To Boat" drill. Sure a rough sea, and the crew members are betting we never make it. There are thirty-seven of us (ships) today. Feeling OK now.

November 26, 1941   Went to sleep this morning at 2:00 a.m. and for all I know died. Awoke at 8:00 a.m. this morning and it's rolling and pitching so bad you can't stand up. Didn't eat breakfast—the stink is so bad you can't eat. Water is breaking over the ship now—I think this clunker is going to break in half. Talked to an engineer last night. Said he'd been to sea for fifty years and had been on a lot of tubs but this is the one. We are on the *Emma Alexander* (450 feet in length, 7,793 tons), which has been in dry dock for light-years and this is her first trip since. It's now noon but I'm going to try and sleep. —5:30 p.m. Have been talking to Reed and Mause—Reed is sick. Just about time for dinner, but not for me. *Mutiny on the Bounty* hasn't anything on this scow.

November 27, 1941   Awoke around 9:00 a.m. The sea had quieted down considerably. We are now right in the middle of the sub zone and also the middle of the damn Atlantic. Haven't had any plane patrol for three days on account of the weather [also the distance was too far from land for any aircraft patrol of convoys in that area of the Atlantic]. It's now 11:30 a.m. I think I'll try to scare up a checker game—not much doing this afternoon. —11:30 p.m. Ready to go to bed—stormy and raining like the devil. This is now the seventh day at sea and have no idea where we may be—keep changing courses.

November 28, 1941   Everything going along pretty good today except I just happened to think that yesterday was Thanksgiving and we had mutton—not like the good dinners my mom always dishes out. —7:00 p.m. The dishes and everything were slid off the table at dinner—sure a mess. It is raining and sleeting—the decks are frozen. I was put on the machine guns for tomorrow, so we are in the danger zone for sure now. What I don't know about machine guns will fill a book, but boy, I'll learn fast. I'll probably be shooting at seagulls and flying fish tomorrow—in fact, anything that even looks like a plane.

Gover needn't have worried about enemy planes or any other use for the machine guns, since the *Emma Alexander* was about fifteen hundred miles east of Halifax and well out of the range of any German aircraft. Obviously, no one told this to Lee and his friends.

November 29, 1941   —9:00 a.m. Eighth day at sea—not much sleep last night, rolling so hard that if you relaxed and tried to sleep you found yourself in the middle of the floor. —1:00 p.m. Just came off duty. Had two hours watch duty on the starboard machine guns—they are twin Marlins and every fourth bullet is a tracer. So let all those Jerries come. Took a nap as I didn't get any sleep last night. —3:30 p.m. Boy, did things happen at 2:25 p.m. I was talking to Jay when we felt two violent jerks, ran out on deck to see the trouble, and saw four of our destroyers racing over to a spot one mile off our port side. Every ship in the convoy cut their motors so the sub couldn't get a sounding on us. As we don't get any news at all on board, except what we see, I don't know how it came out, but the destroyers dropped depth charges and we then speeded up and went on. —9:00 p.m. Well, it's beginning to look bad now. Forty minutes ago one of our tankers in the rear was sunk. We're now zigzagging along at a pretty good clip. I'm not so worried anymore about subs—they either get you or not—but tomorrow we'll be in range for bombers to come out after us, and that's bad. Sure felt good this morning when a fast and sleek destroyer came up through the convoy right beside us and you could see the good old Stars and Stripes flying from her mast. It's now 11:00 p.m. and I'm going to try to hit the hay. We now have orders to sleep in our clothes. It snowed today and the decks are now all white. I just took a last-minute look. There's a really beautiful moon out. Nice night for subs. Damn it!

November 30, 1941 Up at 9:00 a.m. and went to church at 10:20. We are now in the smoker playing cards. It is now 5:30 p.m.—Mause, Reed and I are in Jay's room talking and waiting for the 7:00 dinner bell. —1:30 a.m. It is cold and clear with a beautiful moon out tonight, so I'll hit the hay. This is the tenth day out.

December 1, 1941 Not much doing until 3:00 p.m., when our destroyers dropped depth charges. Their sounding devices spotted two subs. Had some good news this afternoon when our radio reported that a German raider was sunk a few miles off our starboard bow. All ships tried their guns again this morning. It's now 7:00 p.m. and time for dinner.

December 2, 1941 Just came down from breakfast. What a mess. If I ever thought it was rough before, it didn't mean a thing. The dishes were all just thrown off the tables. All parades are canceled, as you can't stand on deck. One man was swept overboard this morning on the ship next to us—poor devil. We set our watches up again tonight. That makes eight times I've done it since leaving San Francisco, and as there is only nine hours' difference between London and San Francisco time, we must be pretty near there. We had a get-together last night and had some pretty good acts. I go on watch at 10:30 a.m. on the starboard machine gun. Boy, I'll drown in this mess. The weather is made to order, though. There's a 70-mph wind blowing and it's foggy, which will stop air attack, and the sea is so rough that no sub can get a good shot for an attack. One o'clock will be the beginning of the twelfth day at sea. —7:30 p.m. Just came down from the dining room. They can't keep anything on the table, so no eats. Didn't have to stand watch today as it was so rough and blowing to around 80 mph. You didn't have a chance to stay on board. One fellow was knocked cold this morning when he was blown down, and a sailor split his head open this afternoon. I think I'll get up a card game.

December 3, 1941   Well, last night took the prize. The boat was thrown around so much that now nothing is where it should be. The fellow across from me in the top bunk, Hancock, was thrown out and down on the floor. Just about killed him. There was no parade this morning or breakfast, as it's still too rough. A British trawler joined the convoy last night. It's now 10:00 a.m. and I'm going to try to get on deck. —2:30 p.m. Our two American destroyers just now left us. They came back through the convoy and headed for Halifax. Sure hated to see them go, as we now have only a British trawler, two destroyers and a light cruiser taking us through.

Gover's disquiet on seeing the American destroyers depart was well founded. Although the convoy was only about four hundred miles from Ireland, many ships had been torpedoed in that area since the beginning of the war.

December 4, 1941   Just came down from breakfast. Not so rough out now but foggy. About ten ships left last night going to Glasgow, I guess. We set watches up another hour last night. — 1:30 p.m. Just came down from lunch. This is the beginning of the fourteenth day at sea. Played red dog [a card game] with Mause and Gilbertson this morning after parade. Got called in front of the whole parade and given hell this morning for shining my shoes on a towel—to hell with them all—I'm sore. —5:30 p.m. Just received word that we will arrive at Liverpool Friday evening unless we're attacked, then we'll make a dash for Glasgow—but we won't get to disembark until Saturday. Boy, Columbus was sure nuts to ride this ocean as long as he did. Guess I'll try to find a magazine to read before dinner. They're getting scarce as hen's teeth.

December 5, 1941 —8:30 a.m. Everything went along pretty well last night. Set our watches up another hour—the last time—we're on London time now. I was on deck this morning but no land in sight. I sneaked up on the bridge last night and talked to the first mate. Talked about torpedoes and such. This is the spot the *Atlantis* was torpedoed at the start of the war. Well, it's about time for breakfast and then I go on watch at 10:30 a.m. Hello, its now 12:45 p.m. and I just came off watch. We sighted land at 10:00 a.m. It was Northern Ireland. About noon we sighted the island of Islay. The first mate said we would be in Liverpool around 10:00 a.m. tomorrow—so now I'll go and eat lunch. Seven of the ships left the convoy headed for Scotland at 10:00 a.m. this morning. It is now just midnight and we are between Ireland and Scotland in the Irish Sea. There are now just five ships and we don't have an escort. We're running along at a good clip trying to make it under the cover of night.

December 6, 1941 —12:00 noon. Went through the Straits this morning and just now picked up a pilot—we are just ten miles out of Liverpool now and everyone is happy as hell. It is pretty foggy also, which is a good deal. Guess what! We anchored at 2:00 p.m. this afternoon. It is now 4:30 and the authorities just came aboard and told us we'd have to stay on board until tomorrow morning, and as we're in the middle of the river, there's nothing we can do about it. The harbor here is just full of wrecked ships, and there are barrage balloons all over the place. It is now 8:00 p.m. I just finished dinner. The city of Liverpool is completely blacked out. I sure hope there is not an air raid tonight, because we'd sure be trapped out in the harbor on this thing. We were told to be ready at 9:00 a.m. in the morning. There are sixteen of us Americans, and we will leave the others. The others consist of twenty-five Australians, twenty-five New Zealanders, and fifty Canadians. We leave them and go on to London, while they go on to some training station.

December 7, 1941   Disembarked at 9:30 a.m. at Wallasey, right across the river from Liverpool. We were taken by bus to the depot and took the train for London. Passed through Rugby at 12:15 and through Northampton at 2:30 p.m. and I'm now playing cards with Mause. Through Bletchley at 3:15 p.m. Arrived in London at 4:08 and taken by cab to the Air Ministry where we signed up, then by cab to the Overseas Club, through a complete blackout. There we got a room and had dinner, and Mause and I are in our room, where we just finished reading our mail. It was sure swell to have letters waiting for you. I was pretty lucky—had five letters. So I'll take a much-needed bath and go to sleep.

The complete blackout in London coupled with the sunken ships and barrage balloons in Liverpool had a very deep impact on Gover and all the Americans who arrived in England. Although they had tried to imagine what England and war would be, they just had no frame of reference. "There is nothing that makes goose bumps all over you as quickly as does the sound of an air raid siren the first time you hear it," Gover reported.

I just had no idea what a huge city and an entire country would be in war, but we sure found out quickly. I was equally amazed during my first evening in London how the activity of the city could proceed with no light. If the German pilots thought that everyone was cowering in fear in the dark, they were greatly mistaken. I saw people going to the movies or to visit friends, coming home from work or just walking around in the total dark. I was impressed.

After their well-deserved bath, and a good night's sleep, Lee and his friends were on their way again. First they returned to the Air Ministry, where they completed the necessary paperwork that would make them officers in the RAF. In place of having to swear allegiance to the King, which would have cost them their U.S. citizenship, each was given a certificate of appointment as an officer in the RAF that was carefully worded to avoid the citizenship issue. It simply stated:

. . . we do hereby command them to obey you as their superior officer and you to observe and follow such orders and directions

25

as from time to time you shall receive from us, or any (who are) your superior officer, according to the rules and discipline of war, in pursuance of the trust hereby reposed in you.

And while there was no accompanying ceremony, each of the Americans was impressed that he was indeed a real member of the RAF and a great deal was expected of him.

Then it was off to Moss Brothers Clothiers, on King Street in Covent Garden, for the rapid transformation from civilians, in their conspicuous California clothes, into well-dressed officers in the RAF. (The uniform each bought with the coupons in his clothing book issued at the Air Ministry included a Class A uniform with tunic and two pair of pants, a raincoat, a greatcoat, an overseas cap, a billed cap, two shirts, two neckties, gloves, black socks and shoes. Each tunic had the wings of an RAF pilot already embroidered above the left breast pocket.) The Americans thought the shirts with button-on collars that could be changed and pants that had to be held up with suspenders because they had no belt loops were odd, but what a thrill it was to look down and see those wings and be identified as one of the great few on whom the defense of Britain depended. Lee summed it up:

> We were so proud that we just strutted down the street. And people were greeting us as soldiers, enlisted men were saluting us, and we really didn't know just what to do. Still, what a great feeling it was, and it sure made the perils of the voyage fade rapidly.

"Well, we're really in the army now," Lee wrote that afternoon.

> This morning's headlines say "Japan Declares War on United States." Now it is 3:30 p.m. and we have just pulled out of Waterloo Station. We are all decked out in our new uniforms and really look swell. Arrived in Bournemouth at 7:30 p.m. and taken to the Metropole Hotel, where we will stay while in Bournemouth. It is now 9:30 and I am in my room unpacking. The city is completely blacked out and I can hear airplanes going over—and so just about ends another very different and exciting day in the life of yours truly.

All the anxious moments on the Atlantic and Lee's initial impressions of war were not part of the news his folks got back home. Just five days after arriving, Lee sent them a Christmas card from Bournemouth, his first note from England.

Arrived OK—had a rough trip. I've crossed England now and the whole country is beautiful. You'd love it. So pretty and green and lots of streams. We are at a reception center now, just waiting to be transferred to an OTU (operational training unit) where new pilots are taught to fly the Spitfire or other advanced combat aircraft. The food is OK except no butter or sugar and not much meat. I priced some grapes today and they want sixteen shillings a pound—that's over three American dollars. Wow! We are now in full uniform and today I was issued my flying outfit and it sure is swell. . . . Everyone here is very kind and tries to help in all the ways he can. I can't say where I am or what goes on but so far so good. Tell everyone to write lots of letters. It broke my heart to give all of my civilian clothes away, but I can't use them now. Anyway, they'd be out of style when I return. Every car over here is just a little thing but pretty snappy.

Arrival in Bournemouth ended the first portion of the adventure that had begun nearly four months earlier, on August 10, with Lee's arrival at Bakersfield for pilot training. The events had exceeded even Lee's wildest thoughts, but he was now a pilot and an officer in the Royal Air Force ready to be assigned to an operational training unit and begin his transition to the Spitfire and, eventually, to fighting the Germans.

2. THE RAF BECOMES A REALITY

THE PACE OF EVENTS DID NOT SLACKEN FOR GOVER AND his friends until Tuesday afternoon. Their third day in England began just as Monday had ended, doing those things that were essential to the process of becoming an officer in the RAF.

Up at 7:15—washed, shaved, breakfast and over to parade at 8:20. After roll call we filled out more papers and had our pictures taken. I was off until 1:40, when I reported for roll call again and was dismissed. Mause, Young, Reed and I then walked around town.

This was the first time the four had the opportunity to reflect on their experiences and what was to come next. And while they all were happy and relieved that the long trip to England was over, the challenges that lay ahead were immense. During the next few weeks they would be assigned to either fighters or bombers and then learn how to fly them. If they were posted to fighters—and all four had been promised that would be the case—they had a lot to learn, because the Spitfire was over twice as powerful and fast as any airplane they had ever flown or even seen. Being in the military was also completely new to each one. They had no military training at all, so did not know how to march or salute and knew nothing of military customs, courtesies or regulations. Breakfast on Tuesday morning, which consisted of hot cereal, toast and tea, had demonstrated that the food was going to be quite different. Many of the items that each had taken for granted while in the United States and Canada, such as eggs, fresh fruit, sugar and meat, were simply not to be found.

There was probably not a better place for Lee to get acquainted with England than Bournemouth. Located on the coast, well south of London, this very old city of 150,000 people was one of Britain's premier summer resorts. The Old World ambience was very evident to Gover during his Tuesday afternoon walk around town. "The English countryside is sure beautiful," he wrote:

and the city of Bournemouth is the most picturesque I've ever seen, with its odd English buildings and all the narrow, winding streets. During the summer the population runs around one and a half million. There are over 450 hotels here, and most of them are supposed to be nice ones. So it's a pretty good city. They have a lot of very pretty parks and places of interest and all the streets just wind around through the town—really swell.

English social life and the efforts of the RAF to entertain the troops also made an impact on each of the Americans. On December 10, Gover's second full day in Bournemouth, he wrote:

Went to parade and then had to go to a tea dance. They sure have some silly customs here. We sat around and looked foolish until about 5:15 and then came on back to the Metropole Hotel. —10:00 p.m. Just came home from the Pavilion—it's a club and pretty nice. Mause came up with four gals and it took the three of us just about three minutes to ditch them. Since the town is completely blacked out, I just stepped into a doorway and I was rid of mine in two seconds. We then went to the Norfolk Hotel Lounge, where we had a good time—a swell place, top hats, tails, orchestra and all. We left at 9:30, which is closing time over here, and groped our way home in the dark.

But for the few Americans among the nearly three thousand RAF personnel at Bournemouth awaiting their initial assignment, the Japanese attack on Pearl Harbor and the subsequent entry of the United States into the war dominated their thoughts and conversation to a much greater degree than did the charm of England. The entries in Gover's diary reveal the real pain he was suffering over the situation. On December 9 he wrote:

> This evening's paper says the American West Coast is all blacked out and heavy losses have been inflicted on the Navy. I sure wish to hell I could just get a crack at those son-of-a-bitch Japs. If anything happens to my family or friends it will take more than the cherry blossoms of Japan to save them. I'm just praying the American government calls me back so I can help from that side, but the British are doing all right, so maybe I'll be able to get a crack at them from Singapore. This whole silly world is sure going to hell fast.

The next day, Lee added, "Just had the bad news about the war over there. Sure is hell that the U.S. just sat on their ass until the Japs caught them napping." Importantly, the Americans realized they were no longer foreigners who were fighting another nation's war but rather the first of that flood of resources from the New World about which Winston Churchill had talked so much.

Still, the Americans were at Bournemouth for only one purpose, and that was to get processed into the RAF and be on their way to a training base. And while the process seemed slow, there were reasons of which Gover and his friends were not aware. The RAF operational training system was saturated, and so it was necessary for the new arrivals, regardless of their origin, to spend up to two weeks in the Bournemouth area until a training slot could be found for them. In addition, the British wanted to be sure that the Americans were fully recuperated from the voyage across the Atlantic, which had been much more taxing than any would care to admit.

On December 11, just three days after his arrival at Bournemouth, Gover was told that his assignment was imminent. All four of the Bakersfield buddies also found that they were assigned to fighters. They made a trip to the Royal Bath Hotel cocktail lounge to celebrate. Jack Mause was absolutely euphoric. "I knew we would all get fighters, just like I said way back in Bakersfield. I'll bet we all get the same operational training unit assignment, too." Jay Reed agreed and even added, "The trip over on the boat wasn't really so bad. I would do it again just to get to those Spitfires." And so it went until the Germans decided to curtail the merriment with a bombing raid that lasted about half an hour. "I was scared, but I guess we will have to get used to bombings," Lee remarked when it was over. "I really take my hat off to these Brits who have been going through this for over a year." And get used to the raids they did, because just two days later they were attacked again.

A week after their arrival at Bournemouth, the four Americans were told to be packed and ready to go the following morning. True to their luck, they were all assigned to the OTU at Llandow, near the village of Llantwitt Major, in Wales. "Ate dinner, played chess with Mause, and, since it's 10:30, I'm going to hit the hay," wrote Gover. "Everyone is pretty serious, since we know that the real purpose of all we have done since May comes together tomorrow."

December 16 dawned cold, rainy and dreary, but emotion was high nonetheless, since the move to the OTU and real flying for the RAF was about to begin. "Mause and I were taken by bus to the railway station at 8:30 a.m.," Gover reported, "but Jay and Don were left behind. Transferred at Southampton, then at Cardiff, Bristol and the fourth time at Barry." Despite the rainy day, the trip to Wales made a very deep impression on Lee. He had already written to his parents about the beauty of England, but he saw much more of it on the trip to the OTU, so his impressions were even more vivid. "I just had never seen countryside like that which passed by the train window," he reminisced.

While California was beautiful, there just weren't the miles of rolling green hills, the unique hedgerows that marked the edges of fields rather than fences, and the trees that were always in sight. It was just so lush compared to the fairly arid area in which I grew up. And we seemed to never be out of sight of a town or village with their quaint buildings and narrow streets. I guess I saw a hundred houses with thatched roofs, but I still just stared at every one of them, they were so different. Maybe it was my work in construction that made me continue to wonder just how that roof was held on and whether it leaked in all the rain. I also got a chance to see the English people as they rode the train and milled around in the stations. The people were so friendly to us, probably because we were RAF pilots, but they really seemed genuine. I got talking to an older English gentleman and when he found that I was from the United States he just bubbled over with appreciation for us coming and helping in their hour of need.

But Lee and Jack found it hard to relax during the long trip, and as the low winter sun gave way to midafternoon dusk, their anticipation grew. Gover later remarked:

We were just so anxious to see and hear a Spitfire that the time seemed to drag by. Of course, we didn't know that we would be living over half a mile from the field and so wouldn't see any of the base until the next day. We also didn't know what to expect as far as the flying program went and so spent a lot of time speculating about it as we rode. At Bournemouth we had heard that they would just give us a couple of rides with an instructor in a Miles Master and then we would be on our own. I guess that if we had thought more about it we would have really been apprehensive, since our first flight in the Spitfire would be solo. Still, I didn't think that we would be allowed to fly the Spitfire without a very thorough evaluation in some other airplane and a lot of instruction in the British way of flying, navigation and the systems operation of the Spitfire.

"We finally arrived at the village of Llantwitt Major at about 10:30 p.m.," Gover wrote.

An army truck came and took us out to the airdrome (RAF Station, Llandow). We had a couple of beers (it is going to be hard to get used to drinking it warm) and some sandwiches and then were taken to our bunks, which are about three fourths of a mile from the field. What a place! It is cold and dreary and about four inches of mud everywhere. There are two of us in this small room, and it must be half a mile to the mess and the showers. The building looks like it is a temporary one made out of boards and tar paper. Maybe it will look better in the daylight. [Lee's description was correct both in the construction of the building

in which they lived and the distance to the mess and showers.]
Jay and Don Young didn't make it, and so now out of the bunch
that were in class in Bakersfield, California, there are just Mause
and myself left.

The fact that Gover and Mause were the ones who made the
trip to Llantwitt Major on the sixteenth was simply the luck of
the draw. When the four reported to leave Bournemouth,
there were only two tickets, so Gover and Mause were the ones
who went.

The two new arrivals expected to go to the flight line first
thing the next day and be able to see, touch and at least sit in
the airplane of their dreams, but that was not to be. With a
sense of resignation, Gover wrote:

Awakened by my batman at 7:00 a.m. and it's still pitch-black
here. Walked forever to get to the mess hall, then to a lecture
hall, where we signed some more papers and were told just what
OTU is all about. The mess here is not at all like Bournemouth.
It was paneled, had a big fireplace, and was just an elegant place.
The one here is just like the barracks, a temporary building. Had
lunch and then back to the lecture room. We were issued our
helmets, goggles, gloves, microphone, etc. so we now have complete flying equipment. There are thirty-five in the squadron and
they are from all countries—France, Poland, Netherlands,
Canada, Australia, New Zealand and we fellows from the USA.

The second session in the lecture room was a short introduction to the Spitfire, and then came the moment that Lee
and Jack Mause had been waiting for since August: the visit to
the flight line and the Spitfire.

Had my first look at the Spitfire this afternoon. What an airplane! It is much bigger than I thought it would be—over thirty
feet long, and I can almost stand up under the wingtip. I just
stood there and looked at it and couldn't say a word. This is the
best fighter in the world, and I am going to fly it. Every moment
of the training and trip was worth it to me, and I'm sure the
other fellows feel the same. It's going to be great to fly—over 400
miles per hour. Well, I sure have my work cut out for me.

But flying also had its hazards, and Gover was introduced to those before his first day at OTU ended.

> It is now 8:00 p.m. and I am up at the Officers' Club, but I think I'll plod through the mud and go to bed. One fellow was killed yesterday. The accident rate here is about four out of ten in training, and when you watch these Spits come in you don't wonder.

Any questions Lee and his squadron mates had about the beginning of flying and how the training would be conducted were answered the following morning. After walking the half mile to shower, shave and have breakfast, all of Gover's class were assigned to flights. Gover was in A Flight and Mause in B Flight, so, for the first time since leaving Bakersfield, Lee knew no one in the unit. This did not dampen the news that "tomorrow is our big day—we take our first flight." Still, the ever-present danger of flying was understandably on Lee's mind, since he had never been in an environment where accidents and death were part of the everyday reality of flying. For him, it had always been a fairly safe undertaking, and even when there were crashes, the pilot was seldom killed. His diary entry for December 18, 1941, his second full day at OTU and the day before he was to take his first flight, reflects his concern.

> The first plane I watched land this morning crashed. Then this afternoon, two more crashed. The Spitfires have such a narrow landing gear and land so hot that it's going to be dynamite. We were told that everyone averages two crack-ups if he lives for the six to eight weeks that he's here—and that's before going on active service with a squadron.

"Well, today was another big day for the little man," began Gover's diary for the next day.

> Went to classes, and they sure shove the information to you—all the secret codes, navigation, rules for flying, etc. Then this afternoon to the field, where the fog was closing in. Only three of us got to go up, but at least I got my first flight since October, and it sure felt good. We take a few hours' dual in the Miles

Master—a two-place, low-wing monoplane of 850 horsepower—
before we go to the Spits. I only got twenty minutes before the
fog covered everything and we were forced down, but at least I
still know how to fly. There were two more crashes today, and
two planes still haven't come in. I got my first look at the country
from the air, and it's sure beautiful. We are only about one mile
from the coast here at Llandow.

There was no flying the next day because of the fog, so Lee
and Jack Mause walked the two miles into town to get their
first look at Llantwitt Major.

Went to a show and I bought four pair of socks. This is the pretti-
est little old Welsh town with narrow winding streets and all with
cobblestone walls. Some of the houses are like little castles, and
some have thatched roofs. Everyone is so friendly to us, and
when they see the USA patch on our shoulders, they go out of
their way to help us. When you see how much these people
appreciate our being here, it sure makes you feel that you made
the right decision in joining the RAF.

"I'll never forget the walk back to the base that day," Lee
reminisced.

Our base commander at Llandow was a Group Captain Ira "Taffy"
Jones. He was a short, heavyset man who stuttered something
awful. He was a World War I fighter pilot and a damn good one—
shot down forty-two German aircraft. Everyone said that he couldn't
land, however, and had destroyed almost as many of his own planes
just getting back on the ground. As Jack and I were walking home,
a car passed us, then stopped, and when we came abreast, "Taffy"
Jones stepped out and gave us hell for not saluting him. I told him
we didn't have eyes in the back of our heads. He took a dim view of
that and proceeded to give us hell all over again. He must have
thought it over, because he became quite friendly from then on and
we talked a lot in the evenings at the mess. He really liked
Americans and appreciated our being in England.

Lee's descriptions of Llantwitt Major were glowing when he
wrote home a few days later.

I can't get over how pretty the country is. All small fields fenced by hedges or cobblestone walls running all directions. I have seen several old places with thatched roofs. There are some really old castles nearby, and we are just a mile from the seashore.

The evening brought a welcome surprise. "Mause and I were playing cards when Reed and Young came walking in. So we are now all four together again." Needless to say, the four were up very late bringing one another up to date on their experiences and giving Reed and Young as much information about OTU as possible. "After all, we were veterans of a flight in the Miles Master," Lee reminisced, "and were therefore real experts on the OTU."

Flying in the English weather dominated Gover's mind. Like most Americans in the RAF, Lee had learned to fly in near-ideal weather conditions. All of their training bases were either in California or Texas, so very few had any experience flying in marginal weather conditions and on instruments. The opposite was true for the British. They had learned to fly in poor weather, so fog and low clouds were nothing new to them. For Gover and most of the other Americans, the entire process of learning to fly the fast and powerful aircraft at OTU was immensely complicated by the weather and learning to fly on instruments.

During the first portion of the OTU curriculum there was a comprehensive ground school for half the day. It included such subjects as radio procedures, aircraft recognition, regulations for flying, and some instruction on the Spitfire and its V-12 Merlin engine. An early and critical subject was escaping from the aircraft both in the air and on the ground. "One topic that was missing, which seemed strange to me, was instruction on firing your guns, how to lead an enemy aircraft and the like. We learned that after we got to our first operational squadron," Gover later wrote. The other half of the day was devoted to flying, but when the weather was too bad to fly there were lots of activities to take up the time. "The fog is still on the ground, so we can't fly," Gover wrote during his first week at the OTU. "I went in and checked out a parachute and got my helmet all fixed up for the microphone and oxygen." Two days later:

Was supposed to fly today but the fog was hanging right on the ground. I went over and took half an hour in the Link trainer. It's the same as flying a ship on instruments, and I can see I'll get plenty of that kind of flying. Then over for another half an hour in the Howardwin trainer. [This was a procedures trainer for the Spitfire.] Then this afternoon we all went to classes. Learned all about the secret codes, signs, heights, etc.

Sunday at war was like any other day, and it was an important one to Lee's flying progress.

Went out to our squadrons at 1:00 p.m. but it was still very foggy. The instructor and I went up to see if it was clearing. We flew up and down the coast and out to sea, but it was still hanging in low, so we came on in. I don't know how these instructors can get down through the clouds and fog so easily, but I guess I am going to have to learn—and fast. About 3:00 we went up again. I just circled up and landed, and the instructor said if I did that again I'd be able to solo. So I just up and did it again. So now I solo the first thing in the morning with just thirty-five minutes of instruction. So I'm not doing so bad.

On December 23, Gover soloed the Miles Master, took his check ride, and was cleared to go to Spitfires. His parents must have shared his excitement when they received his first letter since his arrival at the OTU.

We are given time in a Miles Master, an 850-hp two-place training plane. I soloed it in just thirty-five minutes. That was two days ago. As soon as the weather breaks, I go on to the Spitfire. That's a pretty good jump. Just think, about four months ago I was flying Cubs and now my next flight will be in the world's best airplane. They really are honeys.

This honey of an airplane was first constructed in 1936. Before the end of World War II, over twenty thousand were built. It was not a large airplane for a World War II fighter, but it was huge to Gover and his friends with its wingspan of 36 feet 10 inches and length of 29 feet 11 inches. The Spitfire Lee flew in OTU was the Spit II, which had a V-12 Rolls-Royce

Merlin engine producing 1,175 horsepower. In combat, Gover would fly the Spit V and the Spit IX. While these were the same size as the Spit II, the horsepower of the V was 1,475 and that of the IX 1,650. The aircraft was capable of speeds near 400 miles per hour, depending on the model, and could climb as high as 43,000 feet.

The cockpit was relatively small, and pilots over six feet tall were never very comfortable in it. The pilot sat on his parachute in an armor-plated Bakelite seat with his head almost touching the closed canopy and his shoulders nearly rubbing the sides of the cockpit. The instruments were basic for the time and quite easy to read, with the exception of the compass, which was located near the floor between the pilot's legs. In order to see who was on his tail, the pilot looked in a mirror located outside the top of the canopy.

Control was by use of a spade-grip stick that moved from side to side about halfway up its length to allow better aileron control than the normal straight stick. The spade grip was a circular ring, about eight inches in diameter and an inch thick, on which was located the large brass firing button with a ring around it to arm the guns. There were two sets of rudder pedals. The first set, on the floor of the cockpit, resembled stirrups and had retaining straps that would enable the pilot to still control the rudder if he lost the use of one foot or leg. The second set of pedals, just under the instrument panel, were used during combat to pull the pilot's knees closer to his chest, thus making him more resistant to blackout.

Of particular concern to Spitfire pilots was the canopy, which closed by sliding forward on rails on each side of the cockpit. There was a small door on the left side that, in addition to easing entry, could be put in the slightly open position to lock the canopy open for takeoff and landing. If the pilot had to abandon his aircraft in flight, standard procedure was to release the canopy's two front catches, which would allow the air to lift it off and away. This mechanism was augmented with a small crowbar that could be used to pry the canopy off in an emergency. Quick removal of the canopy was critical, since the main fuel tank was directly in front of the instrument panel and could turn the cockpit into a blazing inferno in seconds if hit by an incendiary bullet.

Directly in front of the pilot was a reflector gunsight, which could be adjusted for distances from 50 to 600 yards. Most pilots kept it set at 250 yards, the distance at which the guns were bore-sighted to concentrate their firepower. The sight was also calibrated for the wingspan of any aircraft. Thus set, when the enemy aircraft was in the circle and its wings within the span line, the pilot knew that his shots had a good chance of striking home. In front of the gunsight was a windshield of bulletproof glass, while the sides and top of the canopy were Plexiglas.

Aside from some difficulty in taxiing because of the narrow spacing of the landing gear, the Spitfire was light and easy to maneuver with a good rate of climb and could turn tighter than any of the other aircraft engaged on the western front. The aircraft lifted off the ground in about one thousand feet at around 100 miles per hour and landed beautifully at around 85 miles per hour. It was a very stable gun platform and also relatively easy to fly on instruments—a necessity, given the English weather. Overall, the Spitfire was as beautiful to fly as it was to see.

The most difficult days that Lee and his friends had since they left the United States were Christmas Eve and Christmas. "Here it is Christmas Eve," Gover wrote.

No word from home and nothing here, so it looks like a bad Christmas. If there was an airplane here that would hold enough gas, I'd fly the son of a bitch clear to California. There's no more wood in camp and so we can't even have a fire in our rooms.

Lee was sick most of Christmas Day but did manage to go to dinner where:

The Doc introduced me to his wife. She's an American from Los Angeles who has been here for two years. They will invite me to dinner sometime. Still, it didn't seem like Christmas with no presents, no letter, no nothing. To top it off, Bill Avery, one of the Bakersfield fellows, was killed yesterday. He had a forced landing and broke his neck. No one to blame but himself. Landed with his wheels down, which just isn't done on a forced landing. Boy, do they drill that into you. That's one of the Bakersfield boys gone. I sometimes wonder just how many of us will come out of this. Well, tomorrow is Boxing Day. Nothing to do with boxing, but an English holiday of some sort. So Merry Christmas to all and to all a good night.

December 27 was a day that Gover would always remember—the day he soloed the Spitfire. Although he had over eight hundred hours of flying time when he entered the RAF, he had never flown any plane larger than the AT-6 with 600 horsepower. The initial flights in the Miles Master had been a challenge, but at least there had been an instructor to shepherd him through them. But now it was the Spitfire, and the first flight in this 1,200-horsepower fighter was solo. Gover had spent about an hour sitting in the cockpit during his first week at the OTU, so he knew the location of all the switches, and his instructor in the Miles Master told him how the flight characteristics of the Miles and the Spitfire differed, but to take one of the fastest planes in the world solo on the first flight was a challenge. "I knew one reason there were so many accidents was that the pilots just weren't ready to handle the Spitfire," Gover reminisced. "I wasn't afraid of the plane, but I sure respected it."

Instruction began as soon as Gover arrived at his plane, since the crew chief had to show him how to strap in, hook up his microphone and headset and get his oxygen mask properly connected. Then came a lesson on how to start the engine and Lee was on his way. "You didn't have to worry much about taxiing the plane, because the airdrome was just one big, square grass field, and so you just lined up into the wind and opened the throttle," he remembered. Lee was surprised at how easily the Spitfire became airborne, but it took some time to get used to the controls, which were much more sensitive than any he had ever experienced. He had flown about thirty minutes and was just beginning to feel comfortable with the ship when the call went out for all aircraft to return to the field, since the fog was coming in. For Gover, the next few minutes were a real test of his flying skills.

Well, today's the day I just about left this world. Was up in the Spit and they called on the radio and said to land immediately as the field was closing in with fog. I started down, let my wheels down, and started to drop my flaps, and they wouldn't come down. Took about four passes at the field, but the field is short and I came in pretty hot without flaps so couldn't land. They called on the radio and told me to land at St. Athans. The only problem was I didn't know where the hell that was. I started down the coast at about 150 feet and 240 miles per hour. I soon spotted an airdrome and circled, then I dropped my wheels again and the damn things would go down but wouldn't lock. So what the hell—I made three passes at the field at about twenty feet and decided to slide it in, as the fog was really getting thick. On the way around the field, it built up enough hydraulic pressure and the wheels snapped locked OK but still no flaps. I drug it in straight for about half a mile, cut the engine and stalled her down as much as possible. Well, she floated quite a bit and then settled to a good landing. But having no air pressure and no brakes, I went about half a mile and was heading straight into a big four-motored bomber when I finally got her stopped, and so ended my first ride in the Spitfire. I learned more on that ride and got more white hair than you can imagine. Another one of my classmates here, not from Bakersfield though, was killed this morning when he ran into a balloon cable and crashed in flames. That's three from this class already.

All the folks at home heard about the flight was:

. . . everything happens to me. On my first flight I had a forced landing seven miles from here. Came out OK though. This airplane sure is fast. The first time I came in I lined up with the field. Then looked down to see if my wheels gauge was showing "down," looked out again, and the damn field was behind me.

As if to set a pattern, Gover's second flight in the Spitfire, two days later, was anything but routine.

Well, here we are on the last day of the year. I just about got the hell scared out of me today. Was up about four thousand feet and about three miles out to sea when I glanced around and there was a Heinkel 111 bearing down on me. I shoved the throttle open so damn quick the plane just about jumped out from under me. Our ships are all carrying machine guns and they are loaded, but I figured I didn't have enough experience to fool around with a ship with three gunners. And besides, I wanted to go to the New Year's party tonight. The German turned outward then, but our interceptors were on the way and it didn't last long. I got back to the airdrome so fast it would make your head swim. I'm not a hero just yet.

The New Year's Eve party was certainly worth returning for. Although there had been very little opportunity for social life during the first two weeks at the OTU, the squadron made up for it on New Year's Eve.

Happy New Year. Boy, what a party—all the wine, women and song you could stand. I got in at 5:00 a.m. Wow, what a time—never saw so much Scotch, wine, gin, roast goose, chicken and everything in my life. The mess must have saved rations for weeks to put on that spread. I danced everything from the Lambeth Walk on up and with the commodore's daughter on down. Boy, what a time. Got up at noon and staggered down to the mess, ate lunch and drank two gallons of water and plunked down in the front of the fire to spend the rest of the day. I would be in real trouble if they had not given us today off. Thank goodness the batmen had cleaned everything up and the place was livable again.

Having a batman was a benefit that went with being an officer in the RAF—and one that Gover and his friends initially found hard to believe. Jack Mause had mentioned it while they were at Bournemouth. "I understand that we have a man or lady who cleans our room, makes the bed, shines our shoes and even wakes us in the morning with hot tea when we get to OTU," he had said. And while the others had heard the same story, they all decided it was too good to be true, especially after the experience they had in Canada making beds and Gover's unhappy episode with shoe shining on the *Emma Alexander*. But the first morning at Llandow each of them had indeed been awakened by a pleasant "Good morning, sir. Would you care for a cup of tea?" And from that point on the batman (sometimes a woman, but still called a batman) became an important part of each officer's life. In addition to paying a nominal amount each week to augment the civilian batman's regular government pay, Gover gave his batman some of the clothes that he had brought with him from California. Most officers also gave their batmen ration coupons and scarce items such as sugar or coffee sent from the United States. In turn, a flier could find that a sweater was mended, socks were darned, a worn scarf replaced or a headache treated. It was not long until the batman became an indispensable part of daily life for Lee and his friends.

Recuperation from the New Year's celebration was rapid, and on January 2, Gover was back in the usual routine.

Warmed up a little today—went to classes this morning and flying this afternoon. Only about one mile visibility and 1,200 feet ceiling, but that is considered excellent flying weather here, while everything would be grounded in the States.

Unfortunately, the accidents also continued with the new year.

Just another rainy day, but I flew just the same. I went together with another ship and we practiced attack procedures using the camera gun. Two of our boys didn't come back and no word this evening, so don't know if they force-landed or what. I called Bournemouth this evening to see if any more of the Bakersfield gang were there. They were, and I talked with O'Hara awhile. I'm glad to hear they arrived. It's just two months ago that I left home. Sure seems longer than that. I have learned more and done more things in this past two months than anytime in my life.

The pace that made time so compressed continued the next day.

Went to classes this morning, still raining. This afternoon I was up for an hour and twenty-five minutes on formation. And do we fly close or do we! Your wingtip tucked in behind his and only four or five feet from his fuselage. And cruising along at 250 miles per hour you really have to keep on the ball. One of the two fellows lost yesterday walked in today. He had force-landed and wasn't hurt. But the other one was found this afternoon. He crashed and burned, and so one more of our bunch has been killed—a swell, quiet little redheaded kid from New Zealand—the fourth one.

The loss was still on Gover's mind the next day, and events did nothing to alleviate the situation.

Everything frozen solid this morning. Went to classes until noon. Got in half an hour in the Link trainer and half an hour in the Howardwin. Another Spitfire was busted all to hell today. Now I see what they meant when we were told on our arrival here that we would average two crack-ups apiece and at least four would be killed. We laughed then, but it's all too true already and we have only been here three weeks.

For the next week the winter weather settled in with a vengeance and Lee's squadron did not do any flying. Any disappointment that the squadron felt was rapidly dispelled on Friday when they were given the weekend off.

Scampered back to the hut and dressed. Walked down to Llantwitt Major and caught the train for Cardiff. This is a fairly good-sized city, so there are a number of hotels and plenty of pubs. Checked in at the Grand Hotel and took in all the night spots.

Saturday was really the first leisurely day Lee had experienced since arriving at the OTU, since he had been sick on Christmas and recuperating on New Year's.

Got up at around 9:30 and went down to breakfast. When you get a room in England you get breakfast along with it. Went downtown and bought some boots and socks and had my picture taken. Had lunch and dinner at the Carlton [another hotel]. They had an orchestra and it was fair. Every bar, or pub as they call them over here, was sold out by 8:00 p.m. because of rationing. Went back to the hotel lounge and met some gals there. We talked, then talked some more, and after awhile we—none of your business.

"Actually, I had good luck with the ladies the few times I was in Cardiff," Gover later wrote.

In fact, a couple of the young ladies kept in touch with me throughout my time in England. One would occasionally meet me in London for a night of romance, and getting to London from Cardiff, Wales, was an all-day train ride. I was flattered and tried to show her the town and a really good time.

Sunday was equally as enjoyable.

After breakfast, Jay and I went over and looked at an old castle—pretty place. Paid my hotel bill, one pound, it was ten shillings a night. Caught the 2:30 train and came back to Llantwitt, then walked to the base. Had a good weekend but now back to work.

Just before he went to Cardiff, Gover wrote his folks describing, as much as the censors would allow, what he was doing in training and requesting everything from chocolate and gum to cookies and candy drops. "We are rationed to one chocolate bar a week," he wrote, "but it tastes like the kind you cook with." Lee's primary concern, however, was the mail and how slow it was in getting to him. This was why he had spent Christmas with no presents, letters or cards.

Just now received your two letters. The one you mailed December 1st was sent to another OTU by mistake. The other one was mailed December 15th. So if things go right, I get your mail in about three weeks. I also received one sent by regular mail, which was postmarked November 28th. So airmail is a couple of weeks faster.

For Gover, and for all of his fellow pilots from other countries, the high point of the day was the arrival of the mail. There was no mail call, so often depicted as typical of World War II; mail for an RAF officer was delivered to his room, generally by his batman, who received it from the mail clerk. Thus, arrival home after a day of flying was always great if there was mail, a letdown if there was none. The sporadic nature of mail delivery was a product of the war. Since the Americans did not have an assignment when they left for England, they were told to have mail sent in care of the London School of Economics. After arrival in England, they changed that address to the American Eagle Club on Charing Cross Road in London. This American Red Cross–operated facility was picked since it was the first place the Americans went when they came into London for any reason. The first address that the folks back home had for sending mail direct was the OTU, and it took at least three weeks for a letter giving that address to get from England to the United States. Thus, it was often over two months before people in the United States had an address that did not require forwarding. Added to this was the fact that unless the sender was willing to pay the extra for airmail, letters and all packages went by ship and took a minimum of four to five weeks for delivery. There are references on many occasions to letters and packages sent but never received. These were generally casualties of the high shipping loss due to the German submarine fleet on the North Atlantic. So, while Gover and his friends often lamented the lack of mail, as Lee did on Christmas, it was not because no one cared. Lee was still receiving Christmas cards and packages in February.

"It is so damn cold I can't get warm," Lee wrote on January 11.

> Last night I had a beer bottle full of water by my bed and this morning it was absolutely frozen solid and there was a good quarter inch of frost on my bed, and I'm not kidding. If the Germans ever got this place they would just freeze to death quick. I have five big wool blankets on my bed now, so I hope I can stay warm.

For a young man who had grown up in California, the penetrating cold of England must have indeed been hard to tolerate. Gover's diary and letters are full of comments about the cold and how difficult it was for him to get warm. Lee described, with some exaggeration, his solution to the cold in a letter to his parents in late January.

> I keep pretty warm by wearing rubber boots, three pair of heavy socks, four pair of underwear (long ones too, boy), my uniform, a

sweater, raincoat, hat and big wool-lined gloves with silk inner liners. At night I just take off my shoes and hat and crawl under five big wool blankets. You should see me when I've got all that on and then my complete flying suit. They just take a crane and drop me into the cockpit.

The Spitfire did not have a cockpit heater, so it was like a refrigerator when the pilot first got in. That soon changed as the aircraft rapidly made its way through the low clouds of winter.

It is so nice to fly, because once you get above the clouds the sun is always beating down on the canopy and you get warm for the only time during the day. I really feel sorry for the poor riggers [mechanics] and fitters [crew chiefs] who have to work in the cold all day and never have a chance to get warm.

Gover flew eighteen times during January for a total of eighteen hours and thirty minutes. The different types of training during these flights illustrate well the curriculum of the OTU. Lee practiced homing with the radio, attack procedures, formation, forced landings, instruments and a height climb to 31,000 feet. The flying was not all routine by any means, however. On January 24, Gover fired his guns for the first time.

Took a little trip across England this morning and out over the Channel—didn't see a thing (which I was glad about). Came back across the Bristol Channel, around the balloons and out to sea on this side. Saw a seagull and had a hell of a fight with him—used up three hundred shells but had a lot of fun. Up again this afternoon on formation, and boy was I hot. I got in so close that the guy next to me kept waving me away. He said afterward he could have reached out and touched my wingtip. One fellow cracked up on landing and another one flew right into him. No one killed, but both planes just chewed all to hell. One other cracked up this morning, so that's three today.

"Hooray for life," began Gover's diary for January 26.

Boy, today was the first day that the sun has been out and there was no wind. And to top it all off, we had the day off. I slept in until 11:00. After lunch, Jay, Mause, Young and I took a hike down to Llantwitt Major. Took pictures of a lot of very old places. The first school in Wales was here, and the town church was built in the tenth century. Took pictures of the place where St. Patrick stayed. Had tea at a little old tearoom that has four-foot-thick walls, built in around 700 A.D. It is a very interesting little village and about the oldest in Wales. Went into a little old billiard room and got a piece of chocolate while we played a game of snooker. Hiked on back to the base, and we are now making soup in a little pail we got. Just about ends the best day I've had here.

If January 26 was the best day Gover had had so far, January 28 was probably the worst.

This must be my bad day—came within an inch of getting killed twice. The first time Jay was in the front [of a Miles Master] on instruments and I was check pilot. A storm came in suddenly and we had to force-land at another base. Came in a little slow and a wing dropped out from under and a big bomber was right under us. I poured the coal to it and just skimmed over him. Then this afternoon I was flying through clouds on instruments and she stalled into a spin and away we went. Got it out of the spin just as I came out of the cloud base, just about five hundred feet up and going straight down. Pulled it out and just cleared some housetops. If the cloud base had been a hundred feet lower I'd never know the diff.

Although Gover was lucky, and probably quite skillful, with his flying, the same could not be said of some of the others from Bakersfield. On December 29, Jack Mause got lost, made a forced landing and destroyed his airplane, although he was not hurt. Just one month later, Gover reported, "Poor old Jay Reed taxied into the gas truck today and tore the right wing all to hell. Was called up to the chief flying instructor and they gave him hell. He says he wants to go home but he'd have to swim." On March 22, "Mause cracked up again but was not hurt much."

Gover's final flight of January was his most enjoyable thus far in the Spitfire, since for the first time he got a chance to explore the real capabilities of the aircraft.

Went on a height climb—went up to 31,000 feet—higher than I have ever been. Rolled it over on its back and had it up to 380 miles per hour. At 25,000, I pulled it out. So when my speed was calculated in accordance with the altitude, I was doing a true ground speed of 480 miles per hour, which is pretty damn fast in any man's army. Then I did spins, slow rolls, loops, Immelmanns, chandelles and lazy eights. Finished up with some cloud flying. Boy, the oxygen sure works swell in the Spitfires, and she just screams at that speed. What an airplane!

It was obvious from his letters home that Gover was becoming more confident in the Spitfire and also more at home in England. Evidently his folks also became more anxious to learn the details of what he did. On January 24, he wrote a very long letter home in which he appealed for chocolate and chewing gum, noted that he had received none of the packages his mother had sent, reported that airmail was taking three weeks to arrive and also commented about his flying equipment and some of the courses he had taken in ground school.

As I fly over lots of water, I wear a life jacket, called a Mae West, and the part of my parachute that was the seat cushion is now filled with a collapsible boat. They sure have some very good things for saving your life. If we could just get the Huns to use wax bullets, I'd be an ace in no time. I've been doing all the flight tactics and slowly getting to be a fighter pilot. I've finished all my ground work, lectures, handling of my machine guns, navigation, operational tactics and such. I have been doing very well in all subjects and also my flying.

Just a day earlier he had written to his parents, "There are a lot of things you ask about, but I can't answer them so you'll just have to wait until the present hostilities cease." Every letter that Lee wrote had to pass the censor, who would simply cut out anything improper with scissors and then seal the letter again with a two-by-three-inch sticker that said "Opened by Examiner [number]." Gover learned very rapidly to keep his comments general and avoid anything that might be classified.

The first week in February, Lee again wrote home talking about his flying.

As far as my flying is concerned, I have now begun to feel a part of the machine, and they really are wonderful machines. Still doing lots of formation, instrument flying (which is sure important), aerobatics, dogfighting and such. My flying outfit is sure swell. It consists of a kapok interliner, heavy flying suit with fur collar, heavy wool socks that come up over your knees, sheepskin-lined leather flying boots, a Mae West, leather gloves with silk interlinings, a swell leather helmet with the earphones and speaking microphone, as well as the oxygen hookup, all together. Then your parachute has a collapsible rubber dinghy in the seat pack, like I told you in my last letter. I sure do fill the seat of the Spitfire.

The final three weeks of OTU were every bit as challenging as the first month had been. During the first week alone, Gover had two flights that tested every bit of his ability in the Spitfire and skill as a pilot. These were rather typical of the situations that many of his classmates got into every day, and that accounted for the high casualty rate. "I think that the reason I survived OTU was that I had a lot of flying experience, before I went into the RAF, that I could fall back on. I never panicked and that is what killed a number of the lads."

"And again I flirted with death," he wrote on February 2.

Started on a cross-country flight. Went out about twenty miles and it was fogged in clear to the deck. Went up through it on instruments and broke out at six thousand feet. When I completed my course and came down again through the clouds there was nothing but water under me. I called the station for a homing [a direction to fly to get to the base]. They took a fix and gave me a vector [course to fly]. I was so far off my preflight course that I was seventy-five miles out at sea. I had to fly at deck level because of fog, and I can't think of anything that will put the creeps up your spine faster than flying over water and being lost at the same time. Your engine starts to sound like it's falling apart. Found out later that there are generally Heinkel 111s out where I was. Boy, I'm still shaking about that. It's just something you feel that's hard to explain.

Just two days later he wrote:

They called on the radio and told me to land at once because of the weather. I came down through the clouds, but they had closed in to about 150 feet. I had to have them direct me home by radio, but it was raining to beat hell and was awfully dark. I didn't see the drome until they shot a red flare up through the clouds. I was flying at sixty feet and throttled back to 160 miles per hour. When I saw the field I never made a turn and pan-caked [landed] so quick in my life. The ambulance was waiting there like a vulture, but once again I fooled them.

Whether flying, attending class or wandering around town, one topic that was always part of the conversation was food. While the fare at the mess was certainly better than that of most Englishmen, it was still a far cry from a normal American menu. As Gover and his classmates went into the small dining room at the mess and plunked themselves down at the tables for four, they could almost always predict what the menu would be. And the young WAAF privates who were responsi-ble for serving were unable to gloss over the fact that there would be some form of Brussels sprouts, potatoes, maybe some fish such as kippers in milk, bread, tea and that was it. But the lack of variety in the menu was not because the British didn't try to serve their pilots the best they could get. There just wasn't enough food. Gover made special mention of breaks in this monotonous diet. "Mause just gave me half a doughnut—the first I've had in England." "Guess what, I had an orange today for lunch. California, here I come."

During the cold of mid-January, Gover decided to walk the two miles into Llantwitt Major "because the gal at the tea room said she could get me an egg—just like the prohibition days in the United States. (You are only allowed one egg a month here.)" Tongue in cheek, Lee wrote his folks, "Boy oh boy, do I eat these days. I even eat soft fried eggs (one a month). Really, you eat what you get, but I'd just about go nuts for ice cream." Almost every letter home asked for candy bars, chewing gum, chocolates, cookies, coffee, tea, sugar and the like. So when the young pilots got into town, the first objective was to see if they could find a steak or, if that failed, maybe an egg. It was not until later that they discovered many of the steaks they were able to get were horsemeat.

Invitations to English homes were welcome because they provided some relief to the diet at the mess, but they also produced a feeling of guilt, because the English usually insisted on serving the best they could to the pilots even if it meant doing without later in the month. To offset this situation, the RAF officers would give some of their ration coupons to the hostess, but even more welcome was some item, such as coffee or sugar, that the British couldn't get. Even an onion was welcome.

When we were on the *Emma Alexander*, I went to the bridge one evening and was talking to the first mate. I asked him what the people in England missed most in the line of food. To my amazement, he said an onion. So I talked one of the cooks out of a large yellow onion and wrapped it up and put it in my suitcase. I packed it to London, down to Bournemouth and clear across England to Llantwitt Major. Then on the 9th of February, Jay Reed and I went to the medical officer's house for dinner. It was a five-mile walk each way, and was it cold. Anyway, he had a homesick American wife and thought our coming to dinner, even if the meal was sparse, would help bolster her morale. I took my onion along, and when I gave it to her you would think that I brought her a ten-pound roast. She actually had tears in her eyes, and not from the onion. We had a swell meal, but the five-mile walk back to the base was sure long, what with guards shouting at us to halt every now and then. I was so tired when I finally arrived back at the base that I couldn't sleep, but I sure felt good about having given that nice lady my onion.

"Shot a game of snooker with Mause, played Ping-Pong with Jay and Don, ate supper and the four of us are now at the hut playing red dog," was a typical entry in Gover's diary. Given the often terrible flying weather during the English winter, time hung heavily on the pilots' hands as they either waited to fly or had only part of the day off. When the entire day was available, most went to a nearby town, no matter how small it was, simply to have something to do. During the first portion of OTU, the students had classes half the day and flew the other half. But in the middle of January, they completed their academics and had longer periods of time available. At Llandow there were no permanent facilities, so activities were at a minimum. The recreation room of the mess, generally the center of nonflying activity at an RAF base, was just a small room with a little fireplace and a few chairs. This precluded having more than one pool table, and even that piece of furniture put a strain on room for any other activity. Further, the Americans were not very interested in the British newspapers and magazines that stocked the mess, and American reading material was almost nonexistent. Thus, cards became the main way to while away the hours. Most games were played for money, and some of the group won considerable amounts, among them Gover. It was not unusual for him to win twenty pounds during a month playing poker, pitch or red dog. (In red dog, each player bets against the dealer, as in blackjack. The bet is that the player has, among the five cards he has been dealt, a higher one of the same suit than the next card the dealer will turn up. Pitch is a more complex game in which six cards are dealt, one suit is named as trump and points are awarded for taking as many tricks as possible in the trump suit.) There was an occasional stage show performed by a traveling company but no theater, so seeing a movie required extra effort. "Mause and I walked the two miles in the mud into town tonight. Bought some tarts but they tasted just like sawdust. Then went to the show. We'd seen it before in the States—*Green Hell*—but it was something to do."

Still, Gover's main attention never strayed far from flying.

Hot dog! Today is a sunny day and I went up in the Spit and just cruised around up above the clouds in the sun. I had a hell of a good dogfight—damn near tore the plane to pieces. One of the boys caught fire and crashed on landing. He has a fractured skull, a broken arm, and a broken wrist and his legs are badly hurt. He was a Canadian sergeant and one swell fellow. We were playing cards together yesterday. I sure hope he makes it. Jay and I are now playing our game of pitch.

A week before graduation from OTU, the base was visited by Air Marshal Sir Sholto Douglas, the chief of the Royal Air Force.

Everything is spic-and-span, for tomorrow is our big day. We'll put on our big fly pass for the big shot himself. The Commander and Chief of the whole RAF will be here. The wing commander here and two squadron leaders will lead the flight. There were nine of us students chosen to fly with them, and I'm the only American. Hurrah for me. I'm getting my shoes shined and pants pressed for tomorrow.

Tuesday, February 17, 1942   Well, today was the big day. The Chief flew in and inspected the whole camp. We put on our air review for him and it really went over swell. The visibility was only about a quarter of a mile and it was a hard job to keep the field in sight. Still, we really did a good job.

As if to capitalize on his flying ability, Lee's last two flights at OTU were formation.

There were four of us and I was flying box and you are really boxed in, too. I had to fly with my prop just back and below the leader's tail wheel, about five feet. It's sure a nice formation, except if either side man slides in or the leader drops, well, you've had it.

"I thought a lot about the Spitfire and what I had learned over the past couple of months during my last day at OTU," Gover remembered.

The first thing that struck most of us about the Spitfire was how small the cockpit really was and how many gauges, switches and instruments there were. For someone who had flown nothing more complicated than an AT-6, the Spitfire cockpit was really something. It was all business. At first I thought it was pretty cramped, since the sides were only a couple of inches from your shoulders and you only had an inch or so of headroom with the canopy closed, but it was actually quite comfortable. It took a few hours of just sitting in the cockpit on the ground before I felt familiar with the whole layout. I think the thing that made me realize that this plane was really a combat fighter was having the gunsight right in front of your face all the time. Even in training, you were conscious of it. I was also awed by the size of the engine. It seemed to stick out in front of the cockpit for yards and yards. Because of the attitude of the plane and the length of the cowling covering the engine, all you could see when you looked straight ahead on the ground was sky.

Getting in the Spitfire also reminded you that this was a high-performance fighter. You really couldn't get all strapped in without the help of the fitter. After you climbed from the wing over the side of the cockpit and sat down on your parachute, he leaned in to help you get the straps right, plug in the microphone and the oxygen, and generally check to see that you were set to go. For a large engine, the Merlin was easy to start; a couple of shots on the primer, hit the starter switch and it would always catch right away. I never ceased to be impressed with how smooth that engine was. There was none of the vibration and shaking that I had come to expect on most planes that I had flown.

In many ways, the toughest part of flying the Spitfire was moving around on the ground. Because of the big engine out in front, you had to turn slightly to the right and the left so you could see what was in front of you. Fortunately, we never had to taxi very far, because most of the fields were grass and we could just point right into the wind and be ready to take off. Besides, you couldn't taxi very long, since the engine would begin to overheat from having so little air flowing through the radiators. The narrow undercarriage added to the challenge, especially on landing. It really wasn't hard to control the plane on the ground, you just had to be careful.

I'll never forget my first takeoff. I gave a little throttle and she started moving forward toward the open field ahead. I had trimmed her to takeoff settings, so I slowly opened the throttle to full power, and how that beautiful Rolls-Royce engine screamed. It was easy to keep her going straight down the field with a little rudder pressure, and as the tail came up it was just a matter of getting enough airspeed to lift her off. At eighty miles per hour, I eased back ever so gently on the control stick and up she went. I pulled my gear and flaps up and adjusted the engine RPM, and as it gained airspeed I kept adjusting the trim tabs so there was no control pressure to maintain. What a beautiful airplane to fly, and she climbed like crazy. I also got the canopy closed right after takeoff, since it was winter. I had flown mostly open-cockpit planes, or ones like the AT-6 where you left the cockpit open for takeoff, so taking off with the canopy open, as we did with the Spit, was not unusual to me. And I think it helped during the first few flights to know that if there was a problem, the canopy was already open so you could get out easily.

She reacted instantly to any movement of the controls. As I turned and banked, climbed and dived, the aircraft made me feel that I was built right into her. She was just part of me, and no matter what you asked her to do, she did it. She was very, very sensitive on the controls but a dream to fly. On my first try at an aileron roll, I moved the spade grip to the side, and before I even knew what was happening, I had gone around twice. But she was also very stable and easy to fly straight and level for instrument work. It was a very predictable plane. Some aircraft do unexpected things when they stall or you try to do certain maneuvers, but not the Spit. She was so smooth and held no surprises in any way. I often marveled at how this plane could be so easy and civilized to fly and yet how it could be such an effective fighter, able to hold its own with any plane in the world.

Landing the Spitfire was also easy. We always flew a 360-degree overhead pattern. This meant that you came in low over the field, sometimes at only ten or twenty feet, and then pulled up in a climbing left turn so you could keep the field in sight. When you lost enough airspeed, you put down the landing gear and, as you turned back toward the field, lowered the flaps. Then it was just a matter of setting up a good descent and, when you were over the runway, leveling out and closing the throttle, and she would settle right in. You did have to work the rudder to keep her straight while you were slowing down, especially in a crosswind, because she could get away from you with that narrow gear. I never had any trouble landing, and after a few flights, the Spit was as easy to handle on the ground as any plane I had flown. I fell in love with the Spitfire immediately.

Gover and his three friends graduated from the operational training unit on February 23, 1942. He had thirty-six hours and fifteen minutes flying time in the Spitfire, and he summed up his thoughts in a letter home.

We have finished here and are to be posted tomorrow. Jay and I were informed this afternoon that we are the two to stay here as instructors. My log book was signed "above average, retained as staff pilot." Mause may also stay but doesn't know yet. We will be here about a month more and will then go to squadrons. So we now say so long to all of the gang we have been with. They all shove off tomorrow for different parts of England. We all get a seven-day leave now, so Jay and I are going to London. We will come back here then and lead formation, dogfights and such with the next bunch, and when they leave, then we are to go to a squadron. There have been a lot of different nationalities represented here—French, Dutch, Belgians, Canadians, Czechs, Poles, South Africans, Australians, New Zealanders, Norwegians and a total of fourteen Americans.

I had to take a taxi back from Cardiff on Sunday and it cost about $7—Wow. Jay bought a bike, and I think I might do the same, since I will be here awhile. I'd buy a car, but you can only get about four gallons of petrol a month. I'd like to have a U.S. motor scooter. I could just put a sponge in the Spit's tank, then run over and squeeze it in my scooter and run a week.

I was flying a new Spitfire today, and you just can't imagine how they go up. Remember, Dad, when we would swoop up about five hundred feet. Well, I can just take off and pull it up like that and just keep on going.

For Gover's class at OTU, the next big adventure began the following afternoon.

Got all ready and at 2:00 p.m. this afternoon we were taken to Bridgend. There we caught the 3:40 train and are just now about to arrive at Paddington Station in London. I don't know where I'll stay, but I have seven days' leave, so who cares. —10:30 p.m. Went to the American Eagle Club, but they were full and so was the Regent Palace Hotel so finally got a room at Hamilton House. It's not so hot, so Jay and I will move tomorrow. I rode my first subway tonight. They just shove you in, slam the door, go like hell and then shove you out again. They really get you where you want to go, though, and in a hurry too. This hotel is right on Piccadilly Circus and in the center of things. All the rest of the boys are now going their separate ways. Sure a bunch of nice fellows, about fifty of them. Hope I see some of them again after the war is over.

As it turned out, Lee saw very few of these friends after the war. Of the forty-three students and instructors who posed for a photograph at the beginning of training (see photo insert), thirty-three were killed. The remainder—except for Lee and four others (two not in the picture)—were so badly wounded in combat or injured in noncombat crashes that they were declared unfit to fly. Such a devastating attrition rate was not unusual for RAF pilots who began flying against the Germans early in the war.

Lee's effort to get acquainted with London began in earnest the next day with his second ride on the underground.

I've had a busy morning. Lost Jay on the subway so don't know when I'll see him again. I started to look for a hotel, but they are all still full. Met two of the fellows from Bakersfield, Bolton and Smith. It was good to see them and tell them a little of what they had waiting for them at OTU. Then ran into Young and Frahm (another friend from OTU) at the American Eagle Club, where I am just ordering a hamburger and a bottle of Coke—can you imagine that. —6:00 p.m. Young and I have finally got a room here at the Regent Palace Hotel. It sure is a swell joint.

Lee described the events of the next day to his folks on beautiful Regent Palace Hotel stationery.

Well, I came in here to take the town and instead it took me. I had my wallet stolen last night to the tune of a hundred and twenty-five bucks (my worldly total) and all my identification papers and such, so I'm a man without a country. I was going to buy you some trinkets, but you'll have to wait. Anyway, there are some pretty buildings and places here that I can see free. This is sure a swell hotel, too. I went to the American Eagle Club and met five of the boys I had known in Bakersfield.

The American Eagle Club, conveniently located at 28 Charing Cross Road, was visited almost daily by most of the American pilots when they were in London. Funded by the American Red Cross, it served as an unofficial headquarters for American pilots in London during the early days of the war. It was generally the first place an American would go when arriving in London, since it was the easiest place to meet your friends and find out who was in town. The club also was one of the few places where one could get a hamburger and Coke and read an American newspaper or magazine. The large main sitting room was furnished with overstuffed chairs and sofas as well as tables for writing letters or playing cards. It provided a good place to relax, plan the next activity in London or just catch up on the news of other Americans. Interestingly, the King of England and members of the Royal Family would occasionally drop into the club to talk to the Americans and thank them for coming to England.   Once a week, a radio broadcast originated from the Eagle Club during which some of the American pilots had the opportunity to talk to the folks back home. If you knew your schedule in advance, it was possible to let your folks in the United States know when to listen for you. Most of the time, however, parents and friends never knew if their son would be talking, so they just listened out of habit.

Gover's diary continues:

—3:00 p.m. I am now at the American Eagle Club on Charing Cross Road and am supposed to broadcast to the States in a little while. —1:30 a.m. Boy, was I nervous at the broadcast. Radio stars there and all, and that little old mike just scared the hell out of me. [Gover did not know in advance that he was making this broadcast, so his folks did not hear it.] Young and I went to see *Blood and Sand* at the Odeon Theater after the broadcast. It was a good show and the theater is beautiful. Had dinner and then took in some of the places. You have to beat the women off with a club.

Friday, February 27, 1942   Got stocked up on money again this morning by going over to Lloyd's of London. They sure were swell about fixing me up—it pays to have my English account with them. Don Young and I went out to Westminster Abbey and looked it over, then through St. James's Park and up Victoria Street. I bought a gramophone on New Bond Street. Had lunch in a little café on Regent Street. Went to a show this afternoon and then to the Eagle Club. Went to the Princess Club tonight, and oh, what a night. Everyone in there bought me a drink—all mixed stuff. I still haven't developed a taste for warm beer. Sure got stinko.

Saturday, February 28, 1942 Still staggering this morning. Boy, what a night. I really got around. That old USA on my sleeve does all right. The phone woke me up this morning. It was one of the gals from last night. They don't give up. Went out to the Thames this morning and took some pictures. Walked over London Bridge, fed the pigeons and seagulls in St. James's Park. It's about time to clean up and eat. Then take up where I left off last night.

Sunday, March 1, 1942 Had a darn good time last night, and this morning I went back out to London Bridge and took some pictures. Went on down to St. Paul's Cathedral. It sure is old and beautiful. Everything is completely bombed flat all around it. One bomb had gone right down through it but otherwise it is all intact. Just had lunch at the Eagle Club and now am going to take a long, hot bath. —Midnight. Had a wonderful time tonight. Met two beautiful gals on the subway as I was on my way out to Temple's for dinner. They gave me their apartment number and I went over there later. They set up drinks and started the music going. When I got back to the hotel, Rose telephoned and wanted me to come on over. You know, I like this town. Having a grand time and wishing you were here but it sure is wicked.

Monday, March 2, 1942 Well, this is the end of my stay in London. Sure had a swell time. Said goodbye to Don Young, who is going to 130 Squadron down at Perranporth in Cornwall, but I'll see him again in London. Caught the 11:55 train out of London. Came on back to camp and who should be there as new pupils but George Middleton and Len Ryerson, two of the boys of my class in Bakersfield, California. Seems funny, I'm to be their instructor.

The next day, Lee wrote home and summed up his week in London but, as usual, omitted any reference to the girls he had met.

Well, I got refinanced in London and really enjoyed it all. I took in some good shows, went all through Westminster Abbey, walked over London Bridge, through St. Paul's Cathedral (boy, it is really big and beautiful), fed the pigeons and ducks in St. James's Park.

Took in all the night spots and hiked around Trafalgar Square and Piccadilly Circus and did just about everything else. Met some of the old gang at the American Eagle Club, had beans on toast, Coca-Cola, hamburgers and chewing gum there. Boy, oh boy. Seems funny to be an instructor when just a couple of months ago I just looked with awe at a Spitfire. Don't worry about me.

Just two days after returning to Llandow, Gover wrote:

I left home four months ago yesterday but it sure seems like a very long time ago. I have decided that I will be staying in the RAF for a while since no one seems to know anything about us transferring to the American Army.

Lee raised the topic of transfer on a number of occasions when writing to his folks, and it was often a subject of conversation around the fire in the mess. There was also a great deal of speculation among the pilots Gover talked with at the Eagle Club while he was in London. Three months earlier, just after Pearl Harbor, a number of Americans in the Eagle Squadrons (Numbers 71, 121 and 133 Squadrons of Fighter Command, which were composed solely of American volunteers) had gone to the American embassy to talk about being transferred to the American forces now that the United States was in the war. They had been told that such a transfer would eventually take place but not in the near future. Apparently this was not well known to those Americans who were in other squadrons, since Gover and his friends at Llandow continued to speculate about the possibility of transfer until March 11, when they were read a letter from the United States saying "they don't intend to bring us back so I guess I'm without a country, but it doesn't bother me a bit now."

Although Lee officially began his duties as an instructor the day after he returned from his leave in London, he did not fly for the next four days because of the weather. However, he soon found that his new position had its rewards.

Thursday, March 5, 1942 Boy, this instructor business is all right. Just sat around at the mess in front of the fire today. About 3:00 p.m., the CO said we (the instructors) could have a bus to go into Cardiff, so twelve of us came on in. [As a student, Lee had had to walk the two miles to the village of Llantwitt Major and then get a train to go the other seven miles to Cardiff.] I even got a steak at the Model Inn. —12:00 midnight. Just arrived back at camp. What a night was had by all. Plenty of women and beer (still warm). It has been snowing all evening and everything is sure pretty and white.

The weather cleared enough for flying on March 7, and Gover flew four times that day and twice the next. As an instructor, he was even more concerned with student accidents. "Two of the new boys cracked up ships today," he wrote. "Another fellow from the senior course went into a spiral dive and was killed. We found his head in a tree and arms and legs here and there. Sure a mess."

On March 11, Lee summed up his job for his parents.

I received my first package the other day. It was the one-pound box of candy that you sent January 20th. I don't know what happened to the others. This instructing business isn't so bad and also isn't so good. I give dual in a two-place ship that has a mere 850 horsepower, which isn't exactly like flying a Cub. The other day one fellow came in fast, hit on the wheels and then yanked back on the stick. There we were looking straight up at about 50 feet and in a dead stall. Then he willingly let me have the airplane. That's the part I don't like. I'll be leaving here on the 24th but won't know where I'm going until the last day. I'm still flying the Spitfire also and I like them better every day but will be glad to get out of this mudhole that I am in now. I was told yesterday that there is now no chance of getting home and transferring to the U.S. forces, so I guess that is that. —5:15 p.m. I've just come in from flying and am having tea. I'm going English, I guess, because I'm beginning to enjoy it. I also received my battle dress today, so I am ready to go. I am now finished giving dual and have all the boys on Spitfires, so will start leading formations and such. Then, when they get a little further advanced, I'll dogfight and such with them. That's the part I like. It is sure fun screaming around up there trying different ways to get them. This war business is just like a game of checkers—you just have to outguess the next one and you use human lives instead of wooden disks.

About the same time that Lee wrote that letter, he received one from his mother, the only letter from her that survived the war.

Received your picture on February 19th, one day less than a month by boat. We were so glad you sent one and all think it's grand. Of course, I think it's beautiful and everyone wants to take a look at it. Your uniform looks pretty spiffy—wish we could see you in person wearing it. Quite often in the newsreel we see some RAF boys but haven't seen you yet.

Well, I feel pretty disgusted over the fact that you have never gotten a package—I've sent six. A lady I met who works in a store in Redwood City sends a package to her mother in England each week and she gets them all, so I'm going to inquire from her as to how she does it. Do they censor my letters to you like they do those you send us? We are all fine, but your dad won't be able to build much from now on as things are getting pretty well frozen around here. Take care of yourself, be careful flying, and write each week.

On March 17, "checked out my last pilot, a classmate of mine in Bakersfield, Len Ryerson." It was also traditional to take some of the ground crew up for a flight in the Miles Master to thank them for all their hard work on the planes. "I did some aerobatics and showed them a good time. They seemed to really like it. I have to treat them nice, since they keep the ships running." Unfortunately, Gover also got the news that another of his classmates from Bakersfield, David Logan, had been killed in an aircraft accident.

Gover's final morning at Llandow was spent leading a formation to check out three OTU students, George Middleton and Lyn Ryerson, who were in his class at Bakersfield, and Pilot Officer Taylor, who was in a later class. "Checked things in and got cleared so I can leave in the morning. Took a WAAF gal to the show, then finished packing."

March 24, 1942 Up at 5:00 a.m. Got a lorry and was taken to Bridgend, where we (Mause, Reed, Martin and myself) caught the train at 7:20. Changed trains at Cardiff and I said goodbye to Mause and Jay Reed (they are posted north to a new Typhoon squadron). It was hard to say "so long" to them after all we have been through together. All I could do was wish them well and hope that we all meet again. Martin and I went on to Bristol, changed trains again, came on down through Exeter, changed again at Plymouth. This is getting to be very nice country and the sun is shining. Came on over to Redruth and said goodbye to Martin. I'm now all alone and on my way to 66 Squadron of RAF Fighter Command.

The months of training with his friends that had started in Bakersfield were over. Lee was an operational fighter pilot in the RAF. Although he knew he was prepared, he could not help being apprehensive about what was to come.

3. SHOOTING REAL BULLETS

WELL, AT LEAST THEY'RE EXPECTING ME, THOUGHT LEE after calling the base at Portreath and being told that a lorry was on its way into Redruth to pick him up. After all, I know the squadron commander from when I was at OTU, so things should work out just fine. That was not to be, however.

> After the short drive to the base, I reported in to the adjutant only to find that the squadron commander, Squadron Leader Cremin, the only one here I knew, and a sergeant pilot had been killed in a midair crash during the afternoon. What a start. I never even got to tell the squadron leader hello. This sure is the real thing. Ate dinner and was shown my room and so to bed. Have sort of a lost feeling tonight.

> **Wednesday, March 25, 1942** Caught the lorry at 7:45 a.m. and came up to the drome. Ate breakfast and went down to the adjutant's office. Signed in and was assigned to A Flight. Looked at the new cannon-armed Spits that they have, came in for dinner, then back out to the flight line. I am now back at the mess. Everything here is sure different from OTU. They are busy on convoy and interception work. I'll bring my gear up and probably start flying tomorrow. It kind of scares a guy to know you are finally in the big show and playing for keeps.

Despite his underlying apprehension, Lee also had a real sense of both pride and accomplishment as he wrote home his second day at Portreath.

It has taken a long time since I signed up in Oakland, but I have finally made the grade and am now an operational fighter pilot. We have brand-new ships and things are beginning to buzz. I am the only American in the squadron and don't know a soul, but they treat me OK. There are nine different nationalities of us pilots, so I'll be talking everything from Rhodesian to New Zealand. I traded in all my equipment today for the latest stuff, which is pretty good. I got a new helmet, goggles, oxygen mask and boots as well as a swell fur-lined flying jacket. The country here is far nicer than Wales. All low rolling country, and we are right on the edge of the sea. It's bad country for a forced landing, but otherwise OK. I had five letters waiting for me when I arrived here. As I was feeling kind of low and lonesome when I got here, they made me feel better. I live in an old English place down by the village and have a batman who wakes me in the mornings, gives me a cup of tea and cleans everything for me, so it's not so bad.

As far as facilities on the base were concerned, Portreath was little different from Llandow. Both the barracks and the mess were wartime buildings with the usual board-and-tar-paper exterior and a very basic interior. The living facilities were located about half a mile from the flight line, which meant a walk each morning and evening. Portreath had a hard-surfaced runway, a feature that many wartime bases in Britain lacked. Because of this runway, the base was used as a staging location for Lockheed Hudson two-engine bombers, which flew as far south as the Bay of Biscay on submarine patrol, and was also home for the only two helicopters in the RAF, both of which crashed while Gover was stationed there. The base itself was located about a mile up a hill from the picturesque village of Redruth, which had several pubs and also staged a number of dances each week. This gave the pilots some diversion when they were not on duty. The entire complex was located right on the ocean with numerous beaches, secluded coves and high cliffs with gorgeous views. No wonder Gover fell in love with the area almost immediately.

Three days after arriving, Lee made his first flight as an operational RAF fighter pilot and also got an initial acquaintance with the local community.

Friday, March 27, 1942   Was up for the first time today, went up in a Spitfire IIA. It was a long-range job with an auxiliary tank under the left wing. They take off differently but fly OK. Stayed up forty-five minutes. Went down around Land's End and back up the coast getting to know the landmarks. Then this afternoon, I was up for another hour getting the feel of the ship and the lay of the land. Had a lot of fun last night at the local pub.

The day after his first flight, Gover was introduced to standing alert, something he would do for countless hours during the remainder of his time in the RAF.

Was at breakfast this morning when I heard an explosion and out on the runway one of the Lockheed Hudsons [two-engine bombers] had crashed and was burning. The crew came tumbling out, but the ship burned to a cinder. I then went to my first session of alert duty. I was on thirty-minute alert when the call came in to scramble as Jerries were approaching. One of our sections went up but returned in about an hour not having made contact. I left the dispersal hut at 5:00 p.m. and walked down the cliff to my quarters.

There were generally three types of alert, although exact procedures varied from squadron to squadron. Unless he had a scheduled mission or an unusual day off, a fighter pilot spent every day on some type of alert.

Cockpit alert was the most trying, since the pilot was either strapped in the aircraft or else sitting on the wing or very near the plane, with the external battery power connected so he could start the engine and give it full power immediately when a red flare was shot into the air indicating a scramble. Either the pilot or the fitter (crew chief) would run the engine periodically so it was always warm. The time allowed to become airborne varied; at Portreath the pilots in Gover's squadron had thirty seconds. Because of the stress involved in having to be ready to go so rapidly, and the boredom of just sitting in the cockpit, a pilot was generally on this duty for two hours, off two hours and back on two hours for the entire duty period of the day.

Lee described the next-lower phase of alert in a letter to his parents a few days after arriving in the squadron.

Now that I'm in an operational squadron things are different. The planes are really taken care of and always warmed up and ready to go. So when we get a call you know it's going to take off. Everything is done right. We are sitting in the dispersal hut and word comes to scramble. While we run to the machine, the crews have it started. Red rockets are shot in the air to warn all ships to clear the field. The crew has your parachute on you and has you strapped in while you put on your helmet. Then you pour on the coal and take off on any runway. From then on your radio does the job. All this is done in a couple of minutes.

On any given day, most of the pilots in the squadron would be on thirty-minute alert. In this status, they were allowed to be at the mess, where they could play cards, shoot pool, read, write letters or even go out skeet shooting. (The last activity was actually encouraged, since it sharpened a pilot's ability to judge the speed of a moving target and lead it more accurately.) Wherever he might be, a pilot would have to get to the flight line in the allotted time, generally to take the place of a pilot who had been upgraded to the next-higher phase of alert. Accounts of the life of RAF fighter pilots often give the mistaken impression that they had little to do—that they sat around the mess all morning and shot skeet or did something similar in the afternoon. This cannot be equated to time off, because on a moment's notice, any pilot could be moved from this thirty-minute status to being next in line to be scrambled after a German aircraft or to meet an oncoming Luftwaffe attack.

One of Gover's favorite places in all of England turned out to be Redruth, the small, quaint village near the base at Portreath. "It was just what anyone would imagine a little old English town to be," he wrote his folks.

The people are so friendly and the old USA on the shoulder always starts a conversation with someone. Most of the men that you meet in the pubs are veterans of World War I and they are always anxious to talk. They don't buy you a beer because they don't have any money, so you buy them one. Was getting my hair cut the other day when the air raid sirens started to blow and the bombs began to fall. Are these people tough! The barber never stopped clipping, but I felt like crawling under the table. Last Sunday, I hiked down to the beach and found the swellest little cottage tucked in a little cove. It is called the Smuggler's Hideout. The most quaint and different place I've ever seen. Had tea and cakes and then on home.

One of the most difficult parts of being in an operational squadron was funerals. While death had become a reality to Gover during OTU, he had been insulated from it to some degree because the students did not have to attend funerals. In an operational squadron all the pilots were required to attend the funeral of one of their comrades. And so only six days after arriving in Number 66 Squadron, Gover was detailed to be a pallbearer for Squadron Leader Cremin's funeral.

Got up at 6:00 a.m., up to breakfast and then down to Redruth, where we took Squadron Leader Cremin's body to the train (we were together at OTU in Llandow). Then this afternoon we buried Sergeant Ritchie in the local churchyard. There are just too damn many fresh graves down there that were our boys of 66 Squadron. It really gets you thinking, and I can tell it bothers a lot of the fellows—thinking that you could be next. I saw some of the boys standing at attention crying during the funeral. I just have to cope with it all and do the best I can and hope that I make it, but it's tough.

As time went on, Lee wrote, "I have learned to cope with the funerals by just trying to not pay attention to what is going on. That's hard to do but it keeps me from thinking."

On the brighter side, the Sunday after he had discovered the Smuggler's Hideout,

I slipped out of camp and went down and sat on the beach and talked to a little fellow who had been bombed out of London. He lives with his mom because his father has "gone to the war." He kind of reminds me of myself because he was so excited at being able to talk to a fighter pilot and he wanted to know all about airplanes and flying. His name is Rex and he has sure been through a lot for a nine-year-old kid.

Over the course of his stay at Portreath, Gover spent a number of hours sitting on the beach talking to Rex.

> He would wait on the cliff or the beach for hours for me to come and talk to him. We talked about all kinds of subjects, but most of the time we talked about flying. I would take him a candy bar now and then and I wrote him a few letters after I left Portreath. I often wonder if he made it through the war and what became of him.

During his first two weeks at Portreath, Lee had been pretty much the new guy and his flying was limited to learning the local area, getting familiar with firing the cannons on the new Spitfires, standing alert and flying combat formation. The RAF generally flew in a four-ship formation, with each aircraft flying directly behind and below the one ahead. This was not a popular formation, especially with the new pilots, such as Gover, since the fledgling was always relegated to the number four, or last, position. This made him able to see the rest of the formation well, but none of the others could see him. Thus he was the most susceptible to being picked off in any surprise attack by the Germans, who often came up on this formation from below and behind. Several new pilots flying in the number four position simply disappeared as they were shot down before anyone else in the formation knew it was being attacked. On April 8,

> I went out to the flight line and up on a formation check with the flight commander. He said I was hot and would start up on the heavy stuff tomorrow, which is both good and bad. Good because I get right into the action and bad for the same reason. Went up again this afternoon and really got right in there. Sure shook up the flight leader, though. He kept screaming at me to get away, but I figured that since we were told that we would have a better chance against the Germans if we kept the formation tight, they could count on me. Walked down to the beach late this afternoon and had an egg on toast at the Smuggler's Hideout. This evening I went into Redruth and took in a little dance at the Ambulance Hall. Met a hell of a swell gal and thoroughly enjoyed myself.

Lee would remember that evening and the young lady for the rest of his service in the RAF.

I would walk down the hill from our air base, which was up on the cliff, to the little town of Redruth, in the evening after flying was called for the night. There were dances in the village two or three nights a week, to occupy both the airmen at the base and the young ladies in the town. I was having a nice time at the dance one evening and had been dancing a lot with a very cute, short, well-built brunette named Liz. As we danced and talked it was obvious that we were both kind of lonely people who had been put in unusual circumstances by the war. For me, it was being in England and just beginning to fly combat with all the uncertainties that such duty entailed. For her, it was having her father in the army in North Africa and her mother working in an aircraft factory near London and not knowing if any of the young men from the village would ever come home from the war.

As the dancing and the talk got more intimate, she very shyly asked me if I would like to come to her house. She was very attractive and seemed so sincere and it was so nice to have her close to me that I accepted with no hesitation. As we talked, I could tell that she was a very frightened young lady who had no idea what tomorrow might bring. After a little while it was obvious that we were going to become very intimate and I suggested that she turn out the light. She said she couldn't do that, for reasons I don't know, so I put my service hat over the light bulb. We spent a long time making love and finding peace, comfort and release in each other's arms. The war and all the upheaval it had brought seemed far away for a few hours. When I reluctantly departed, after we agreed to meet at the next dance, I noticed that my hat felt very warm. The light bulb had burned through the leather hatband. We met a couple more times, but a few weeks later our squadron got transferred to Ibsley and so I never saw her again. Throughout the rest of my RAF days, however, I was reminded of the young lady and a lovely evening when I forgot about the war, every time I put on my service hat.

Lee's first real operational mission was on April 14, when he flew an hour and a half on convoy patrol, one of the most boring but dangerous missions that a fighter squadron had to fill. Lee remembered:

> Operations would call the squadron and tell us they wanted a patrol sent out (always two planes). They would give us a vector and away we would go. When we saw the ships we would establish radio contact and give them our position, because if we surprised them we could get shot at. Patrols usually lasted about one hour and thirty minutes. We would fly about a hundred feet off the water, round and round the convoy. Sometimes I'd get tired of going one way so I'd do a 180-degree turn and go the other way just to break the monotony.
>
> You had to be damn careful, because the weather was always treacherous, and when it was hazy, there was no horizon, and many a pilot flew into the sea. And while flying round and round was boring, it was better than listening to that little voice reminding you that survival in the water was always difficult, even with a dinghy. Engine failure at that low altitude meant you probably could not glide to land and so you had to either ditch, and face an almost certain death on impact, or bail out, and take your unfavorable chances of surviving in that big body of hostile water.
>
> The Germans always knew about the convoys and would send out JU-88s to bomb them when conditions were right. That's why we were there. We all hated convoy duty because it was so boring but it could also be very dangerous.

The next day, as if to ensure that Gover had all his new operational experiences quickly, he had his first scramble and contact with a German aircraft. Lee later wrote:

> On April 15, I met my first enemy aircraft. Two FW-190s came in on a low flight and strafed the streets of Redruth. I flew as number two man on the interception, we made contact and I fired away. I thought I saw hits, but it was probably just smoke as he gave full throttle to get away. I felt good about at least having a crack at those Germans, because they were coming over all the time and dropping their bombs or machine-gunning the streets and then going right out over the water on the deck and you couldn't get them. I think that getting to know some people in

Redruth, the old men at the pubs, the girls at the dances and little Rex, made the attacks on Redruth a more personal thing to me.

Gover flew only two more operational missions while the squadron was at Portreath, but they were enough to establish him as an experienced member of the squadron.

April 22, 1942   Darn busy today with five and a half hours on readiness, then did a cannon test on a new kite [the British referred to an airplane as a kite] and flew two convoy patrols. Three JU-88s attacked the convoy, but we were able to keep them from hitting anything. Chased a plane halfway to France but couldn't get it. Off duty at 8:00 p.m. Came home, cleaned up and went to the dance in the village. Liz was there, so it was a good evening.

April 24, 1942   On readiness this morning and got a scramble for six Jerries off of Portreath. They stayed on the deck and the visibility was so bad that we never found them, so no combat. Got separated from my partner in the clouds so began looking for a place to land. Off to my right I saw an aircraft going my direction, so I thought that I'd just join up on him and hope that he was more experienced than I was and knew where he was going, because I sure didn't. As I got closer, I looked hard at the plane but couldn't see a propeller. I then thought it might be a German but saw the British rondel but still no prop. He saw me about then and pulled right away and lost me. After I got a vector back to base, I told the intelligence officer what I saw and he said I was to say no more about it. [What Gover had seen was Britain's first jet aircraft] Went into Redruth to the show and then to a dance. Met Jean, a cute WAAF, and we took the bus back to the base, hiked down to the beach and stayed a couple of hours. We leave for a base up near Bournemouth on Monday. We are taking the place of a squadron which has lost most of its pilots so we're to take a try at it—sweeps to France every day.

April 27, 1942   Up at 7:00 a.m. Got everything organized and caught the train. Arrived at Ibsley at 8:00 p.m. and on up to the billets. The squadron whose place we are taking has lost eleven men in twenty-four hours and fifty in the last two weeks. We are definitely in the front line of the action. Boy oh boy.

The base at Ibsley was quite a different environment from that at Portreath. Ibsley itself was rather isolated, and there was no transportation available for the pilots. When 66 Squadron arrived at Ibsley, most of the eighteen pilots were sergeants and had quarters very near the base. Since there were only eight officers, they had a four-bedroom farmhouse about half a mile from the base. (The RAF had a large number of noncommissioned officers who were pilots. Because they were not officers, the sergeant pilots had separate living and dining facilities, although they flew the same aircraft in the same formations as the officers. The formation was always led by an officer, however. This system was often criticized, because isolating the sergeant pilots kept them from sharing in all the combat experiences of the unit. Discussions about a certain mission or new tactic usually took place at the officers' mess, since the flight leader was always an officer.)

Since there were only six to eight officer pilots in the squadron at any one time, they could live comfortably in the house, which also was the site of the mess. As at Llandow, going to the base meant a walk unless the lorry was not being used by the squadron commander, in which case it could be dispatched to bring the pilots to the flight line. Ibsley also had a hard-surfaced runway, but with a very unusual feature. At the end of the runway was a huge net, about sixty feet wide and seventy-five feet high. This net, which was normally in the collapsed position at the end of the runway, could be shot into the air in case of a strafing attack in hopes of snagging some of the German aircraft and causing them to crash.

"There were absolutely no recreational facilities on the base," Gover later said. "We did not have a pool table or even a dart board. Boy, did we get bored." While the base was situated close to the large city of Bournemouth, there was no railroad connection with Ibsley, so it was almost impossible to get to town unless you had an entire day available. "It is nice to have a large city close by, but I know I'll miss Redruth," Gover wrote. "I thought the village was so quaint and the people so nice. I really became attached to that little place in the month we were there."

April 28, 1942 Awakened this morning by the air raid siren. Two of the boys were sent up after seven Huns. —11:00 a.m.

There's a hell of a racket outside and the guns are all barking. What a mess.

April 29, 1942   We're on readiness this morning. One of our sections just got a call to take off. When you are on readiness here, you sit in your machine, all strapped in and on the end of the runway. When a red rocket is fired, you have to be in the air in thirty seconds. Boy, they sure mean business here.

That same day, Lee wrote home evidently describing the move and what he was doing at Ibsley. When the letter arrived in San Carlos, so much of it had been cut out by the censor's scissors that it was just a blue paper border framing the air, signed "Love, Lee."

"The last time I was in Bournemouth was when we were just processing into the RAF," Lee wrote. "It is so different to be an operational fighter pilot that all us officers decided to go into town and see who we still knew."

About 6:00 p.m. the phone rang and it was Fighter Command releasing us until dawn. We hurried back to the house and Vic Nissen said, "Let's try to get the CO's lorry and go to Bournemouth. I haven't been there since I left for OTU, and I know this great little bar." Got into our uniforms and the six of us [all officers who lived in the little house at Ibsley] jumped into the lorry and took off for Bournemouth. It was raining and there was mud everywhere. Parked the lorry behind Vic's little pub and had just started walking around the building when we heard an aircraft coming. Thought nothing of it until a bomb hit about sixty yards in front of us. We all hit the ground, and when we got up we were covered with mud. We looked at each other, turned around, got back in the lorry and came home. So goes our big night in Bournemouth. I can't wait to find the Jerry who dropped that bomb.

One of the requirements levied on the squadron at Ibsley was to provide a pilot to ferry aircraft throughout England for various purposes. Probably because he was one of the least experienced combat pilots in the squadron, on May 1, Lee was detailed for three weeks in that duty.

May Day and a very nice and sunny one at that. Caught a bus into Salisbury, then the train to Bristol. Then had to take the bus into Bath because the railway was all blown to hell. Arrived in Bath and what a mess it is—all bombed to hell. This happened last night. People are all homeless and on the move. It sure shakes you to see something like that. Caught another bus to Bathampton and a train from there to Box. Nice officers' mess where I have just cleaned up and had dinner.

After his first day of ferry duty, during which he got lost and had an engine failure, he wrote a long description of his impressions of the job to his folks.

Guess what I'm doing. Ferry work. Don't know what made them think I could do it. I hadn't been out to the delivery flight fifteen minutes when I was handed the papers and a ship to be delivered to Northern Ireland. Boy, that trip shook me. It's a long way and lots of water. I have to fly all types of aircraft. One hour you are flying a trainer that lands at 60 miles per hour and the next one is a fighter that comes in at 120. I have to fly both single- and twin-engine craft.

I was taken by car to another drome yesterday and picked up a ship and started out. Wound up lost and had to force-land at a navy drome. The fog was down on the deck. Got a bearing and went on to where I was supposed to go. Had to wait a couple of hours for a ship to come and pick me up. We just got off the ground and one motor cut out, but plunked it down OK. Waited for it to be fixed and finally arrived back here at 2:00 a.m.

Boy, you have to be one-quarter owl, one-quarter blood-hound, and half crazy for this work. Whoever says ferry work is easy and safe can have my share. The RAF just assumes that you can fly any airplane there is. It's like being a traveling salesman, except you don't have time to meet any farmer's daughters.

There is a very nice mess here at Colerne and my room is in the same building, with lights and hot and cold water, and the food is very good. Only trouble is I don't get to stay at the mess enough. Speaking of food, we each get a jigger of sugar a month, so each morning you take a pinch and put it on your mush. Just before I left Ibsley, I took my whole ounce of sugar and poured it all on my bowl of mush. The guys looked at me like I was nuts. I just wanted to be sure that if I didn't get back from this ferrying job, no one would get the rest of my sugar.

It's so easy to get lost here, because all the fields are very small, all odd shapes, and all look alike. Just thousands of little villages and railroads in all directions, so you are never sure which is what. When I got lost in the squadron, they always brought you home by radio, but we're not allowed to use radio in this work, so that's not so good. I fly some of the big shots around, and boy, if they only knew.

On May 9, when he was about half finished with his ferry duty, Gover wrote another very informative letter home. "I guess when I had more time and no one to talk with, I just wrote better letters," Gover commented later.

Another day, another trip around England. Boy, am I having fun. Sure wish this job would last. Went down to Bath last night with a Czechoslovakian pilot in his little car. Boy, he drives just like all Czechs fly—wide open, wild and reckless. Sure glad to get home in one piece.

Just before I came up here we were on a sweep and now the fellows sing the words to the song "The White Cliffs of Dover" as "There were one-oh-nines [ME-109s, German fighters] over, all over Mr. Gover . . ." There's always something funny that makes you laugh even though you're flirting with death. One day, some silly jerk in the bunch called on the radio and said, "Don't look now, but you're being shot at." It is amazing there wasn't a midair crash with everybody dodging every direction to get away. Another time two of us were sent on an interception and about ten miles out we were called and told there were seven enemy aircraft dead to port. This other fellow called back and said, "How many?" The answer came back, "Seven." My partner said, "Oh, that's what I thought you said." I thought I'd laugh to death. Anyway, we missed them. I've met some of the U.S. Air Corps boys in my travels and they will soon be in on the fighting. The sooner the better, but the good old RAF has sure been giving the Huns hell lately.

During his nearly three weeks of ferry duty, Lee flew the Miles Master (a trainer), Miles Magister (another trainer),

Spitfire, Tiger Moth (a small biplane), Defiant (a fighter), and Hurricane (a fighter); he crossed all of England, including going to Northern Ireland and Scotland, and had two forced landings because of engine failure. He also managed to spend two days in London, where "I met one of the pilots I knew from Bakersfield who said that a couple more of our boys had been shot down. Took in a few places and then met an actress in the Regent Lounge and so another day."

"The Regent Lounge was one of the best places in London to meet some of the more high-class ladies," Gover remembered.

It was really very nice, with paneled walls, thick carpet and plenty of places to sit and talk. It was not unusual to go there during the evening and have a young lady come right up and look to see if you were wearing wings. If you were a pilot you were set. Many a memorable evening began at the Regent Lounge.

On May 19, "packed my gear and was flown back to my squadron at Ibsley." Gover's reward for having been gone three weeks on "easy duty" was his first extended taste of combat. The day after he arrived back at Ibsley, while on a reconnaissance mission near Cherbourg, France, Gover shot down his first German aircraft, an ME-109. Of the party that followed, Lee simply wrote, "How we got home, no one will ever know." The action continued, and just four days later, on May 24:

Went on another shipping reconnaissance to France, but this one began in an unusual manner. The squadron leader was Flight Lieutenant Peter Simpson, a veteran of the Battle of Britain. He is a great guy and I have been anxious to fly with him. After we flew across the north end of the Isle of Wight and to Portsmouth, he signaled us to go into a landing formation. We landed and asked him what was wrong. He said it was teatime and as we were on a fighter sweep, it didn't matter when we got over France, so he thought a spot of tea would do us all good. We went into the mess, had our tea and then flew the mission. Saw six German ships and flew down the coast of France for five minutes. Came home wide open with Jerries on our tail. I got a cannon shell in my wing for my trouble, so I now have a German plane but they almost got me. Boy oh boy.

Lee's first note of any apprehension about combat came on May 29. "Going over France again tomorrow. Boy oh boy, I hope I don't get bumped off, as I go on leave in three days."

May 30, 1942 What did I tell you. I was over France and back before breakfast this morning. One of our boys went in the drink (there were four of us) and ME-109s and FW-190s chased us clear to the English coast.

On May 31, Lee thought that all his concerns about living to go on leave were justified when he embarked on the most ill-fated mission of his career in the RAF. "I was Red Two and we were strapped in our Spitfires on cockpit alert on the edge of the runway," he remembered.

Shortly after the alert period began, a red flare sailed through the sky and off we flew. Right after takeoff, Red One called and said he had to abort as he had a bad surge in power. Control then vectored me toward the Huns at Angels two zero [twenty thousand feet]. I saw them, two ME-109s about one half mile ahead, flying line abreast about two hundred feet apart. I was closing at a pretty good rate. Just as I got in range, the one on my left started a steep turn to the left and the one on my right started a steep turn to the right. I caught on too late to what they were doing. All I could do was to go after one of them. I had no sooner latched onto the one on my left when the one on my right swung in right behind me. I was now between a rock and a hard place. We went round and round, but one of them hit my engine and that's all she wrote.

I had no choice but to bail out, so I jettisoned the canopy, unbuckled my shoulder harness, took off my helmet, climbed out on the wing and away I went. If I had stayed with the plane and crash-landed with no power, I am sure I would have been killed. The Germans circled me once and then headed back toward France. I landed OK and was soon taken back to the base and given a medical checkup, and was flying missions the next day. The old-timers gave me a good-humored "bad time" for falling for the "old squeeze play." My only consolation was that I got strikes on one of them. Sixty seconds earlier I had visions of sneaking up on them and shooting both of them down. What a difference a minute makes. I was a much wiser fighter pilot after that day.

This account was written after the war, because Gover did not want to put things in his diary that might cause his parents concern if they read it. Both of Lee's sisters, Juanita and Betty, said that Lee's mother was terrified about his being in combat and was quite convinced that he would be killed. In his diary Lee simply wrote, "Was sent out twice on scrambles. One time to 27,000 feet after a Jerry and another time to 23,000 feet. We chased them awhile and then they would chase us." The entry in his log book notes, "Shot down by two ME-109s. Bailed out near the coast at Bournemouth."

"I knew that my mother was always very worried about me," Lee remembered.

I would have liked to tell my folks about all our survival equipment, because it might have made them worry less. On the other hand it could have caused them to worry more about my being shot down. Each of us had a personal bail-out or escape kit in our breast pocket. It had silk maps of France and the Low Countries, a file, several kinds of currency to use if you were able to evade capture, a compass, a box of waterproof matches and a three-inch knife you carried in your boot. The knife was interesting because it had one blade and a long needle in it. The needle was to puncture your dinghy in case it accidentally inflated on crash-landing or in combat and kept you from being able to move in the cockpit or get out of the airplane. We actually had three compasses. One was just a plain navigation compass in the kit. The second was a collar button on your shirt. You could take it off, scrape off the paint on the back of the button, and there was a compass. The third was a small one that could be inserted into any body orifice to hide it for future use. These kits were so good that most of us used them for the remainder of the war. A lot of us added a small flask—I filled mine with brandy—for use if you needed to steady your nerves after bailing out or crash-landing.

June 1, 1942 Now I know why the squadron that we replaced at Ibsley lost all of its pilots. This afternoon our whole wing here (three squadrons and thirty-six planes) flew up to Redhill, refueled and were briefed. Took off at 6:00 p.m. and went over France at fifteen thousand feet. The flak was sure popping around us, and how. The Calais Silk Factory, where they make parachutes, was the target. We were out for an hour and thirty minutes. This sure is a nerve-racking business. Arrived back at Ibsley at 10:35 p.m. When I checked out my machine, I found nine holes from flak. They are really after me.

When Gover departed for his week in London on June 2, he did not know that he would not fly again until July 21. He was not thinking of the future, however, and began his leave on a high note.

Tuesday, June 2, 1942 Happy days. Packed a kit and arrived in London at 4:00 p.m., checked in at the Regent Palace. Went to the Eagle Club and met Tabb [a friend from Bakersfield], had a hamburger and went out with a little actress this evening. Really did all right my first night in town.

Wednesday, June 3, 1942 Met Tabb at the Eagle Club and we went to a leg show at the Windmill at 12:30. We were invited to the Palladium at 7:15 and were the guests of Bebe Daniels and Ben Lyon. [Daniels and Lyon were well-known American entertainers before World War II.] We were in her dressing room for an hour having drinks and talking with them. Then we went out front and saw the show, "Gangway." Was sure good. She sang "Night and Day" for me. We met them after the show and had a party. They're from Santa Monica, so we had a lot to talk about.

Thursday, June 4, 1942 Went out to lunch with Jacky, one of the gals in a show here. Then this evening I met Hancock (a fellow from California). We made the rounds. Jim Barow and Bob Fraham [students at Bakersfield but not in Lee's class] were killed. Not many of us left.

On Friday, Gover took time to write his folks about London and his activities.

I finally got my leave and here I am in London again. I've seen a few of the boys, but the majority have been posted to heaven. Night before last I was the guest of Bebe Daniels and Ben Lyon. They are the ones who host the radio broadcast to the United States every week from the Eagle Club. Was in her dressing room for an hour having a couple of drinks and talking about Santa Monica and such. We then went out front and had a box all to ourselves. Saw the show, and it was sure good. We were quite the celebrities with spotlights and such. They sure treated us swell. Then went out with some of the chorus girls. The Eagle Club manages to get us into any show, and it's sure swell having such a place. I was very glad to get leave, as we have been damn busy lately and a little of that goes a long way. I was surprised at the number of U.S. boys over here now. I've seen all branches of the service here in the last two days, and things should really get hot soon.

My Spitfire is being overhauled while I'm away. I just about killed the poor thing one day and it hasn't been the same. But we're good pals and I sure put all my hopes in the old iron. This stuff of flying through flak is not as much fun as the movies make out. [This is as close as Gover came to telling his folks about his having to bail out or having his plane shot full of holes from flak.] P.S. There hadn't been an air raid in London for seven months until the night I arrived, and boy, I was the first into the shelter.

Lee's leave ended unexpectedly the next day.

Saturday, June 6, 1942   Got up around 10:00 a.m., had breakfast and went to the Eagle Club. There was a telegram there instructing me to report back to the squadron, so there goes my leave, shot to hell.

Ever since his arrival in England, Lee had been plagued by sore throats and periods of not feeling very well. While he was at OTU, the problem had been diagnosed as his tonsils, and he had been scheduled to have them removed while he was at Llandow. The hospital had not been able to take him, however, so he had been put on the waiting list. As luck would have it, his name came up while he was on leave in London, and so three days after his arrival back at Ibsley, Lee began his trip to the hospital.

Caught a bus and went into Salisbury, got the 12:30 p.m. train to Trowbridge, transferred and came on to Swindon. Got a room, went into town and had tea, then to a show, where I saw *One of Our Aircraft Is Missing*. It was pretty good.

June 11, 1942   Caught a bus to Wroughton and walked about five miles out to the hospital. Ate lunch and then sat around in the sun until supper. All set for tomorrow—I think—anyway, I sure have a beautiful nurse.

The operation was postponed, however, for Lee had developed another cold. He sat around the hospital for the next week waiting for his cold to clear up so he could have the problem tonsils removed.

Friday, June 19, 1942   Well, today's the day. I had a cup of tea and one piece of toast at 6:00 a.m. It is just now 8:00 a.m., so I'll soon be getting the old shot and wheeled away.

Friday, June 26, 1942   Boy, a lot of things have happened since the 19th, but I've been too weak to move, let alone write. I went on the table at 11:00 a.m. that morning and for four days didn't know or care whether I lived or died. I had a temperature of 104 degrees for those first four days, and they had to keep me going on oxygen during the second night. Didn't eat a thing for six days and couldn't even drink. This is going on the eighth day now, and I feel fairly well. I got up for the first time this afternoon to take a bath and couldn't even stand by myself. So if this is something they do to kids, there should be a law against it.

The same day he wrote a reassuring letter to his folks telling them, "They give you wonderful care here and they really have the best docs in the world on these stations." He also talked about having a couple of weeks of sick leave, "which I asked to spend with a quiet old couple at some wooded estate in the country, maybe near Redruth. They said it could be arranged—they sure do everything they can for you here."

Saturday, June 27, 1942 Feeling pretty good today but still very weak. The Red Cross was in to see me the other day, and this morning a can of "Texas" grapefruit juice, a can of pears and a jar of honey arrived for me. They sure look after us fellows in trouble. The American Red Cross lady was in to see me again today and gave me some candy and gum.

Gover continued to progress satisfactorily, and on Monday, July 6,

Got transport to Swindon, changed trains and came on to Redruth, where I was met by Mr. Rickard, at whose home I am to spend a few days. There are only he and his wife, since their two sons are away in the service. It is sure nice of these people to open their homes to recuperating pilots. As soon as I arrived they sat me down to a big steak, carrots, peas, onions and potatoes. Boy, did that taste good. It was my first real meal in over two weeks.

Lee had asked to recuperate near Redruth because of his love for the little village, so, on Tuesday, after a breakfast of ham and eggs in bed, he rode his host's bike to town. There he saw his former batman and talked with his little friend Rex, but was unable to find Liz.

Wednesday, July 8, was a day that Gover would always remember. He described it in a letter to his parents.

This afternoon I went with Mr. Rickard to the munitions factory he runs. It was a big day for him, because the Duke of Kent, the King's brother, was scheduled to visit. I was just standing off to one side watching the Duke inspect the place when he saw me and came over to where I was. He asked me what part of the States I was from, how long I had been here, how I liked it, what squadron I was in and a lot of other things. He had on his air force uniform (air commodore). He was damn nice and you feel pretty good that he would come to talk to you.

About six weeks later the conversation made the front page of the *San Carlos Enquirer*. Under the caption "LeRoy Gover and

Duke of Kent" was a four-by-eight-inch picture of the Duke talking to Lee and a short summary of the occasion.

> This photo, taken on July 10th, arrived in San Carlos on Tuesday, the very day on which the Duke of Kent, youngest brother of King George IV, was killed in the crash of a Sunderland flying boat north of Scotland. The picture shows LeRoy Gover, son of City Councilman and Mrs. Roy Gover, in conversation with the Duke of Kent. LeRoy is with the American Eagle Squadron attached to the RAF.

Actually, Gover was not a member of one of the Eagle Squadrons until August 1942. Because the three Eagle Squadrons were made up solely of Americans, it was common for the press and public to assume every American fighter pilot in the RAF was a member of one of these squadrons. Lee had even written to his parents in early April explaining to them that he was not in one of the Eagle Squadrons.

Lee's remaining days at the Rickard estate were filled with walks on the beach and the cliffs overlooking the ocean, dances in Redruth and just enjoying the town. He determined that he would spend the second week of his sick leave in London "to rest, relax and get back into the swing of a normal life." Sleeping late, seeing the sights, enjoying the shows, and having a few drinks with both male and female friends occupied his time. "It seems like everyone I see that I know talks about someone who has been killed," Gover lamented.

> Went to the Eagle Club this morning [Sunday] and met Taylor. He said Bill Arends, Fletcher Hancock and George Teicheira [all from his class at Bakersfield] had been killed. Ray Doyle was sent home but torpedoed and killed on the way. What luck.

> **Wednesday, July 15, 1942** Went out to Biggin Hill today to the Eagle Squadron Number 133. Saw Lambert, Middleton, Beaty, Gudmundsen, Gray and a few others I knew in the States. Stayed for tea and a game of pool—then on back to town. Saw Len Ryerson, Snuffy Smith, Hively, Osborne and Wright [all American pilots in the RAF] in the Regent Bar. Good to see the

old boys. But there are always so many missing every time I come to town. Bolton [a classmate from Bakersfield] was killed a while back.

By Friday, Gover was his old self again, and his last three days in London were more bent on "getting back to a normal life" than they were on "rest and recuperation."

Friday, July 17, 1942   I was up at 8:15 and down to breakfast in the hotel. (This is the first morning I really have had much energy.) Went down and bought some records. Took a walk up Oxford Street. Stopped in at the Peel Boot Company to pick up the gloves that I had ordered. [Because Lee had suffered frostbite to his hands when he was a kid, he always had trouble keeping his hands warm. The RAF-issue gloves with silk liners just didn't do the job, so he ordered a fur-lined pair to wear when he wasn't in combat.] It started raining, so I came on back to the Eagle Club. Met Lambert and Middleton about 8:00 p.m. in the Regent. Also saw Hively. Went over to the Crackers Club and then back to the Regent, where I met a cute little number. Picked up a major there because we were out of dough and he had five pounds so kept him in tow.

Saturday, July 18, 1942   Met Middleton and Lambert at the Eagle Club about noon. Had something to eat, then we and Kearney went to the show. I left the boys after, cleaned up and met Dorothy [a lovely brunette with whom Lee spent a great deal of time when he was in London] and we started around on a tour of having a good time in general. Saw the boys again. Lambert tried to kick my door in about 4:00 a.m. this morning. I told him to go away as I was talking to a friend. Really, I was in bed with Dorothy.

Sunday, July 19, 1942   Up at 10:00 and down to the Eagle Club for breakfast. Saw Peck [another American pilot] and talked with the boys for a couple of hours. Dorothy and her sis came in about 4:30. Went to St. James's Park for a while and then to the Pam Pam for eats. Took them home about 9:00 and then met Don Young in the Regent Bar. Gabbed awhile, then went for eats. Came back to the Crackers Club and then over to the Regent again. Sat around until 1:00 a.m. and then hit the hay. I have to report back to the squadron tomorrow. What a life.

Gover arrived back at Ibsley on Monday evening, ". . . and what a change here. Five of the boys posted east, the CO and my flight commander have been posted to other squadrons, so it's not like the old days." Lee may have thought he was back to 100 percent, but his first flight since being in the hospital "left me tired as hell when I came down." Lee's sister Betty got more details of the flight a few days later.

I went up this morning to just do some practice breakaway maneuvers when an American in a Mustang (P-51—they look just like an ME-109) dived on me. Shook me to the core until I recognized it. So I pulled up hard and banked her over and was soon on his tail—blacked myself out doing it. And then we went at it. I used my camera gun on him and really shot the hell out of him. He couldn't shake me at all. He'd do 400 and then stall at 100, but I hung on. I let him get on my tail and in a couple of turns I was on his again. Boy, you can't beat the old Spitfire for all-around fighting. He finally put his wheels down, which signaled that we quit, and so I came on back. I was sure tired after being off flying for so long, but I can't wait to see my film.

Everything was routine with convoy patrol and generally getting used to flying again until the following Monday, when Gover saw his first action with the enemy in nearly two months.

Went on a shipping reconnaissance to France today. Came in at Cape de la Hague and flew along the coast to Cherbourg. Saw a couple of small boats in the harbor at Cherbourg, but they weren't large enough to attack. About thirty enemy aircraft came up to meet us and I got hits on an ME-109 in the action but he went into the clouds streaming smoke, so I don't know if he got back or crashed.

Just four days later, July 31, was "another day to remember."

Boy, was there a job on and how. Our wing here (thirty-six planes) flew down to Bolt Head, refueled and teamed up with other squadrons. We then escorted Boston bombers over to St. Malo, France. We flew at sea level until within thirty miles of the target. Then we climbed rapidly up to ten thousand—and can those Bostons go. We jettisoned our long-range tanks right before we got to the target. The bombers dropped their eggs right on the target. There wasn't very much flak. Then we brought the Bostons back right along the whole Cherbourg Peninsula and by the Jersey Islands. There were diversion sweeps along the coast with 250 aircraft taking part. By the time we got to the Jersey Islands, Jerry fighters were swarming all over us. Eleven Jerries were shot down and we lost eight, but I didn't get a good shot. It was a very successful raid. We crossed 130 miles of water to get there, which made me nervous, but the old Rolls-Royce motor just kept on humming.

There was no letup in the action with the coming of August. During the first six days of the month, Gover flew ten missions, in the course of which he damaged two ME-109s and destroyed one. Rain, fog and clouds were the order of the day through the weekend, but things brightened again on Monday when Lee and several of his friends were given a forty-eight-hour leave.

Monday, August 10, 1942   Was given a forty-eight-hour leave, so jumped on the 10 a.m. bus and went into Salisbury. Then caught the 12:30 train and arrived at Waterloo Station at 2:30 p.m. Checked in at the Regent Palace and went down to the Eagle Club. Saw Tabb, Harden and Quinn. Went to a few bars in the evening and ended at the Grove Club on Piccadilly after sending old Deytrikh home. [Deytrikh was a squadron mate who lived in London.]

Tuesday, August 11, 1942   Slept most of the morning. Met Deytrikh at 1:00 p.m. and went to see *Eagle Squadron*. It was pretty fair. [This movie was about the Eagle Squadrons, to which Gover would soon be assigned. Most of the members of those squadrons walked out of the film because they thought Hollywood had done such a bad job with the picture.] We went to Deytrikh's home and met his mom and sister (very nice too). Then back to the Regent, where I met Dorothy, took in a few beers—boy, I wish they would learn to serve them cold over here—and back to Manor House on the subway.

Wednesday, August 12, 1942 Checked out of the Regent at 11:00 a.m. and went to the Eagle Club for dinner and to a show, *Pardon My Sarong*. It was funny as hell. Caught the 5:00 p.m. train for Salisbury and so back to Ibsley.

"Well, what do you know, we are back where we left off," Lee wrote the next day. "Up early, on patrol, see the Jerries, chase them into the cloud and lose them. Nuts." To his dad he wrote that "this situation annoys me no end."

No, Dad, it's no secret what heights we fly—the Jerries do the same—if it's cloudy and low, we fly low, no clouds, then anywhere up to 35,000 feet. The only catch is that no matter what height you fly, they are above you. You know, it's funny, but here I am looking out the window at a peaceful little valley and a farmer picking apples. It reminds me that I'd like to see your garden and orchard. But someday— Bye for now.

On August 15, "We were told this evening to pack and be ready to leave for Tangmere at dawn tomorrow morning. Something big is coming off."

Sunday, August 16, 1942 Up at dawn and down to the flight. Got ready and took off for Tangmere. Arrived after two of the boys taxied into each other and chewed their tails off, so we're now down to ten planes. Was put up in an old house. We ate supper and then all went down to Chichester to the pub for a few beers. Still don't know what's on.

"Still in the dark as to what's happening," Gover wrote on Monday, "but there are six squadrons here on this field now." But late in the day on Tuesday, the entry in his diary reflects both relief and some concern at knowing what was to come. "This evening we were told we were not allowed off camp under any circumstances. We were then told that a commando raid was coming off in the morning at Dieppe. So we're to be on readiness at 4:00 a.m."

Lee was typical of every other pilot in the squadron as he and his squadron mates Vic Nissen and Tommy Tomblin talked well into the evening about what the next day might bring. There had certainly been a great deal of talk about some kind of big operation being in the offing, and some had even speculated that it might be an invasion of France. But Lee and most of his buddies had put that thought out of their minds, because it was just too early in the war, and they had seen the might of the German defenses in France on their almost daily missions across the Channel. So when the word came that it would be in support of a landing at Dieppe, in France, the mission took on a new seriousness. The danger of the day was certainly not lost on any of the young pilots, as they realized that the Luftwaffe would put up everything it had to show the British that any invasion of the Continent was simply too costly.

"I wonder why we are trying an invasion now," said Vic. "I don't see any way that we can be successful. We can't protect the troops on the ground, because we will be too busy fighting for our lives in the air."

"I think this is just a small fake invasion to keep the Germans on their toes and it won't last more than one day," mused Tommy Tomblin.

"But the losses to those poor guys on the ground could be horrible, and I agree that we don't have a chance of protecting them," added Lee.

Actually, the three were pretty accurate, because the one-day operation was planned by the British to test the Germans' defenses and keep them off guard. Lee was also right when he commented on the casualties, for they were to run nearly 50 percent among the commandos who made the raid.

"The action of August 19, 1942, was my most memorable combat experience while in the RAF," Gover reminisced. It is also one of the longest entries in his diary.

Boy, this been a very exciting and also sad day. Our Ibsley Wing—66, 501, and 118 Squadrons—had to escort twelve Hurri-bombers over to Dieppe this morning at first light. We all flew at sea level the entire mission. We took them in through flak that cannot be described. There were hundreds of planes screaming through the sky. Dozens of dogfights going on. Planes plummeting to earth on fire. Pilots who had been shot down were floating in their dinghies. I saw nine or ten Spitfires just shooting hell out of a Jerry Dornier. We fought off attacks on the Hurricanes, but four were shot down by the shore batteries. We were attacked twice more by Messerschmitt 109s as we crossed back out over the coast of France. I got strikes on a Messerschmitt 109, but I was flying about fifty feet off the water and couldn't maneuver to finish him off. Three of our Spitfires were so badly shot up they were out of the fight, but did manage to fly back to England.

There were five planes left in our squadron for the second mission at 11:00 a.m., and we went back across the Channel to shoot up any gun emplacements we came across. By this time Dieppe was a real mess. The Germans were sending Dornier 217s to bomb the landing craft that were now trying to take men off the beach. Seven Focke-Wulf 190s attacked us as we hit the French coast. The only advantage we had was to outturn them. I got strikes on two, but did no real damage. We lost two more of our Spitfires. I was now out of ammo, so broke away and headed home.

This afternoon our squadron, which now consisted of three aircraft, was detailed to fly close escort on four Bostons, who were to lay a smoke screen along the shore to cover the withdrawal of the commandos. We went in at sea level, and two of the Bostons were shot down right in front of me. I was about 250 yards from shore and the German machine guns were spraying hell out of things. Large cannon shells were bursting all around, and cannon shells were hitting the water and shooting up tall columns of water. As the Bostons finished laying their smoke, one more was shot down. As I was now being shot up, I lost track of the other Boston and do not know his fate. The beach was covered with fallen commandos. About two miles out on the way home we were jumped by a gaggle of Focke-Wulf 190s. One was right on me and getting hits, so I pushed full left rudder and his bullets struck the water beside me. He turned and shot my number two, Vic Nissen from South Africa, straight into the sea. Then the third man in our threesome was shot down, and I was now all alone. I weaved to beat hell and came home balls out. Saw three more pilots in the water in their little yellow dinghies.

They sure looked lonely bobbing about in that mess. Boats that had been sent in to pick up the commandos were leaving the beach with three or four commandos. Most all were dead on the beach or couldn't break out because of the terrible shelling directed at them.

Then this evening I had the only aircraft available and, although it had many bullet holes, serviceable to fly. I was put on alert, and sure enough, a Jerry Junkers 88 came over and bombed the field. I couldn't get off the ground, but the field defense guns brought him down, right near the mess hall. I'm hitting the hay, one very tired and lonely fighter pilot.

What Gover, a very modest man, failed to report was that he destroyed an FW-190 on his first mission of the day and damaged an ME-109 on the second. There were about seventy German aircraft destroyed or damaged during the day, while the British lost nearly one hundred. Gover's speculation about the casualties on the ground proved prophetic. Of the nearly five thousand Canadian commandos who embarked, some one thousand were killed and another two thousand became prisoners. Still, the raid was classed as a success, for it forced the Germans to diversify their defenses in France and gave notice that the British were not ready to sit back and let Hitler have his way in Europe.

The day after Dieppe, Lee was told that he "was posted to the EAGLE SQUADRON (Number 133), so took my Spitfire back to Ibsley, packed up my few belongings and we went out on a beer binge to celebrate." (The orders for Gover's transfer had actually come to his squadron on August 15, but the squadron commander had not told Lee because he feared that a transfer would mean that Gover would miss Dieppe.) Lee capitalized "Eagle Squadron" in his diary because he had never really thought he would belong to one of the famed units. He had written to his parents in May:

All the USA fellows are being posted to the Eagle Squadron, but I haven't been notified of anything, so imagine they have forgotten I am still here. I don't care much either way except the Eagle Squadrons are all close to London (just a half hour train ride) and you have someplace to go during time off.

Despite this diary entry, Gover later admitted that he was excited about his transfer, because it meant flying with many of his friends and having the distinction of being an Eagle. Certainly this transfer was not accompanied by the apprehension Lee had felt a few months earlier when he left OTU for 66 Squadron and his first operational assignment.

4. AN AMERICAN EAGLE

FRIDAY, AUGUST 21, 1942 CAUGHT THE TRAIN AT RINGWOOD this morning and came into London. Decided to stay in town for the night, so checked in at the Regent and then went over to the Crackers Club for a beer. Don Blakeslee was the acting commander of 133 Squadron. He and most of the pilots were at the Crackers Club when I walked in, so I reported in unofficially as present and accounted for. Don bought me a beer, said, "Welcome aboard," and I was an Eagle. It was great to be joining a unit where I already knew most of the fellows. After that I took Natalie out for a few drinks and called it a day.

The Crackers Club and the Regent Palace Hotel were both special places for Lee during his entire time in England. He later wrote:

Whenever we went to London, most of us headed for the Regent Palace Hotel. It was just a few feet off Piccadilly Circus and handy to everything, like the Windmill Theater, with its dancing girls, and the Eagle Club. My favorite, and that of most of the Eagles, was the Crackers Club, a small bar in a cellar about two hundred feet from Piccadilly. It probably had been used for storage prior to the war. As you entered the dimly lit room, the bar, with eight or ten stools, was on the left and there were three or four tables set about. There wasn't much decoration, just a few posters on the walls. The entire place was perhaps eighteen by twenty feet. Crackers was owned by Marie, an olive-skinned, slightly plump lady who had escaped from Malta at the start of the war and opened this little bar. She had a young girl named Madeleine who helped her. Marie treated us all like a mother hen, even though she was not that much older than some of the fellows. She always said that we'd all have a reunion in New York City after the war, but this was not to be. I'll never forget the north wall in the club, because all the members of the three Eagle Squadrons signed their names on it. I was in the Crackers Club the night Wing Commander Guy Gibson, one of the most decorated pilots in the RAF, came in to celebrate receiving the Victoria Cross from the King [the highest award an RAF pilot could receive for heroism]. Many a pint flowed that night. He became known as the dam buster because he successfully bombed several German hydroelectric plants, but he was later reported missing in action and was never found. The place was full of very pleasant memories for me. Unfortunately, it was destroyed by a German buzz bomb late in the war. I never heard what happened to Marie.

Back to the Regent Palace. Whenever we came in, I'd walk up and the gal behind the cage would hand me a room key. The other guys would hang around for hours waiting for a room to open up, sometimes with no luck at all. When they asked me how come I always got a room, I just told them that "I'm lucky, I guess." The guys never did know that I was seeing Margaret, the girl in charge of rooms. She would come up to the room when her shift was over and we would have a great time. Years later, I told my good friend Mick Lambert about Margaret and he said that he knew there was something going on but just couldn't figure out how it all worked.

Although he had "unofficially" reported in at the Crackers Club, Lee was expected at Number 133 Squadron's headquarters at Biggin Hill the next day. "Went down to the Eagle Club to check the mail, then caught the train to Bromley South and a taxi to Biggin Hill. Met the gang and was told we were leaving in two hours for gunnery practice at Martlesham Heath." Gover felt very much at home when he signed in at Biggin Hill, because of the twenty or so pilots in the squadron, four were his classmates at Bakersfield and several others had been there at the same time but in different classes.

Because the British required that any pilot coming into the RAF from a foreign source be able to go directly into the British OTU system, those pilots recruited by the Clayton Knight Committee, as Gover was, had to complete a basic flying training program. Training facilities in Canada were completely saturated, so Knight established several private contract schools in the United States, among them the one that Gover attended in Bakersfield.

By August 1941, the RAF had established three Fighter Command squadrons, Numbers 71, 121 and 133, as exclusively American units. These three squadrons were known as the Eagle Squadrons and were to gain considerable fame in the history of World War II. Most of the pilots in these three squadrons were recruited by the Clayton Knight organization and given their training at one of the contract schools in the United States. Thus, a good number of the Americans in the RAF knew one another from having trained at the same school or through mutual friends.

Moving 133 Squadron to Martlesham Heath for gunnery practice served two purposes. First, since combat was sporadic, some members of the squadron could possibly go for several days, or even weeks, without having occasion to fire their guns. Practice shooting at a drogue (a cloth sock) towed behind a plane gave them the chance to sharpen their gunnery skills. The move also gave the unit a few days to relax without the pressure of alert and constant combat missions. Thus, for the first week that Lee was an Eagle, he got a well-deserved break from combat and spent his time getting used to the squadron's new aircraft, the Spitfire IX, which had a more powerful engine and significantly greater performance than the Spit V he had been flying, and discovering another English city, Ipswich.

Sunday, August 23, 1942   Up at 7:00 a.m. and down to breakfast and then out to the flight line. I'm in B flight with quite a few of the old Bakersfield gang. Did air firing and got the best score of the day. Spent some time looking at a neat book they have in dispersal called *Forget-Me-Nots for Fighters*. It has all sorts of points about air fighting. Most of them are illustrated by cartoons— pretty funny, but I think they will be very helpful in combat.

This very cleverly illustrated book contains scores of ideas. "Never follow down a machine you have shot; there may be a kick still left in the air gunner, or he may have a pal in an ME-109 just behind you." "Flying boots, leather gloves and goggles will protect you if your clothing or the cockpit should catch fire. Your gloves are most important, as if your right hand were to get burnt you would not be able to feel the rip cord." "Remember that the sun can be your best friend and your worst enemy. Used correctly he is your friend; neglected he can be your worst enemy." This rule is illustrated by one sun bearing the likeness of Winston Churchill, the other that of Adolf Hitler. These are but three of scores of points for fighter pilots.

Monday, August 24, 1942 Took life easy this morning and went into Ipswich to the show this afternoon. Went to the White Horse Hotel bar afterward and met some of the gang. Couple of rounds of beer—it is warm here, too—and on home. Wrote a couple of long-overdue letters and now to bed.

One of the letters was to his folks, the first since before the Dieppe raid.

I'm late in writing this week, but things have been happening so fast I just haven't been able to. First, we were whisked away to another field, stayed there a couple of days, and then came the big raid at Dieppe. I was over [censored] and it was really a pretty big show and the RAF really did all right. Never saw so many airplanes in my life, but I imagine you read all about it. Well, after the raid, the adjutant told me that I was posted to the Eagle Squadron. So I jumped in my Spit and came on back to our own drome. Caught the train into London and the next morning came out to the squadron to meet the gang. There are quite a few I know from Bakersfield. Our base is only about twelve miles south of London, so it is sure a handy place for getting into town. I sure hated leaving the old Number 66 Squadron. I had worked my way up and was number one man in our flight and was section leader, but so it goes. By the way, I had christened my old Spitfire before the Dieppe show. It was called *Sondra Lee* in nice printing on the side. [Sondra Lee was Lee's niece, his sister Juanita's daughter.]

Don't know if I told you that we fighter pilots always keep the top button of our blouse undone. It comes from the Battle of Britain and it sure sets you apart. Well, the other day a pilot came into the Eagle Club with all his buttons undone and said, "If you fighter guys can keep one button open when you fly with one engine, then I can keep all four undone, since I have four engines." What a clown. I'd better close now and go out and keep up my top shooting score. By the way, I received a letter in just ten days when it was sent to the Eagle Club, so that works out OK. [When he began ferry pilot duty, Gover had told his folks to send all his mail to the Eagle Club since he moved around so much and it sometimes took over a month to get to him. He maintained that practice until after his transfer to the U.S. Army Air Forces.]

Wednesday, August 26, 1942 Did a little drogue shooting today and into Ipswich to the show later this afternoon. Over to the White Horse after. Left the boys and took in a few pubs until I found the one I wanted, then spent the evening there. Lots of wine, women and song.

On Thursday, Lee made one of the most important entries ever in his diary. "Oh yes, I took my physical examination yesterday for transfer to the U.S. Air Corps and passed with flying colors." Lee's initial optimism was ill-founded, however, because he learned a few days later that it was only a preliminary physical and the Americans wanted to do some further tests on his lungs. This made his acceptance into the Army Air Forces conditional at that point. Actually, the whole process came as a surprise to Gover, since he knew nothing of the impending transfer to the U.S. forces until his arrival in 133 Squadron. Since he had been the only American in 66 Squadron, there was no talk of any transfer or any interest in it—all the rest of his squadron mates were in the RAF for the duration of the war. However, on his arrival at 133, one of the first comments that his old pal Mick Lambert made centered on transfer. "Isn't the news about our transfer to the U.S.

Army Air Forces great?" Lambert had asked. "I don't know when it will take place, but I hear that it will be soon. I really like the British, but think of all that money."

"I don't know what you're talking about," was Lee's reply. "I thought we weren't going to get to transfer, and besides, I like the RAF. I'm not so sure that I really want to move." That was the end of it until the August 26 physical.

A week later, Gover wrote to his folks telling them all about the projected move.

Here it is September 3 and ten months since I left home. It seems the U.S. Air Corps wants the Eagles back and we all took physicals for transfer and I passed A-1 so I must be in good health. They must think we are pretty good boys, 'cause they (the U.S. government) are paying the RAF 50,000 bucks apiece for us fellows. [There is no evidence that any such payment was ever made. It is logical that it might have been, however, since the British had paid for all the Americans' training and transport to England, and were losing a proven combat resource.] Don't know just when we go in or what the deal is, but boy will I have dough when I start to get that two hundred to three hundred bucks per month instead of the fifty-eight I get now. I received the paper smacker [dollar bill] that you sent and I'm having all the boys here sign their names on it. I'll send it back for you to put in a little frame for me. [Gover still had the dollar bill fifty years after he came back from Europe.] Tell Dr. Ross hello and that I've had compliments from every dentist I've been to here on his exceptionally good work, so he's now world-famous.

Gover's relief at passing his physical was still apparent on Friday.

Friday, August 28, 1942 Some more air firing this morning and into Ipswich again this afternoon. I had seen all four shows in town so came back out to camp. We have been bombed here for the last three nights, but it is just now 10:00 p.m. and our bombers are streaming over the coast toward Germany. Good luck to them all. A Wellington [bomber] crash-landed here last night all shot full of holes and on fire. Walked down the road about a mile this evening to the Red Lion Pub and had a couple of beers, then to a fish-and-chip joint for a bag of chips and then home. Did one of the dumbest things in my life yesterday. We were at the White Horse for a few beers. After walking about five or six minutes on our way back to camp, we saw a couple of men up ahead. It turned out to be a bomb disposal team and they were preparing to disarm a bomb a plane had dropped but it hadn't gone off, or had a delayed fuse. We were feeling no pain, so we sat down on the edge of the crater and watched them do their job. The men doing the work did not say a word to us. I guess misery loves company, and we didn't think of the danger, or just didn't give a damn. After a bit they got the fuse out and we got up and walked on back to the base. Boy oh boy, were we dumb.

For some time, Lee's mother had been asking him about the food and, with typical motherly concern, if he was getting enough to eat. The questions were quite logical, since newsreels in the United States continually publicized the lack of everything, including food, in England and the difficult time everyone was having finding the daily necessities of life. Since Saturday was a no-flying day for Lee, he used the time to pack for Sunday's return trip to Biggin Hill and to give his folks a rather detailed account of his daily diet.

Well, as you know, I am now with the Eagle Squadron and like it OK. Lots of the old gang are here and it makes it pretty nice. We will be going back to our drome tomorrow. We have been having better food here, and yes, I am getting enough to eat. One morning a week we get bacon and an egg (with 66 Squadron it was no bacon and one egg a month). Other mornings it's sausage, fried tomatoes, potatoes and toast with marmalade, plus a glass of canned orange juice, milk, tea or coffee. It's really swell.

Sometimes for breakfast we get what they call "bubble and squeak." They take the potatoes and Brussels sprouts left over from dinner the day before and combine them, make them into patties, much like hamburger patties. They fry them and serve them hot with the rest of breakfast. I think they are pretty good. But when you fly, "bubble and squeak" has a different meaning. It forms gas, and as we get to higher altitudes, the gas expands and the bubbles bubble and we squeak.

For lunch we usually get roast beef or cold Spam, salad, potatoes and string beans or Brussels sprouts, and tea or coffee, plus some dessert or a sweet as they call it over here. Then at teatime its tea, toast and marmalade. At dinner it's about the same as lunch. Ever since I've been on operations, I've always fared pretty well for food. [Gover wrote this exaggerated description of his diet because his mother continually expressed concern about his health. In fact, there was often little, if any, meat, few eggs, seldom coffee or canned juice, and Gover's weight was as low as 130 pounds on occasion while he was in the RAF.]

You realize the difference when you go on leave and just don't get much at all. When we first got here we were invited out to eat at English homes and they really fed us well. It wasn't until we were more familiar with the food situation that we realized these families were using up an entire week's ration coupons just to give us a good meal (they only get one egg and one ounce of sugar a month for each person). We save up our coupons now and give them to families if we are invited to dinner, but the easiest way to keep this from happening is to just not accept the invitations.

How did you like our effort at Dieppe? I suppose you saw the newsreels of it. Sure was a fast moving affair, but we sure kept 'em covered. It seems, just at the moment, that I am back at Bakersfield as Middleton, Beaty and Ryerson are asleep on the lawn. We have all new Spitfires now and those old 1,650 horses sure get you along. My health is very good and I still have control of the old nerves, so who could ask for anything more.

Lee later reflected on the problem of not being able to control your nerves.

Most of us thought about our nerves at one time or another while flying combat. The constant pressure and being in life-or-death situations several times every day eventually got to some of the pilots. One of the first problems you would see was that they started to drink heavily just trying to unwind after a tough mission. Many would also become chain-smokers. A night of drinking and they were in that much worse shape the next day, so the combat was even more challenging and it was more difficult to unwind. This led to more drinking and the cycle just got worse. Eventually a pilot either asked to be taken off combat, like my good friend Mick Lambert, got the shakes so bad that it was obvious he couldn't fly safely, or got shot down.

A lot of us were careful not to drink too much, especially if we were going to fly the next day, because that seemed to me to be the thing that compounded the nerve problem more than anything else. Overall, most of the pilots were able to find ways to cope with the pressure and complete their tours, but the nerve problem did get to some.

The week of gunnery practice was over on Sunday and the squadron flew back to Biggin Hill. Because he was the new man in the unit, Gover had to shepherd some enlisted men back to Biggin Hill on the train. On Wednesday, Lee flew his first operational mission in his new Spit IX and was greatly impressed. "Boy, these new planes go right on up to forty thousand feet like nothing and do about 410 miles per hour up there straight and level!" The following two days he was on alert, but on Sunday, Monday and Tuesday, he had one of the most intense periods of action of his RAF career.

Sunday, September 6, 1942 Escorted thirty-six Flying Fortresses over to Méaulte, France. When we reached the French coast we were attacked by FW-190s and had combats all the way in and out. Spike Miley was having trouble with his power and was lagging behind. An FW-190 was stalking him, so I broke formation and went back to help him. I had turned left to be in the sun so the Hun would have less chance of seeing me. He didn't see me and I came around and hit him good. Pieces started flying off his plane and he turned right, going down in a steep turn. I was sure he was finished and I caught up with Spike and we were able to rejoin the squadron. About then all hell broke loose as fifteen FW-190s hit us. Two of the Fortresses were shot down and we lost two planes, Doorly and Gudmundsen. I arrived back at base with seven gallons of petrol.

Monday, September 7, 1942 We took off and went to Martlesham Heath, where we refueled and were briefed for a sweep to Rotterdam, Holland. We escorted thirty-six B-17 Flying Fortresses. We were attacked by a gaggle of FW-190s over the target. After the attacks were broken up, the Forts dropped their eggs and we all turned for home. We were about twenty-five miles inside the Dutch coast when my engine began to surge and run very rough and only make about 50 percent power. I began to lag behind and soon lost sight of the squadron. Our controller in England heard me calling to the squadron for help and said they had six enemy fighters plotted on their scope between me and the coast. They were just milling around, waiting for me, since my squadron was already well west of them in mid-Channel. I was now all alone and on my own.

I soon saw the Germans and tried to figure out how to get by them. I remembered that my dad always told me that if a fight was going to happen, strike the first blow as hard as you could and you have the other guy mentally whipped. I had about three thousand feet of altitude on them, so I put the Spitfire into a shallow dive and built up all the speed I could. I dove right for them with all guns blazing. I gave a little left rudder and then a little right rudder so my bullets would spray them and maybe make them scatter.

Sure enough, they broke every which way as I went through them. I just kept right on going, since my engine was not running right, I had no more ammunition and I was very low on fuel. One good thing on my side was that we were over the Dutch coast by now and the Jerries weren't going to come very far over the Channel. I made it home with three gallons of petrol and no ammo.

Always ready for news about its hometown hero, the *San Carlos Enquirer* ran a front-page article on Lee's escapade. The headline read: "Gover, Trapped by Six Nazi Planes, Escapes." Directly under the headline was a three-by-five-inch picture of Gover standing on the wing of his Spitfire *Sondra Lee* and a fourteen-inch, single-column article detailing the adventure. While the main facts were from a letter Gover wrote describing the event, the paper typically increased the speeds, altitudes and drama. The article concluded by summarizing Gover's mission to Méaulte on Sunday and mentioning his action during the Dieppe raid.

Tuesday, September 8, 1942 My fitter told me this morning that they had to change three barrels on my guns because they were warped from all the continuous firing yesterday. Escorted nineteen P-38 Lightnings over the Cherbourg Peninsula (my old stamping grounds when I was in 66 Squadron). We then went up the coast by Le Havre and on back to Tangmere. I was worried because we were over Abbeville, where the yellow-nosed ME-109s, the best in the Luftwaffe, were stationed. After we turned for home, about ten or twelve ME-109s came right through our formation, which was fairly spread out. There was one bright blue ME-109 that ended up coming head on to me. We never missed by more than ten feet. With a closing speed of well over 700 miles per hour, I'm sure they didn't see us until the last moment, because they never fired a shot and neither did we. It all happened in one or two seconds. They just kept going, and so did we. It just scared the hell out of us, and most likely them too.

Years later Gover remarked, "I have never forgotten that near miss and I've always wondered who was flying that beautiful light blue Messerschmitt. It was the only one painted blue, so it must have been the commander of the outfit. Every month or so I still think of that day over Abbeville, and I'll bet he does too."

Although Gover had anticipated a very busy flying month in September, his flight on the eighth was his last combat mission with the RAF. The squadron was greeted with "fog right on the ground" on Wednesday, and the weather remained too bad for flying for the remainder of the week. On Saturday, "Caught the 2:00 p.m. train for London and checked in at the Regent. Took some film to be developed and then took in the show at the Chez Marcelle when Dorothy came in. I was always happy to see Dorothy."

"It was about this time that we began a new tradition that lasted pretty much until I left England," Gover reminisced.

We always had a problem with some of the guys drinking too much or going out and spending all their money and then not being able to get back to the base. One time on our way to London, I told Lambert and Middleton to each put a pound in my breast pocket so they would have money to get breakfast and get back to Biggin Hill. While I always had as great a time as anyone in London, I never did drink so much that I ran out of money, so they thought it was a great idea. I soon had eight or ten of the boys giving me a pound to keep for them. It worked out well, and often that pound was all that stood between them and being flat broke.

Gover was one of the few pilots with a camera or an interest in photography. During his time in England, he came to know the man who operated the photography studio directly beneath the Eagle Club on Charing Cross Road quite well. "I took a lot of pictures to send home, because my mother kept a large scrapbook about me and the folks really liked my photos," Lee remembered.

The studio was a convenient place to drop off film, and they always did a good job of developing my pictures. On one occasion, the owner even gave me a beautiful handmade photo album, because, he said, I should take more pictures, since mine were so good. I expect that he told all the Americans the same thing. It wasn't until quite late in the war that I found out why he encouraged me so. When Roy Evans [another Eagle and friend of Gover's throughout the war] was shot down in early 1945, his Luftwaffe interrogator produced a lot of pictures of Evans and all the guys that I took. Roy said, "My mouth just dropped open when I saw them." I am sure that the photography studio was run by the Germans and they were making duplicate pictures and sending them to Germany throughout the war. I just thought it was a nice place to do business.

By the middle of September, the impending transfer to the American forces was utmost on everyone's mind in 133 Squadron. Lee wrote to his folks on September 9 that he would be transferred on the seventeenth and reminded them to send his mail to the Eagle Club, since he did not know where he would be stationed. But Lee's transfer was kept on hold because of his need to take an additional physical. On Wednesday, September 16, "Up at 6:00 a.m. and came into London to take my physical for transfer to the U.S. Air Corps. I hope that everything is OK, because I really haven't been feeling 100 percent."

Transferring to the American forces had been an objective of most of the Americans in the RAF since Pearl Harbor. The American forces wanted them, at least those in the three Eagle Squadrons, since they were operational fighter units and there were no such American units in Europe in the summer of 1942. Still, there were several problems that had to be overcome before transfer could take place. The first of these was the Americans' rank. The solution was, in most cases, to assign the equivalent of that held in the RAF. A number of the Americans, including Gover, believed that their experience entitled them to higher rank than lieutenant, but only one of the group actually held out for higher rank as a condition of transfer. "We should have all done that," Gover remarked, "because he won and transferred as a major." A second problem was that none of the Eagles had graduated from an Army-accredited flying training program and had therefore never been awarded American pilot wings. This issue was resolved with the awarding of American wings when transfer took place.

Still another concern was the unit to which the Americans would be assigned. Some key U.S. officers, including General Carl Spaatz, commander of the Eighth Air Force, wanted to assign a few Eagles to each of a number of American units to provide a seasoned combat-tested resource. The Eagles, on the other hand, were determined to stay together as squadrons. This produced an interesting standoff during which the Eagles threatened not to transfer at all if their units were to be fragmented. Since they had signed up with the RAF for the duration of the war, there was no way the Americans could be forced to transfer, and so the Eighth Air Force eventually backed down.

A final issue was airplanes. Gover wrote in his diary on September 19 that they would be getting P-47 Thunderbolts when the transfer took place. This was obviously a rumor, because there were no acceptable American fighters available in Europe until very late in 1942. If the Americans were going to transfer and be operational units, they were going to have to take their Spitfires with them. In the end, the British agreed to give the United States two hundred Spitfires in exchange for a future transfer of two hundred P-51 Mustangs to the RAF.

All of these issues took time to resolve, but by early September all was in readiness and transfers began.

For Lee, as for most of the other members of his squadron, operations continued at a normal pace as they waited to transfer. He was on alert or grounded for weather during the third week in September. On September 19, he made a short flight to check out his guns, which proved to be his last as an RAF pilot.

I was given a brand-new Spitfire IX this morning. Took it out about ten miles south of Beachy Head and tested my cannons. One jammed, but she flies very nice. A new boy joined up with us two days ago and was killed this morning. They don't last long in this business.

The following day he wrote a "good news" letter home.

I was accepted in the U.S. Air Corps. Go back to London this Wednesday and get sworn in and then get decked out in a new uniform. Got another new plane. This one has 1,750 horsepower and a four-blade prop. It sure is pretty. If they get much bigger motors, we'll soon just strap a saddle on the motor and away we'll go. Saw a funny poem on the wall in the dispersal hut today called "You Can Tell a Fighter Pilot."

> By the ring around his eyeball
> You can tell a bombardier,
> And you can tell a bomber pilot
> By the spread across his rear.
> You can tell a navigator
> By his sextants, maps and such,
> You can tell a fighter pilot
> *But you can't tell him much!*

The members of Lee's squadron had been going into London, two or three at a time, for several days to complete their transfer to the American forces. This had to be done by everyone before the transfer ceremony scheduled for September 29. So, after two more days on readiness but without flying, it was off to London and the big day for Gover. (Gover was among the last in the squadron to transfer because of the problems he had with his physical.)

Tuesday, September 22, 1942   On readiness again until 1:00 p.m. I caught the 5:00 p.m. bus into Bromley South. Jumped the train and came on into London and checked in at the Regent. Then went to the Crackers Club, where I saw Jackson, Baker, Miley and Lambert [all squadron mates].

Wednesday, September 23, 1942   Down to Pen House at 9:00 a.m. Was sworn into the U.S. Army Air Force by Colonel Ayling and then taken out to a U.S. Army camp and given a bunch of papers to sign.

Among the papers that Gover received, three stand out. The first was his appointment as a second lieutenant.

SUBJECT: Appointment
TO: Second Lieutenant LeRoy Gover, AUS.

   1. The Secretary of War has directed the Theater Commander to inform you that the President has appointed and commissioned you a temporary Second Lieutenant in the Army of the United States effective 23 September 1942. This appointment may be vacated at any time by the President and, unless sooner terminated, is for the duration of the present emergency and six months thereafter. Your serial number is 0885183 and you will rank from 23 September 1942.

   2. This letter should be retained by you as evidence of your appointment as no commissions will be issued during the period of the war.

   By command of Lieutenant General EISENHOWER

Also included were orders designating him a pilot and another set placing him on flying status. Everything about the move was not good, however. Lee and the other Americans got no credit for their service in the RAF for pay or time in the service. They also were not given official credit for enemy aircraft destroyed, although their combat time counted. One concession was that they could wear their RAF wings over the right breast pocket of their U.S. uniform.

"Well, I'm in the Army now for sure," wrote Lee on September 24. "Back out to sign more papers and get $150 for my uniform allowance. Then back into town, where Lambert and I bought our uniforms. Then to the tailors." On Friday, "I went back out again and fixed up my $10,000 insurance papers. Jay Reed, Jack Mause and I went out on a spree." (The $10,000 free life insurance was very important to all of the Americans, and some of those who were not sure if they should transfer were convinced because of this factor. While in the RAF they had no insurance of any kind.) The next morning, Gover wrote his folks with the news.

Just a short note saying that I have transferred over and am now in the U.S. Army Air Forces. This was a few days ago, but I have been pretty busy signing papers, so I haven't written. I saw Jay last night, first time since we left OTU. Mause was in also, so we celebrated. I'm having my new uniform tailored and have to go get it tonight. Hate to get out of the old blue job. It has treated me pretty good. I really hated to leave the RAF. They made me a lieutenant, but promised a promotion in a month, so you just watch my smoke. My new address is Lieut. LeRoy Gover, 8th AF Fighter Command HQS, APO 637, New York, N.Y. I know it sounds like a silly address, but mail will get to me in six or seven days, since it all goes airmail.

Gover and his friends were a happy lot as they celebrated on Saturday night. Little did they know that while they were enjoying the day in London, the greatest tragedy they would see in the entire war was taking place with their squadron over France. Early on that Saturday morning, 133 Squadron had departed Biggin Hill for Bolt Head, where they refueled and were briefed for a normal mission escorting B-17s on a raid over France. The fighters were to rendezvous with the bombers over the Channel, but the two groups never found each other. While the fighter pilots had been briefed that they would have a wind of 35 miles per hour from the south, it was actually over 100 miles per hour from the north. The squadron was soon blown out of both radio and radar range. After searching for the B-17s for over an hour, Flight Lieutenant Brettell, an Englishman who was leading the unit because the usual commander, Carroll McColpin, was in London with Gover being sworn into the American forces, decided to go down through the clouds and look for a familiar landmark, since fuel was becoming critical. Given the forecast wind, Brettell thought they would be over England and it would be easy to find London and Biggin Hill. Instead, they found that they were over one of the most heavily defended ports in France, Brest. The ensuing barrage of flak, coupled with the fuel crisis, caused the loss of the entire squadron. Gover's account conveys his feelings.

Sunday, September 27, 1942 Miley and I caught the train out at 1:00 p.m. and came on up to our new station at Great Sampford. [The squadron was moved the day before in preparation for a ceremony transferring the Eagle Squadrons to the U.S. Army Air Forces.] Met McColpin and came out to the mess, where we heard the worst news possible. Our squadron had gone on a sweep to Brest, France, yesterday escorting Flying Fortresses, and our entire squadron was wiped out save one, Beaty, who crash-landed on the coast and is in the hospital. The Fortresses overshot the target and our boys ran out of fuel on the way back. Two bailed out in the Channel, and the rest bailed out or crash-landed in France. So there are just six of us left. Those lost were F/Lt Jackson, F/Lt Brettell, F/O Cook, F/O Baker, who had received the Distinguished Flying Cross two days ago, F/O Sperry, P/O Wright, P/O Neville, P/O Middleton, P/O Ryerson, P/O R.E. Smith, P/O D.P. Smith. So this is a sad place tonight around here. It is so quiet and empty. And it's raining hard.

Ryerson, Middleton and Beaty had been in Gover's class at Bakersfield. Of the eleven who bailed out or crashed, Sperry, Brettell, Jackson, Cook, Middleton and Wright were taken prisoner. All but Brettell survived the war. He was one of the fifty prisoners executed by the Germans for planning and executing the "Great Escape." Baker, Ryerson, Neville and Dennis Smith were killed. Robert Smith was able to evade capture and eventually returned to England through Spain. Gover's log book reflects how deeply he felt the losses. Next to the heading "The Eleven that went to Heaven" he lists each of the pilots who were lost and their fate.

The official transfer of the three Eagle Squadrons to the U.S. Army Air Forces, with accompanying pomp and ceremony, was scheduled for Tuesday, September 29, at Debden, which would be the base of the new American Fourth Fighter Group. But for all three squadrons, it was far from a happy day. The officers of 71 and 121 Squadrons, the other two Eagle Squadrons, also knew those who had been lost on Saturday, and even 133's eleven rapidly acquired replacements could sense the sadness the event brought to everyone. Nonetheless, the ceremony went as planned, but Gover's account shows his preoccupation with his lost friends.

> Well, we did our stuff for General Spaatz, General Hunter, Air Marshal Douglas and the other big shots and were officially welcomed into the U.S. Air Corps, with newsmen and newsreel boys all over the place. We received word tonight that Jackson, Sperry, Cook and Brettell are now prisoners of war. Those who jumped over the Channel have been given up as lost. No news of the others as yet. Hope they all made it OK and can make their way to Spain and escape.

Although Gover's description is brief, the ceremony was very important, for it not only marked the end of the American squadrons in the RAF, it also signaled the existence of a large enough American force in Europe to assume a major role in the offensive against the Luftwaffe. At the ceremony, Air Chief Marshal Sir Sholto Douglas noted the significance of the day.

> We of Fighter Command deeply regret this parting, for in the course of the past eighteen months, we have seen the stuff of which you are made and we could not ask for better companions with whom to see this fight through to the finish. It is with deep personal regret that I today say "Goodbye" to you whom it has been my privilege to command. You joined us readily and of your own free will when our need was greatest. There are those of your number who are not here today—those sons of the United States who were first to give their lives for their country. We of the RAF no less than yourselves will always remember them with pride. . . . Goodbye and thank you, Eagle Squadrons, and good hunting to you, Squadrons of the Eighth U.S. Air Force.

Life and *Time* magazines, which had followed the Americans in the RAF since the first squadron was announced in

October 1940, carried major articles on the ceremony and its significance to both Britain and the United States. Of the Eagles, *Life* wrote, "Only four of the original thirty-four pilots were on hand. One hundred men were missing—killed in action or by accident, or prisoners of the Axis." While *Life's* numbers were a little high, the units had certainly sacrificed a great deal for the cause of freedom. There had been 244 Americans in the Eagle Squadrons, and of this number 77 had been killed and another 16 were prisoners of war. It was from *Time*, *Life* and the news accounts that Gover's parents had to get the details of the transfer, because, typically not interested in any type of ceremony, he never wrote home with the details. A week later he simply wrote, "We had a parade when we changed armies, with newsreels and all. It was pretty nice and we are to receive a medal for our work in the Eagle Squadron."

Lee's tour in the RAF ended with the ceremony. He was awarded his American pilot wings, donned his U.S. Army Air Forces uniform, and began a new chapter in his life at war. Since entering the RAF, he had flown over one hundred hours in the Spitfire, the aircraft of his dreams, and become an experienced and proficient combat pilot.

5. SPITFIRES WITH STARS

With their transfer to the U.S. Army Air Forces (USAAF), the men of the three Eagle Squadrons made more history than they knew. Not only had they assured themselves a place of honor by having been among the first Americans to fly in combat in World War II, they were now almost the entire fighter contingent of the Eighth Air Force.

Because the American Army Air Corps emphasized strategic bombing during the latter part of the 1930s, the United States was able to provide some heavy bombers, primarily the B-17 Flying Fortress but also a few B-24 Liberators, to the European theater by early 1942. The numbers were small, however, and nearly all of the bombing was done by the RAF. But the interest in bombers meant that fighters were almost forgotten prior to the war, so the U.S. fighter inventory was in sad shape when the storm clouds gathered and France fell to the Germans. The fighters that were the backbone of the force at the beginning of the war, the Curtiss P-40 and the Bell P-39 Airacobra, were no match for the primary German fighter, the Messerschmitt ME-109. Added to these first-line U.S. fighters were such relics as the Curtiss P-36 Hawk, the older P-26, and the Brewster Buffalo, all of which were far too slow and lightly armed to be suitable for any combat.

The first effective long-range American fighter, the P-47 Thunderbolt, did not fly in production form until March 1942, and it was late summer before an American squadron equipped with eighteen of the earliest version of this aircraft arrived in England. The P-47 underwent further development and was not ready to assume the burden of being the primary U.S. fighter until January 1943. The P-51 Mustang, which proved to be the best fighter of the war, did not become operational in the Eighth Air Force until December 1943. (The P-51 with which Gover reported his simulated combat in July was an early version that was not put into combat production because of serious engine problems.) So if the Americans were to have a fighter that could hold its own against the Luftwaffe and perform the demanding escort mission for the B-17 in late 1942, it had to be the Spitfire, and the initial source of both pilots and aircraft was the RAF.

Since there were a relatively small number of bombers available, the flying duties for the pilots of the Fourth Fighter Group differed significantly from those they had while in the RAF. With the exception of having American uniforms and being paid nearly four times as much, however, the rest of their lives remained about the same. The units were still stationed at RAF bases, eating British food and flying Spitfires, often with RAF squadrons on the same mission and under RAF control. The first missions flown by the Fourth were still led by Wing Commander Duke-Woolley, who commanded the wing when it was still in the RAF. Even the fitter and rigger, the key to any pilot's success in combat, were British. "Without a good ground crew, you might as well never take off," Lee remarked.

These guys worked day and night, in freezing winter or hot summer, to make sure that your plane was always in top shape. I was happy to have my old fitter and rigger working on my plane after we transferred, and I must admit that I was a bit uneasy when the American crew chiefs took over.

The Americanization process was slow, and it would be early 1943 before it was completed. After all, the Army Air Forces was not getting spit-and-polish military men. Most of the former RAF pilots did not even know how to march. Lee remembered:

When we first came into the American Army Air Force, we were a raunchy bunch of pilots. We wore our RAF turtleneck sweaters, big fur-lined boots with a hunting knife stuck down in one of them, and an assortment of flying jackets. Our clothes hadn't been pressed for months. We were just a ratty bunch. The spic-and-span American pilots had all gone through flying school and were sharp dressers who complied with regulations. It didn't take them long to nickname the Fourth the "Sweatshirt Brigade." Every American pilot in England thought we were a rag-tag outfit. Our base commander, the first commanding officer of the Fourth, was Colonel E. W. Anderson. He was a Stanford graduate and also a West Pointer and was a perfect master at slowly getting us turned around. He never gave us hell or showed his authority. He just quietly made us realize the value of being a sharp outfit. Within three months he had us wearing our uniforms into the mess in the evening for dinner and looking in the mirror. He made a fairly decent bunch of pilots out of us, since we wound up the war as the highest-scoring group in any theater of operations with 1,052 enemy aircraft destroyed.

Upon their arrival in 336 Squadron, Gover, and each of the squadron members who had been an Eagle, received a personal letter from Major General Carl Spaatz, the commanding general of the Eighth Air Force. It said, in part, "There is attached to this letter a communication from Air Chief Marshal Portal, in which he thanks you and all your associates of the Eagle Squadrons for your services while members of the RAF." The letter is a significant tribute to each of the Americans who flew for the RAF.

On the occasion of the merging of the Eagle Squadrons with the USAAF, I would like to thank them, through you, for all they have done for us during the past two years. The RAD-RAF will never forget how the members of the Eagle Squadrons came spontaneously to this country eager to help us in the critical weeks and months during and after the Battle of Britain. We have admired their fine offensive spirit and their many successes bear witness to their skill. We are sorry to lose them, but we realize that it is in the best interests of the United Nations that they should now serve with their own country's Air Force. On behalf of the RAF, I heartily thank them and wish them continued success in the future.

There was no flying on September 30, because the British insignia, the rondel, had to be replaced by an American star on the Spitfires. Lee's thoughts, and those of the rest of the new

336th Fighter Squadron, did not stray far from the fate of their friends who had been lost four days earlier. "Received word that Jackson and Brettell are both wounded and prisoners but still no word of the other seven boys. Not much to do, as our new planes aren't ready. Won seven pounds playing poker." The following day, "flew our first squadron formation with our American Spitfires and the new guys (those who were assigned to take the place of the eleven lost last week) seemed to do OK." The same day he wrote about the transfer to his parents.

As you know, we're now working for Uncle Sam. Middleton and Ryerson were posted to heaven a few days ago [Gover's parents knew them from Lee's class at Bakersfield]. I'm on my eighth Spit now and it had an internal glycol [engine coolant] leak yesterday so they're putting in another motor. We are still known as the Eagle Squadron and get to wear our RAF wings over our right breast pocket, besides the U.S. wings on the left. A lot of us are supposed to get another medal of some sort for taking part in the Battle of Dieppe, another for being under fire, and still another one for being in the war before the States came in. So I'll just be full of them. [That these medals would be forthcoming was only a rumor, and they never materialized.]

I'm glad that I was in the RAF, because it gave me a way of looking at the war that the American forces just don't get. We were really treated as Brits and got to know them a lot better than most U.S. fellows do. We also were able to go to their homes and see the problems they have making it through the day and how really brave they are. It always amazes me every time I see an air warden standing outside in a bombing attack waiting to do whatever is needed to help out.

Three days after transferring, the squadron was unexpectedly sent from its base at Great Sampford to a satellite base at Gravesend. "Wait until you see the place," Mick Lambert had told Lee. "It is huge and the most beautiful house and grounds you've ever seen. We can just land on the lawn and taxi right up to the house if we want to." Gover was not disappointed.

Came down to Gravesend this noon and then went up for forty-five minutes to do a little tail chasing—me, Miller, Foster and

Robinson. Called back after forty-five minutes as the weather
was closing in. We are billeted in an old mansion on a very beautiful old estate.

Lee described the estate in great detail to his parents.

I'm now living in a big old castle and it is sure some place. It was
built in 1400 and belongs to Lord Darnley. I'm in the library
now, and it's a mere sixty by thirty feet. I'm sleeping in the Blue
Room. Queen Elizabeth, Henry III and some of those folks are
supposed to have slept here. There are hand-painted pictures
here that are ten by twenty feet, and the books in the library
must be worth a fortune. Some of them are even written in long-
hand. There's a bathtub that's made of marble and is four feet
deep, ten feet long and about four feet wide. Damn near can
swim in it. There are eight hundred and some acres in the estate,
with such spacious lawns and fountains around. The walls are
four feet thick, and it's really put together. You should see the
wallpaper. It must be hand-painted. The bathrooms are so damn
big that while one fellow was taking a bath and two were shaving,
five of us were around a table in the corner playing poker.
Lambert tried on a suit of armor, fell down and couldn't get back
up. He looked just like a beetle on its back. We just let him
holler for a while. When we use his estate, Lord Darnley moves
into one wing of the mansion and we use the other. The RAF
brings the food over from Gravesend for us.

Lord Darnley was no stranger to having pilots staying on his
estate. Because the Spitfire could operate easily off grass fields,
the RAF often used his estate as overflow from Gravesend
when there was a big mission in the offing. Occasionally, the
estate was also used to hide the Spitfires under the trees so
they would not be the target of a German strafing mission.
Lee continued his long letter:

We're in the U.S. Army now but we stayed together as an Eagle
Squadron, which suits us fine. We saw ourselves in the newsreel
the other day when they showed the transfer. There were eighty-
four Eagles that transferred. Not such a big number, but we've
been doing damn good. Do any of the old gang ever come up to

the house and ask how things are? Do the papers there ever mention the Eagles? If they do, send me some clippings now and then. P.S. Just received your letter saying you would put one buck away for me with every one I sent home, Dad. Is that a promise? Because I won $32 today playing poker.

"I think that England has the world's record for fog," Gover confided in his diary after his flight on Friday. "You can never plan on flying, so it's good that London is nearby."

Saturday, October 3, 1942   Fogged in tighter than hell. Released at 1:00 p.m. and went into town for the first time in an American uniform. What a change! Saw Mause and Reed at the Eagle Club. They are both about to leave for Africa—bad deal. Went to the Crackers Club and at 11:00 p.m. met Margaret and took a walk in the park. Stayed at the Regent and came back to Gravesend Sunday morning.

Gover later wrote about the change that he noticed when he went into London that Saturday.

Being in an American uniform was not a big thing for the people that we knew in London, since most of them knew about the transfer. But it was still strange to go into the Eagle Club and the Crackers Club and not see any RAF uniforms when a week before there were no American uniforms. Outside our familiar haunts, the difference was amazing. When we were in the RAF we were treated as being British even though we had a USA or Eagle patch on our shoulder. The people were always saying how glad they were that we had volunteered to come to England. But that was not the case with the American uniform. There were so many Americans in London every night that the British really got tired of their behavior. That is where the saying "overpaid, oversexed and over here" came from. In fact, there were occasions when the British were unfriendly until they saw our RAF wings. We made so much more money in the U.S. Army that prices which put things completely out of reach a few weeks earlier seemed very low to us after the transfer. We could seldom afford a cab while in the RAF but could take them all the time in the U.S. Army. I could tell that lots of the prices were raised for the Americans, but I don't blame the British, because we had so much more money than they had. I was really embarrassed with the behavior of some of the Americans. They just didn't understand England or the British way of doing things and didn't bother to learn. Those of us who had been in the RAF tried to tell them about getting along and how the British felt, but I don't think it did much good. The new boys in the squadron got a good course on how to behave and we didn't have much trouble with them, but most units didn't have a bunch of former RAF pilots in them.

Lee's first real operational mission as a USAAF pilot was convoy patrol on Tuesday, October 6, with Mick Lambert. Gover and Lambert always remembered the flight.

We had been flying convoy patrol for about an hour when we were called back to the base because of the weather. The clouds were very low and we were flying right on the deck. Somewhere along the way, Lambert hit a telephone line and a piece of telephone wire about 150 feet long got caught on his tail wheel, which didn't retract. I called him and said, "Mick, you've got a couple hundred feet of wire on your tail wheel." All he heard was "You've got a couple on your tail." Lambert went into all kinds of gyrations and started yelling over the radio. I lost sight of him in all his actions and landed first. He landed and came into the mess all steamed up. "Why wouldn't you help me when I was fighting off those two Germans?" he asked. "All you did was fly off and leave me." Everyone in the mess had a real laugh over that one when we figured out what happened.

The reason for the transfer to Gravesend became apparent when Lee's squadron was called back from an afternoon in London on Thursday and prepared for a major mission.

Friday, October 9, 1942 Up at 6:30 and down to breakfast. Then we were briefed to take 118 B-17 Flying Fortresses into Lille, France. There were five hundred fighters escorting them, both British and American. It was the biggest daylight bombing raid of the war so far. We lost four Fortresses, but not a single fighter. They sure tried to get me, though. I got a nice hole clear through my wing from flak—too close for comfort. [Not only was this mission the largest for the Eighth Air Force to date, it was the only one of that size during all of 1942.] At 1:00 p.m., we packed up and flew on back to our own base at Great Sampford. My ground crew was sure not happy to see the hole in my kite, but they are good boys and will have it all ready to go tomorrow. [Gover was enough impressed by the flak hole that he pasted a picture of it in his log book.]

Escort missions brought with them a number of problems for a fighter pilot. The first of these was evident with the 133 Squadron disaster of September 26—rendezvous with the bombers. Because of fuel capacity, fighter escorts never went with the bombers all the way to the target and back. Rather, they would rendezvous with the bombers and escort them through areas of high danger from enemy fighters and then break off and return home. Thus, any rendezvous time had to be precise for the fighters, because they were always operating on the margin of fuel availability. For the bombers, on the other hand, a few minutes one way or the other was not significant on a mission that would last for six to eight hours and on which fuel was seldom a problem.

The young, eager and inexperienced gunners on the bombers presented another challenge. It is difficult to recognize various types of aircraft in a combat situation without a great deal of experience. Often the gunners on the B-17s would mistake a Spitfire for an ME-109 and begin to fire on their own planes. This could cause the fighters to break off the escort in order to keep from getting hit themselves. The Eighth Air Force had to resort to distinctive paint schemes, such as white bands around the fuselage, in order to help the gunners discriminate between friend and foe.

Taking the fight to the enemy is the credo of a fighter pilot, and he was always ready to go after a German aircraft whenever he saw one. This trait was often used to their own advantage by the Luftwaffe pilots. They would fly in the vicinity of the bomber formation, or even make a small-scale attack on it, simply to draw the fighters away from the bombers. The main German force would then attack the bombers and inflict serious damage before the escort aircraft could rejoin the formation. This made it necessary to instruct the fighters to stay with the formation and only engage those aircraft that were directly attacking the bombers—a difficult thing for an aggressive fighter pilot.

Any excitement that went with the transfer to the USAAF had worn off by mid-October and the boredom of daily life was taking its toll. Lee explained the problem in a letter home. "We are just doing the same thing day after day and the cold, damp weather is getting everyone down." Gover's diary entries also become more brief.

Sunday, October 11, 1942   Did some practice flying today and took in the show that was held on camp this evening, then back to bed. Pretty cold and dark out these nights.

Monday, October 12, 1942   On readiness again and then we did some formation flying.

Tuesday, October 13, 1942   Readiness again and more local flying. Played cards again this evening and won twelve pounds—not bad.

Wednesday, October 14, 1942   More readiness and more cards. Won another two pounds. Getting colder these days.

The one bright spot in the whole situation was the time to play cards. "It is so great to be able to play poker instead of red dog, hearts and pitch," Mick Lambert remarked. "I think I can make some real money now." Lee agreed and added, "I wish we had been able to get up some good poker games when we were in the RAF. We would have cleaned up." He later explained that "we didn't play poker while in the RAF because no one had much money, there were no poker chips and the Brits were not interested in learning the game." While Lambert never reported his success, during the first week after transfer Gover won over $100 playing poker, and before October ended, he recorded that he had made over $200 for the month. The poker games paled, however, when compared to "the big crap shoot." Gover recalled the action.

When we transferred to the U.S. Army Air Forces, our pay jumped by over four times. Instead of about $58 a month we were getting nearly $300. So instead of playing hearts or pitch for a shilling, a big crap game started. There were over two hundred officers on the base, about one hundred pilots and then all the support people. There were thousands of dollars in cash ready to be gambled. The snooker table became the casino room, and on payday everyone tried out the crap table to see how he could do. By the second night, those who were winners from the night before shot it out, so on about the fourth night after payday, eight or ten of the fellows had all the money and the big-stakes game really got going. I watched all this for about three paydays, then decided I'd take $500 and go for broke.

Right in the middle of every game was Snuffy Smith, an ex-Eagle pilot. He really was a good crap shooter, and I decided to wait until he got a hot streak and then ride along with him. I won a few hundred dollars on payday night, and on the second night I did real well and had won a few thousand dollars. On the fourth night, I had built it up to $12,000. The dice came around to me and it was my turn to roll. I told myself that no matter what, I was going to quit with $10,000. I put $2,000 on the table and it was covered. I threw the dice and up came an eight. I took a deep breath, rolled, and a three and a five came up. I picked up my $14,000 and went to my room.

I had never seen that much money in my life, so the next day I sent $12,000 home and asked my dad to invest it in property. The other $2,000 I took, along with my friend Don Gentile, to London town. I bought Don a handful of big cigars, since he enjoyed one now and then. We hit every nightspot in town, bought everyone a drink or two and spent two days at the Savoy Hotel. We had a hell of a good time. The $12,000 I sent to my dad paid for a small building on El Camino Real in the heart of San Carlos. My dad fixed it up and rented it to a fellow that opened a bar, called the Patio Club. I never laid another dollar on the crap table, but I sure played a lot of poker.

Despite having transferred to the USAAF, Lee's squadron still had the use of a Tiger Moth (a small English biplane) when going to another base or if a couple of the pilots wanted to go somewhere together. "It was fun to just go up on a nice day and see the countryside," Lee reminisced. "The little machine only went about 100 miles per hour and it was the easiest thing to fly there ever was."

Thursday, October 15, 1942 Went up for a hop in the Tiger Moth. Was just flying around and enjoying the beautiful countryside when I saw green flares being shot up (the signal to land). I came down and was told to hop in my Spit as we were off to a show. Flew down to Thorney Island and were briefed and refueled. Then we escorted twelve Bostons over and bombed Le Havre, France. We were only at eight thousand feet and then went down to five thousand, so we dodged about in the flak for most of the way out. Came on back to Great Sampford without loss to the Bostons or ourselves. This was the first show for a couple of the new boys, and they were kind of shook by the flak. They ain't seen nothin' yet! So, another show is over.

As usual, a three-day pass for the long weekend meant a trip into London, the Regent Hotel and the Crackers Club. By Sunday Lee "was tired of London (meaning I was out of money), so caught the 1:00 train at Liverpool Street Station and came back to camp. Took in a movie." The week continued with readiness, formation flying and gun camera work, the latter two because the squadron was getting so few operational missions. The contrast with the action while still in the RAF was striking. "I wish that we would get more missions over France," Carl Miley remarked as the unit sat around on readiness waiting for something to happen. "I don't know why we aren't getting more action."

"I guess it just isn't our turn," replied Mick Lambert. "Maybe the American commanders don't think we can fly and we need more practice. I don't mind some, but it sure doesn't substitute for being up against a bunch of Huns."

Neither Miley nor Lambert had the right explanation, however. While in the RAF, the squadron was used almost daily on sweeps over France, for convoy patrol or on alert for the defense of England. But the USAAF was not responsible for either the defense mission or convoy protection, so that part of the flying was, with rare exceptions, taken away. Further, since there were so few American fighters in Europe, they were needed for use primarily as escorts for American bombers. Given the shortage of these aircraft, there were few missions, so practice was the order of the day—practice and long weekends in London.

Friday, October 23, 1942 Caught the 11:27 train out of Audley End and came on in to London. Checked in at the Regent Palace Hotel and did a little shopping. Went down to the Crackers Club and talked until 9:30, when I met Margaret. We hit a few of the spots and then back to the Regent and to bed.

Margaret was one of the first women that Lee had met after coming to England. "I'll never forget the first time I saw Margaret," Lee remembered.

"The Regent Palace is the place to stay," the fellows told me over at the Eagle Club. "It is really nice and the location is great—right off Piccadilly and close to everything." Because the streets run off of Piccadilly like spokes, a lot of the buildings, including the Regent, are pie-shaped, so I missed the narrow entrance the first time. But after I found the door, I was impressed. The place just kept getting larger the farther you walked in. It was all paneled in wood and looked like the nicest places in San Francisco. Off to the left was a stairway that took you down to the bar, and to the right was the lobby. The room was spacious, with lots of chairs and sofas and the registration desk on the right side. I walked over and asked for a room. "I'm sorry, we are full for the night," said the trim brunette behind the desk. "I really wish I could find a room for you, but I'm just out of them." I left and found a room in another hotel but came back the next day, both to find a room and to talk to the girl behind the desk. I found that her name was Margaret, and since she was a looker, I asked her if she would meet me after she got off work. We met and had a really good time seeing the sights and hitting a few nightspots. When I left she told me to be sure to come to the Regent next time I was in town and I would have a room.

My next visit to London took me straight to the Regent, and sure enough, there was Margaret and I had a room. We met after she got off work again and one thing led to another. I suggested that we go to my room in her hotel, and she agreed. I'll tell you she was a well-built woman and gave me a night to remember. After that, I would always get a room at the Regent, and Margaret shared it with me lots of nights. She was a neat lady even when we weren't in bed, and I just enjoyed her company. I went out with

Early in his flying career, Lee Gover learned that the ladies always liked a pilot: With a friend and an Eagle Rock biplane at Cooley Field, San Carlos, California, in 1930.

Gover and his Cub in 1936, before he modified it with wheel pants and a propeller spinner.

With his instructor, Herb Tansey,
Gover narrowly escaped death
when they crashed their PT-17 in
August 1941.

Gover's flying buddies at Meadows Field (the Bakersfield, California, airport) in August 1941. Don Young (opposite bottom) flew in the Eagles and the 4th Fighter Group with Gover. He was the only other member of Gover's class at Bakersfield to continue operational flying throughout the war. Jack Mause (top left) was seriously injured in a plane crash in Africa and sent back to the States as unfit to fly. Jay Reed (top right) transferred to the USAAF and flew during the invasion of Africa. He returned to the United States in early 1943. Mick Lambert (bottom left) flew with Gover in 133 Eagle Squadron, but shortly after transfer to the USAAF he was removed from combat flying and sent to instructor duty. During the years after World War II, he was Gover's best friend. George Middleton (bottom right) was shot down in his Spitfire in September 1942 and was a prisoner in Stalag Luft III for the remainder of the war.

Mick Lambert (lead plane), George Middleton (middle) and
Gover in August 1941 on their first dangerous mission: to buzz
Clark Gable's duck pond.

Gable (in sunglasses) asked Gover and his friends not to do it again—
and then bought them root beer.

Gover's class at the Bakersfield RAF Refresher Course in 1941 (Gover standing, sixth from right). Just half the class survived the war, with only Gover and Don Young left in operational flying at the end of 1943.

Dec. 1941

Gover's operational training unit class at the Llandow RAF Base in December 1941. Gover (front row, fifth from left) and two others (excluding the administrative staff) were the only ones not later killed in combat (the *X*'s) or hurt so badly in crashes that they never flew again (the *O*'s).

In a village near his training base in Wales in December 1941. The young Californian's diary and letters home reflected admiration for the British people and appreciation of their country's beauty.

X = Killed
O = Crashed & Unfit
To Fly Again

Like most of his fellow pilots, Gover spent much of his leave time escaping the war in the clubs of London—although it was here that he was very nearly killed in an air raid in 1944.

With a Spitfire VB on alert at the Portreath RAF Base in April 1942.

The first picture to his parents from England, March 1942.

Mission briefing for the 66, 118 and 501 squadrons of Ibsley wing in July 1942. Arrow indicates Gover.

Gover in the cockpit of his Spitfire, Ibsley RAF Base, July 1942. Note the small bar on the cockpit door, used to pry off the canopy if its release mechanism failed.

Gover meets the Duke of Kent at a munitions factory near Redruth, England, in July 1942. Less than six weeks later, the duke was killed in an aircraft accident.

Gover's Spitfire VB with bullet holes. If the hits had been three feet further toward the nose, Gover's war would have been over.

Gover's ground crew with his Spitfire VB at the Tangmere RAF Base just prior to the famous Dieppe raid of August 1942.

Eleanor Roosevelt visiting the 4th Fighter Group in November 1942 at the Debden RAF Base. Gover is at left. Several of the pilots had just returned from flying, the reason for their motley attire.

The *Sondra Lee*, named after Gover's niece.

Glenn Smart, World War I ace Eddie Rickenbacker, and Gover
at Debden in July 1943.

The first two-hundred-gallon belly tanks for the P-47, Debden, July 1943.
Their addition increased the P-47s' range so they could escort B-17s into
Germany. The first time they were used, the Germans attacked the
bomber formation, still thinking the escorts must be low on fuel.

The *Miss San Carlos.*

Gover getting into his P-47.

Don Gentile, one of the highest-scoring USAAF aces of World War II, and Gover at Debden in 1943. Gentile later crashed a P-51 while making a low-level pass for reporters and was sent home. He and Gover remained in close contact until Gentile was killed in an aircraft accident in 1951.

Photo of Gover in his P-47, the *Miss San Carlos*, taken from a disabled B-17 he was escorting, 1943.

Gover after receiving the Silver Star and Distinguished Flying Cross at Debden on July 9, 1943. He was the first pilot in the 4th Fighter Group to receive the Silver Star.

Lee Gover is still active in flying at age eighty.

her off and on all the time I was in England, and I never had to worry about getting a room in that most popular hotel.

Lee's diary continues.

Sunday, October 25, 1942 Just fooled around the Eagle Club this morning. Beaty and I went to see *Bomber Command* this afternoon. It was very good. Went to the Georgian House for a while and then to the Princess. Beaty met a little gal and I cracked off to the Regent and guess who.

While he was lounging around the Eagle Club, Gover wrote his folks about his activities in London, the description of which contrasts sharply with what he confided in his diary.

I have a couple of days off, so came into London hoping to see some of the boys. Did a little shopping this morning. Bought myself a pair of brown fur-lined flying boots for $30 and a very nice trench coat. It should be nice, it cost $74, and that ain't hay. There are a lot of people in town these days, but I usually get fed up in this place and go back to the squadron early and take a hop in my kite, here and there, just having fun. As I told you before, I received the swell wristwatch, but no sign of the fountain pen. [Lee had asked his folks to send him one several months earlier.] I met a ferry pilot here at the Eagle Club a little while ago and he gave me his new Parker pen. He's going back to New York in the morning and insisted I take his pen, as he can get another. Pretty nice of him, since I had never seen him before. He flies the big Liberators over, and his wife is his copilot—ain't that something. So, if the pen you sent doesn't arrive, I'll be OK. This one is a honey. [The letter is nicely written, evidently with the new pen.] Is Dad still going to put a buck with every one I send home, and how much is he going to sell the Cadillac to me for? How about a hundred bucks under blue book?

Lee's tangible memories of his time in the RAF came to an end the following Tuesday when he flew for an hour and then "went over to my room and packed all my Royal Air Force clothes, which I'm going to try and send home—Happy Memories." Two days later, ". . . hopped a train to London. Went to a party at the Eagle Club to celebrate our transfer to the USAAF. Gabbed awhile with Bebe and Ben Lyon. Was a pretty good party and lots of fun." Gover later wrote:

> The Eagle Club was a second home to us. Mrs. Dexter and Barbara Blake worked so hard to make us feel welcome that everyone tried their best to get to the party. I saw some of the guys who were not in the Fourth Fighter Group but who had been at the Eagle Club a lot. There were several American civilians there also. Since it was run by the Red Cross, there was no alcohol allowed, but no one seemed to mind. Besides, we all went out and had another party afterward.

With the party at the Eagle Club and another day in London, Gover's first month in the U.S. Army Air Forces came to an end. "Overall, it was pretty boring and we really didn't have much to do," Gover remembered.

> I think that the Eighth Air Force hadn't figured out how to use us yet, and since there weren't many U.S. bombing raids, we sat around a lot. I spent an awful lot of time in London, but the account evened out when the going got tough in 1943.

Although he flew nearly sixteen hours in October, only four flights, totaling six hours and fifteen minutes, were classed as combat missions.

The 336th began November by moving to Debden, a large permanent base about two hours by train from the heart of London. Since his arrival in England, less than a year before, Lee had moved nine times, but he stayed at Debden for the remainder of his tour in Europe. The other two squadrons of the Fourth, 334 and 335, had been stationed at Debden since before the Eagles left the RAF, so now the group was complete and all at the same base. Debden had two hard-surfaced runways, approximately 90 degrees to each other. The runway complex was completely circled by taxiways next to which the aircraft were parked. On the east side of the runway complex were the maintenance buildings, then the various support groups, and behind them the officers' mess and pilots' housing. Gover remembered:

The living quarters were very nice, since it was a permanent base. There were four or five houses fifty yards or so from the main officers' mess. Each house had several rooms in which the pilots were billeted. There were also a large number of rooms in the mess. I roomed in one of the houses for a couple of months with Spike Miley until Oscar Coen, who lived in the mess building, lost his roommate and asked me to move in with him. It was great to be in the main building. We were only fifty feet down the hall from the dining room, lounge, bar and poolroom. We were on the first floor with a bathroom and showers right across the hall. I stayed there the rest of my tour in England.

Gover's initial reaction to Debden was "It is not a bad place but cold as hell."

On November 3, the anniversary of Lee's departure for England, he wrote a rather nostalgic letter home.

Well, today makes exactly one year since I left home. I received your letter of October 9th a couple of days ago. The mail situation hasn't been so good of late, but you haven't been getting any either, so I guess we're even there. I was in town [London] for a couple of days last week. I went to a party at the Eagle Club that was given for us fellows that transferred. It was a pretty nice affair. Bebe Daniels and Ben Lyon were there, the American newsreels took movies and there was a photographer from *Life* magazine. So you may see it over there. I went to a movie here last night, and what should I see but a picture on *Young America Flies*. It was taken at Palo Alto, and it sure was good to see the old field and some aerial shots of Stanford. All those little old Cubs flying around. All us fellows got a big kick out of seeing the troubles the kids went through to learn to fly. It all looks so simple now that we've gone this far in the flying game. But there's probably not a one of us that could jump in a little Cub and fly it the way it's supposed to be done. It was bad news for me that Grandma had died. Just how did Grandpa take it and what is he doing? We thought a while ago that we might be going to come home but that's out. [This was another rumor that proved to be false.] So I'll be seeing you in another year if everything goes OK. I believe Jay and Mause have gone abroad, but Young and I are still with the Eagles as before. [Gover continued to refer to his squadron as the Eagles for several months after he transferred out of the RAF.]

The bad weather of the first few days of November cleared on the fourth, just in time for a visit by Eleanor Roosevelt, the President's wife. The entire squadron put on a thirty-minute air show for the occasion, and after they landed, they had the opportunity to meet the First Lady.

We all lined up and Colonel Anderson introduced each of us to Mrs. Roosevelt. Later in the day there was also a tea in her honor. We were all impressed that she would come to our squadron and then take the time to talk to each of us. She asked me where I was from, made some nice remarks about California and thanked me for all I was doing in the war. I'm sure that she said about the same thing to everyone, but I was still flattered that she talked with me.

Gover later revealed that when the Eagles transferred to the USAAF, almost none of them knew how to march, since they had not learned in the RAF. When they heard that Mrs. Roosevelt would review the squadron, the adjutant was assigned to draw a faint line on the tarmac so the unit would be in a straight line and would look good for the First Lady. Neither she nor the generals accompanying her knew that the lineup and the dismissal after the review were simply chaos. "If anyone had asked us to do something like pass in review, we would have all been dead ducks," Gover wrote.

The day following the visit by the First Lady, Lee finally saw some action again. Even though the "weather was lousy," he led his flight on convoy patrol, a mission seldom performed by the Fourth. The convoy was huge, over sixty ships, and they were attacked by two ME-109s.

They must have been crazy to try to do anything to the convoy in that weather. I think they were just going home on the deck and stumbled onto the ships. Anyway, we chased them and I got a short burst off, but they disappeared into the clouds. Was out for an hour and forty-five minutes and we got back with no problem.

Had his aircraft problems of the next day occurred while he was on convoy patrol, Gover would have been in real trouble.

Friday, November 6, 1942   There was a sweep to Le Havre scheduled today. We went down to Ford and refueled. Just after we took off, my instruments went all haywire and I couldn't continue on the mission, so I came back to Debden. It is a good thing my instruments went bad when they did, because everyone on the sweep got caught in the fog and was asking for a homing to find the base. I still am mad that I didn't get to go on the sweep.

Sunday, November 8, 1942   Finally had a sweep to Calais this noon. We took eighteen Fortresses to Lille, France. There was a lot of flak and the FW-190s really came up after us. We lost one Fortress but also six fighters. I got the hell shot out of me by an FW-190 I didn't see. He came in from the side and got me right behind the cockpit. A few feet farther forward I would be history. Overall, the mission was a big shambles.

In his log book, Gover included a picture taken of his Spitfire after this mission. The bullet holes make a clean line from top to bottom right behind the cockpit.

As with most intense action in which he was involved, Lee wrote nothing about this mission to his parents. He did get upset when his mother wrote she had heard that men over twenty-eight years old were being kept out of combat.

No, we fellows over twenty-eight are still at it. That's all hooey. We are right in the front-line fighters and can show these new guys plenty. I'm still alive after a year of it and I've seen plenty come and go. I've had some good gos and get right in there. Just use the old bean and you have a good chance. Well, Mom, I'll close for now and hit the hay.

On Tuesday, Lee was off to London on a five-day pass. "Checked in at the Regent and hopped over to the Crackers Club. Sure dark out tonight." Lee often mentioned the darkness and how hard it was to get around in London with the total blackout. "If there was no moon, you really had a time," he wrote.

You just had to know your way and get what light you could. Some of the new guys really got lost on a dark night, but if you knew the town and how to use the subway, you could get around just fine.

Wednesday, November 11, 1942 Armistice Day and we are at war again. What a world! Rose called this morning. Did a little shopping and met her at 6:00 p.m. Went to the Princess Bar for a few drinks and then to dinner. Went out to her apartment after and gabbed awhile. I missed the last train back to town, ahem— so I went back and stayed there. Sure glad her husband is out east these days.

Of all the women whom Gover went out with while he was in England, Rose was the one for whom he developed the deepest feeling. She was married to a British army officer who was stationed in the Middle East. "Meeting a married woman was not at all unusual. A great number of them went out with other men during the war. I think we all just lived for the moment," Gover reminisced.

I met her one night when I was at a pub having a beer. She was there with another guy. I guess she was attracted to me, because she got up, came over and opened my greatcoat to see if I had wings. When she saw them, she dumped the other guy, fortunately without getting me in a fight, and I had her. She was pretty, about my age, maybe a little on the chubby side, but most of the excess was in the right places. She was about five feet five, brunette, and really a lot of fun. That first night I met her we went to her apartment, and wow, did I learn some things. Anyway, the last train left the station near her apartment at 10:00, so I often missed it. It was just fine with me to stay with her all night, but I always had to sneak out in the morning, because she didn't want her neighbors to know that she was "entertaining" a male friend. She would often call me at Debden and ask me to come in or else call me at the Regent, since she knew I always stayed there. We did a lot of things over the time I knew her, and she was just fun to be with. We had the same interests and could shop and see the sights for hours, even though both of us had seen them before. I was really very happy when I was with her. I don't know what happened to Rose. It was a sad day for us both when I left England, because I think we knew in our hearts that we would not meet again. She was truly a lovely lady and I remember her fondly.

Gover's diary continues:

Thursday, November 12, 1942   Got up at 6:00 a.m. and beat it back to town. You know how people talk. Then went down to the Eagle Club. They asked me to broadcast, so I talked home this afternoon.

Although, once again, Gover's parents did not hear the broadcast, the Red Cross sent them a transcript, which generated big stories in both the Redwood City and San Carlos newspapers. Under the headline "San Carlos Flier Broadcasts from England" was a picture of Gover speaking into a BBC microphone. The Redwood City article recaps Gover's experiences during the past few months while that in the San Carlos paper simply notes, "Photograph of Lieutenant LeRoy Gover of 616 Cedar Street, San Carlos, received from London this week, showing him speaking into the BBC microphone during a weekly broadcast to America from the American Red Cross Eagle Club in London, England."

Saturday, November 14, 1942   Don Young and I ran about town this morning, and did we have a time. We were casually walking across London Bridge, taking pictures and looking at the sights. All of a sudden a female voice screamed, "Attention!" Damn near blew my eardrums out. We could tell rank by now, and there stood two female lieutenant colonels. They wanted to know why we didn't salute superior officers. There was an MP nearby and she called him over to check our identification. She wrote down our names and such and said they were from General Eisenhower's office and we would hear about this. She then asked us what we were doing in London when there was a war on. Don Young just said, "I suppose they'll have us sent to combat." That was all there was to it. Came on back to the Eagle Club and had a big laugh over the whole thing. On back to camp and so ends a lovely weekend.

Typical late-fall weather continued at Debden. The day after returning from his latest foray into London, Lee got caught above the clouds.

Was up flying this afternoon and the fog closed in tight. Had to ask for a homing, and the clouds were so damn thick that I went right over the field and didn't see it. They vectored me back near Debden and shot rockets up through the clouds. I just spiraled down where the rockets had come up and, sure enough, there was the field. I was sure glad to get back. Went to the show and then to bed.

The same situation was repeated all week, and although Gover got a couple of flights, he spent most of the time waiting for weather good enough for a takeoff. Lectures on enemy aircraft, security, how to conduct yourself if you were captured, and how to escape took up some of the time. Snooker, movies and writing letters rounded out the days.

On Wednesday, November 25, Lee began a two-week air firing course at Debden. "Spent the day learning how to assess combat films and shooting at a lot of clay pigeons. Did some flying and attacks this evening."

Thursday, November 26, 1942   Thanksgiving Day. Did some cine gun today [making attacks on other aircraft using cameras rather than guns]. The fog closed in and caught a bunch of us up. Three fellows landed at another field. I just arrived and barely got in with a ceiling of fifty feet. Two fellows collided, and Captain Sprague of 334 Squadron spun in and was killed. The other fellow came back to the field here and crash-landed. Another kite was washed out this morning by my number two man, Mitchellweis, so that's three planes and one life today. We had a pretty fair supper of roast pork and apple sauce, but I'll take Mom's any day. This evening Hively, Miley, Nee and I went into Saffron Walden for a few beers.

Met Major Coen, Captain Stepp and Lieutenant Ross and had a few more. Then back to the mess.

Having to fly only thirty minutes on the day after Thanksgiving gave Lee time to write a very long and thoughtful letter to his folks.

We had a pretty good Thanksgiving dinner last night of roast pork and apple sauce. Only we couldn't have an extra helping. Enclosed are a couple of clippings you can put in your scrapbook. And now, Dad, here's where you come in. I'm taking you up on that dollar-for-dollar deal, and as soon as I get to London after the 1st of December, I'm going to send you a money order for $1,000. So you just put it together with the one you just received and buy me two $1,000 war bonds. That will leave $500, as they cost $750 apiece. Just save it until I send you the other $250 for another $1,000 bond. Make them out to me and yourself as the beneficiary. Then if anything happens to me they are yours without any red tape. If anything should go wrong that you should need this money to live on, you just pull the bonds out and sell them. You're plenty welcome to them, and I owe you folks more than money could ever buy. I came into the U.S. Air Corps as a second lieutenant on September 23, 1942, and the CO told me that he has sent in my name and in a day or so now I will be a first lieutenant. I believe I can be a captain in six months now. I have a good record and try to do right and tend to my job. In this business, you have to or else. Dick Beaty was a happy kid last week when he left here for home. He was with me at Bakersfield and has had a couple of crack-ups and it scared the kid pretty bad. Lambert is sitting here beside me now reading the paper. He, Young and I are the only ones left of the Bakersfield gang.

"For some reason the weather cooperated while I was at gun camera school and I flew every day," Gover wrote.

Tuesday, December 1, 1942 Still leading the class. Captain DuFour asked me if I'd stay and be his assistant. Said I'd get a captaincy out of it. I'm also getting pretty good on my skeet shooting these days. Still damn foggy around here.

Wednesday, December 2, 1942 Finished the course today. Major Coen said I was needed in the squadron and asked what I wanted to do. When I thought about being off operations if I went as an instructor, I decided to stay and keep up with the fight. Probably be killed if I stay on fighting, but that's what I came over to do—fight.

And fight was just what Lee was to do as soon as he got back to the squadron.

Friday, December 4, 1942 We had a sweep today—Captain Stepp wasn't here so I took charge and led A Flight. We went in at Calais, France, and to Gravelines. It was a good show and lots of fun being the leader. There were only about twelve Jerries up after us. I got one in my sights and got a couple of good bursts at him. I saw that I was hitting him but don't know if he crashed, so I'll have to be content with one FW-190 damaged. Another Jerry got even with me by putting a few machine-gun bullets right through my rudder.

Sunday, December 6, 1942 Again I led A Flight on a sweep. We were escort to a bunch of Fortresses and went in to bomb near Lille, France. We were at 25,000 feet and it was cold as hell. About thirty FW-190s came up but we drove them off. Then this p.m. I took another pilot out and we did a convoy patrol for fifty-five minutes. The weather was so damn bad we had to leave and ask for a vector home. If it wasn't for radio over here we would all have been lost and killed long ago, and I don't mean maybe either. I also received my first lieutenant's bars today.

In another letter home, Lee summed up his very busy week.

I went on a show this afternoon and damn near froze to death. I sure wish the Spitfire had a heater. In fact, my oxygen tube would freeze and when I'd squeeze it, ice crystals would blow into my mask and slap me in the face. Very refreshing when its about 40 below, very. Got a card from George Middleton and was very happy to hear he is well even though he is a prisoner of war in Germany. I wrote you earlier that he had been posted to heaven. I got a kick out of his card. He started off by saying,

"First thing you guys can do is put back all my stuff, 'cause I'm very much alive." Anyway, he was right; we've divided all his stuff. I'm going to write back and ask him what he's going to do about it. He's a great guy. Our captain was gone today and so I led our flight. I'm slowly going up the old ladder.

I finished my air firing course in first place and was asked if I would take a job as an instructor and was told I'd make captain if I did. Sounded OK until I realized I would be off of operations and no more fighting. Maybe I was wrong, but I just couldn't do without the old squadron life. Dawn patrols, convoy patrols, scrambles, sweeps and the old scared feeling when you're starting out on a do. My CO got wind of it and went to the colonel and told him I was needed in the squadron. He then put me as sub–flight commander and told me not to worry about a captaincy as it would just be a matter of a few months. So I'd rather be a captain in a fighter squadron than a general in a soft job. By the way, just what did I say on that radio broadcast? I can't help it if I forgot.

Lee had Thursday and Friday off and, as usual, went to London.

Found out at the Eagle Club that Jack Mause is back from Africa. He was shot down and is here in the hospital with a fractured skull. So I hope I get to see him. Took in a show this afternoon with Don Nee and Mick Lambert. Saw Tabb and some of the boys at the Eagle Club. Then stepped out with Rose this evening. Went to dinner at the Princess and then out for a few drinks. She sure is fun.

Friday, December 11, 1942 Was called back to the drome today, so something must be cooking. And just when I had begun to get going here in town.

Whenever it was necessary to contact one of the American fliers when they were in London, a telegram was sent to the Eagle Club, since many of the Americans dropped by there at least once a day. Even if they did not come by the club, the word was passed along and would soon be all over town that they had a message. "The system worked well, and I don't know of anyone going more than a few hours without getting the word," Gover remembered.

Saturday, December 12, 1942 Was called to briefing about 10:00 a.m. and then our group (thirty-six planes) took off and escorted Liberators to Abbeville, France. [In the RAF, three squadrons was a wing; in the USAAF, three squadrons was a group.] We bombed the airdrome there, which is where the crack German fighter pilots are based. And did the little dears come up or did they? Just like a bunch of mad hornets when you stir the nest. Alexander's motor cut going over the Channel, but he made it back to Manston airdrome in England. We mixed it up for a while and then beat it for home. I got a couple of bursts but didn't hit anything. We have to stay close to the bombers so can't chase the Huns very far. I was on readiness then in the afternoon and was sent out to patrol a convoy. It was very hazy and no visibility, so just flew round and round the convoy for an hour and a half and came home. Played pool and went to the cinema this evening.

As Christmas approached, Lee's thoughts turned more toward home. Although this was his second Christmas season in England, everything had been so new to him that he hadn't thought much about home a year before. Now he had been in combat, lost several of his friends and learned the reality of war. In thinking back to that second Christmas season in England, Lee wrote:

I always thought that the Christmas season would really be something in England, the land of *A Christmas Carol* and all. But with everything blacked out and bombs dropping periodically, London didn't seem much like a Christmas city, and the war pretty well dampened everyone's Christmas spirit. I think that made me focus more on home. I wasn't homesick, but I just thought a lot more about everyone.

Lee's letters reflect that general spirit.

December 7, 1942 I just received your Christmas package, and thanks. Not being exactly sure of my being here on Christmas [this is the closest Lee ever came to speculating that he might be killed], I opened it and am very glad to get the things. I just received another card from Middleton, from his prison camp in Germany. In fact, I'll send it along for you to put in your scrapbook. I've just finished writing him a letter. I should just drop it down to him and save the postage. Sorry I haven't sent any Christmas presents, but there isn't much to send. But my best wishes and all my love will be with you. Don't worry about me, as I'm taking very good care of your boy LeRoy.

The same tone was evident ten days later.

December 17, 1942   Greetings. I'm sitting here in my little old room just chewing away on some caramel candy that belongs to my roommate and looking at my new sweater that Grace knit and sent me for Christmas. I'm enclosing a picture of George Quinn. He was with me at Bakersfield. Anyway, he received the Distinguished Flying Cross awhile back but has been killed since. I want you to take a picture of the Cadillac from in front and one from the side with no one in the picture, and a half-dozen different views of the house as well as one of each of you and send them to me—but quick. There was a broadcast at the Eagle Club and party tonight celebrating its second anniversary. I was invited but couldn't make it. Don't let the post office kid you. You can send me packages of over two pounds and as many as you want through my APO address. So I would like some "Chok-Full-A-Almond" bars, maybe a box of chocolate-covered nuts, and another box full of those "Russian tea cakes" that Aunt Jean used to make. If all this is too much trouble, then never mind. We were told that we don't get off for a leave to go home until we have served eighteen months, and my thirteen in the RAF don't count. Just the time since we transferred. So, I'm afraid I won't be seeing you until the summer of 1944. I'm not homesick or anything like that but would like a couple of weeks home. This way, I'll have three years in this damn war, and it's a pretty big-time war from where I'm sitting. But someone has to do it. All I hope is that when it's over we get a chance at a good job there and those chickens who stayed there don't get all the gravy.

Christmas season or no Christmas season, the war went on, and so did Gover's combat activity.

Sunday, December 20, 1942 Escorted ninety Fortresses that bombed near Paris, France, today. We went in at Dunkirk at twenty thousand feet. We didn't get any flak but there were over seventy FW-190s up at us. Not a good day, since we lost eleven bombers, but forty-four FW-190s were shot down. I got my piece of the action. When they came in at the bombers I picked one and got deflection on him with no trouble. I shot the hell out of him, but the pilot never bailed out (I think he was probably dead). There were so many Germans coming at those bombers that I couldn't follow the 190 down so don't know if he crashed or not. It was a good day for our fighters but a bad one for those poor bomber boys. This evening Tiger Booth and I went to the show.

Tuesday, December 22, 1942 I was duty pilot today and all night tonight. Fog closed in and I took over the ground radio and got them all in safely. Just one thing after another today.

Wednesday, December 23, 1942 Finished up my tour as duty pilot at 6:00 this evening. Sure is a bind. The complete drome is under your control and you're responsible for all aircraft and there was night flying on last night. What a workout.

Friday, December 25, 1942 Merry Christmas. I was on readiness until 1:00 p.m. Then just sat in front of the fire until supper. Had roast pork (cut with a razor blade), potatoes and Brussels sprouts, so we'll have bubble and squeak for breakfast.

Fog, clouds, rain and snow were the order of the day for the remainder of 1942. The snow was cleared from the runways so Gover could take some of the new pilots in the squadron up for some cloud flying on twenty-ninth. He also took the time to sit in front of the fire in the mess and write to his parents.

Well, it looks as if another year has just about slipped by. Doing quite a bit of flying these days and keeping very much alive. I received word that Mause is back in London so will run in tomorrow and see him, as he is on his way back home. Jay is still OK, but is still in Africa. The flight commander is back and I'm taking a couple of days off, so I will be in London for New Year's

Eve. O'Hara is the latest casualty of the Bakersfield gang. I believe I told you Quinn also had it. Lambert's nerves are shot, so he is being sent away to some nonoperational unit. That leaves Young and me the only ones left. We had roast pork, Brussels sprouts and potatoes for Christmas dinner. Sure didn't compare with Mom's, but I have no complaints at all. I've just been going over our December flying times and find that I have the most time and have made more sweeps than any other pilot in the squadron. Tell everyone hello and Happy New Year.

"Throughout the war, people in London would send invitations to the Eagle Club for an American pilot to be their guest at a dinner or a party," Lee remembered.

I went to several of those but most of the boys didn't like to go. I guess they would rather drink and chase girls. Mrs. Dexter at the Eagle Club even asked me one day why more of the invitations weren't taken, because, she said, there were really some nice parties available. I guess I was one of the few who enjoyed going to some of the things, and besides, I really didn't have much else to do, especially if one of my ladies wasn't available. I remember once going to see *Arsenic and Old Lace* with General Montgomery. There were four or five of us, but I was the only American. We sat in the best box and all. I never got to talk to him other than to say hello.

Thursday, December 31, 1942   New Year's Eve. Went into the Eagle Club this morning and Barbara Blake had an invitation for what she thought would be a very good New Year's Eve party, so I decided to go. She gave me a little card that said the invitation was from Mr. G. B. Morgan, Flat 32, 55 Park Lane, which sounded pretty exclusive to me. The card said I would be picked up at 7:30, and what do you know, a chauffeur-driven Rolls-Royce pulled up in front of the Jules Club to get me. The chauffeur said he was to take me to Mr. Morgan's party at the Landsdowne Club, one of the most exclusive in London. When I got there I found it was in honor of Lord Louis Mountbatten, the commander of all the forces in India. There were six gals and six fellows in our group. My escort was a pretty little thing, about three or four years younger than me. I really felt self-conscious, but everyone tried to make me feel at home. Lots of people wanted to know about being a fighter pilot and combat, and since I was the only pilot there, they talked to me. I even sat and talked with Lord Mountbatten for ten or fifteen minutes. They served a dinner with things to eat I had never seen before in England and so much silverware and so many glasses that I didn't know when to use them all. They even had waiters wearing white gloves. I just watched my escort and did what she did and got along OK. At 11:30 we went to the Embassy Club and helped the New Year in. At about 4:00 a.m. I breezed back to the hotel in the Rolls-Royce limousine. It was a damn good party and nothing but champagne, and the gals were damn pretty too.

Friday, January 1, 1943   Happy New Year. I got up late and my head even later, so I didn't do a hell of a lot today. Took in a show and went to the Savoy in the evening to throw a little do for Glenn Smart, who is getting married tomorrow.

"Mr. and Mrs. F. Barratt request the pleasure of the company of Lieut. LeRoy Gover at the Marriage of their daughter Marjorie to Lieut. Glenn Smart at Holy Trinity Church S.W. 17, on Saturday Jan 2nd 1943 at 1-15 o'clock. R.S.V.P. 11, Fircrop Rd. S.W. 17."

"A number of the fellows married English girls," Lee noted.

There were a lot of young ladies available, and many of them certainly thought that marrying an American was a good thing to do. I'm not saying that they were not sincere, because most of those marriages lasted for a long time. Glenn Smart had been going with Marjorie for quite some time, and everyone assumed they would get married. She was very nice and quite attractive, and I know Glenn was happy to be marrying her.

Saturday, January 2, 1943   Slept late this morning, and at 11:30 I met Don Nee, Fred Keene, Henry Ayres and Glenn Smart at the Eagle Club. We then took the tube out to Tooting, where we went to the bride's house. Had a couple of gin and oranges and then hiked up to the Trinity Church. It was a small wedding with very few people in attendance, but they had a very nice ceremony. Afterward, we went to a small reception at Marjorie's parents' home. Then Fred Keene, Don Nee and I came back to London and took in a show, after which we caught the train back to camp.

There was no flying at Debden until the following Friday, because the base was snowed in. On January 7, Gover was made operations officer of his squadron, with responsibility for manning the unit's missions. "Spent the day at dispersal getting things in order," he wrote. Two days of routine flying broke the monotony, but on January 10, the fog and snow came in again, and it did not lift until the thirteenth.

Wednesday, January 13, 1943 We were close escort to twelve Bostons and we bombed the airdrome at St. Omer, France, from ten thousand feet. There was a hell of a lot of flak, and they opened up with a lot of the white, heavy flak. But we had no trouble with fighters. Then this afternoon we escorted eighty Fortresses that bombed Lille, France. We were about twenty-two thousand feet and there were plenty of smoke trails [contrails]. Thirty FW-190s came up but we could see their trails and had no trouble with them.

Thursday, January 14, 1943 This was about my last day on this earth. I took two fellows (Lieutenant Peterson and Lieutenant Mirsch) on a rhubarb [two-to-four ship low-level missions to destroy enemy trains, ships and other ground targets]. We went across the North Sea at zero feet and crossed the French coast above Le Tréport. Swooped inland and turned right, all the time right on the deck and hopping over houses and trees. I spotted a train and shot hell out of it. Then I attacked a group of soldiers and splattered them good. I was so low that mud and guts slopped all over my windscreen. I then turned to come back out and came right over Dunkirk. The ground defenses were shooting like mad now. I saw a gun post straight ahead shooting at me, so I dived on it and poured a long burst of cannon and silenced it. Then a factory was in front so I blasted that. I had just reached the harbor then and dived on a boat ahead. I was just then hit from behind by cannon and I thought I'd had it. One went right through the tail, hit the radio, and blew it all to pieces. Another shell came through right behind my ear, and what a racket. I then skidded to the left as I saw their tracers closing in on my starboard. I was soon out of range and hit a course for England. The fog had closed in and I couldn't see a damn thing. Lieutenant Peterson had his right wheel shot up and a big hole through his wing. He crash-landed at Bradwell Bay. Lieutenant Mirsch crashed on landing also. I came on and was about to take to the silk when I spotted North Weald and landed with five gallons of petrol. I had been airborne for two hours and ten minutes, a long time in a Spitfire with no external tank. When I looked at the plane I also found a hole in the propeller. I ate lunch there and, when the fog lifted, I came on home. It was a hard flight because I was afraid that if I changed the speed of the prop it might break where it had the hole. I just flew nice and easy and got back with no trouble.

Gover was awarded the Air Medal for this mission, his last combat flight in a Spitfire.

"Saturday, January 16, 1943. There were twenty-four of us picked to go over to P-47 Thunderbolts today." In his log book, Lee pasted a picture of his Spitfire with the note "Kissed my old Spitfire *Sondra Lee IX* good-bye and transferred over to Republic P-47C Thunderbolts." It had been a year and twenty days since Lee's first flight in the Spitfire. In that time, he flew 158 hours and 20 minutes in this aircraft of his dreams, 57 hours and 45 minutes of it on his forty-seven combat missions. It was now time to fly an American fighter.

6. THE THUNDERBOLTS ARE HERE

THE FIRST FEW DAYS AFTER KISSING *SONDRA LEE IX* good-bye were difficult for Lee. The 334th Squadron was to be the first to transition into the P-47 and so stopped flying combat missions on January 15. Those from the 335th and 336th who were picked to fly the new plane were transferred to the 334th, and some of the pilots from that unit were moved to the other two squadrons of the Fourth Fighter Group so they would be able to continue to fly their Spitfires at full strength. While this change in squadrons did not require a physical move for the pilots, it did cause Lee to have to watch a period of heavy action for his old unit, the 336th, from the sidelines. The entries in his diary read almost as though he were on the missions, and he obviously shared the anguish of the rest of the squadron when someone was killed. Gover remembered that "it was really hard for me to watch the Spits go off on a show and not be able to go along. During those first few days, I wished that I hadn't been picked to go to Thunderbolts."

The day following his move to the 334th, ". . . took my first hop in a P-47. Seems to be a pretty fair ship." It is a testament to the ability of Gover and his fellow pilots that they could almost immediately move from the Spitfire to the Thunderbolt with very little ground school or preparation. There were no two-seat P-47s, so the first flight was solo. Gover summed it up.

They gave us some manuals to read and checked us out on the cockpit and away we went. It was a lot different to fly than the

Spitfire, but I didn't have any problems. There were several things that you just had to get used to. It was so much bigger than the Spit and there was that huge 2,300-horsepower engine out in front of you swinging a four-blade prop. You had to turn all the time you were taxiing, kind of go like an S, so you could see out in front. You were always aware of that great big engine. The "Jug" [the pilot's nickname for the P-47] was also a lot heavier than the Spitfire and it performed very differently. It didn't glide as well, so landing it was not the same and if you got it going straight down, watch out. Sometimes it was almost impossible to pull out of a steep dive. The cockpit was much larger than the Spit's and it had a heater, so you didn't have to dress like a polar bear to fly. After awhile, I got to really like the plane.

The Republic P-47 was a much larger airplane than the Spitfire in every way. It had a wingspan of over forty feet, was thirty-six feet long and weighed almost fifteen thousand pounds fully loaded. In sharp contrast to the liquid-cooled V-12 engine of the Spitfire, the Thunderbolt had a twin-row, eighteen-cylinder, air-cooled Pratt & Whitney radial engine that produced between 2,300 and 2,500 horsepower, depending on the model, almost 1,000 horsepower more than the Spitfire. Pulling the aircraft to a top speed of over 430 miles per hour was a four-blade propeller that was over twelve feet in diameter. With a service ceiling of 42,000 feet and a range of from twelve hundred to nineteen hundred miles, depending on the external fuel tank, it was far superior as an escort fighter. The Thunderbolt was also a deadly machine, with standard armament of eight .50 caliber Browning machine guns and external racks on the wings for various types of bombs and rockets.

The Thunderbolt's cockpit was not only much larger but more sophisticated than that of the Spitfire. The spade-grip control column was replaced by a stick, the two sets of rudder pedals gave way to one, the instruments were more logically placed and easier to read, and the Plexiglas canopy gave better visibility than had been the case in the Spitfire. Whatever the former Spitfire pilots thought about the P-47 in general, almost all of them had to admit that it was a much more comfortable plane to fly. Over fifteen thousand P-47s were built, the highest number of any American fighter, and it saw action in every theater of the war.

Gover's diary entries for the next four days paint a graphic picture of life at Debden.

Tuesday, January 19, 1943   About ninety Huns came over the estuary this afternoon and the flight went up (without me). Steve crashed on takeoff. Bob Mirsch was flying my Spitfire, *Sondra Lee*, and he came in too high and crashed it all to hell—so that's the end of another one. And I had just had all the bullet holes patched up. What a business.

Wednesday, January 20, 1943   Everything OK today but it sure was a shambles yesterday. The Jerries machine-gunned the hell out of things, and plenty of people were killed. Took in the movie tonight.

Thursday, January 21, 1943   Took a couple of hops in the Thunderbolt today and like it less each time. There was a show on this afternoon to Caen, France. Took Venturas over and bombed. Plenty of flak and fighters up. [Gover was not on this mission, but he was obviously there in his heart.] Coen and DuFour got a crack at two FW-190s coming out. Went to the movies with Don Young tonight.

Friday, January 22, 1943   There was a sweep to the St. Omer airdrome today. The squadron was met by seventy-plus FW-190s and it turned into a dogfight. Almost everyone got a crack at a Hun. Tiger Booth had about ten on him but got home. The squadron escorted Bostons, and there were four Bostons and six Spitfires shot down. Seven Jerries were knocked down. Lieutenant Grimm went into the sea, and Mirsch was shot up; so were Boehle and Anderson. Bishop crashed on landing back here at Debden, and I just had to watch from the sidelines. There was quite a piss-up (beer party) at the mess tonight.

Gover flew the P-47 each day until the twenty-seventh.

Bad weather today, so we caught the 11:27 a.m. train and went into London. Took in a movie and then went to the Crackers

Club. Don Nee and I then went over to the Princess for a few drinks. Met Margaret at 11:45 at the Regent.

January 28, 1943   Caught the 7:00 a.m. train but damn near everyone missed it. Came on back to camp and the old routine. Last night proved to be a night to remember. The Regent has a house detective who just walks around to see that everything is OK. He is really a pain in the ass, because we have to sneak girls into our rooms if we want a little romance. I have to be doubly careful because Margaret works at the reservation desk and will lose her job if she gets caught in my room. I guess Margaret and I were making a bit too much noise and the house "dick" must have heard us, because when I went down to check out this morning, they wanted to charge me for two people. I argued with the desk clerk until I looked over and saw Margaret at the reservation desk. She had an early shift and was sitting there grinning like a fox eating hornets. Neither of us said a word, but I paid the bill and got out fast, as I was about to crack up laughing.

There are losses in any training program, as Lee had learned so well when he was at Spitfire OTU. The checkout in the P-47 was no exception.

Friday, January 29, 1943   We lost our first P-47 today when Lieutenant Foster crashed in a field at Northampton. The plane was washed out but he was unhurt.

Saturday, January 30, 1943   We lost our second P-47 today when yours truly applied the brakes to keep from hitting a damn truck that drove out on the runway. She nosed over, busted the prop, screwed up the motor and when she came down busted her back and tail end. So ends another one. They just towed it to the scrap heap. Man, I felt bad.

By the end of January, Lee had flown ten hours in the Thunderbolt and "I am beginning to feel at home in the 'Jug.' I still miss the Spitfire, but maybe the P-47 will be OK."

One of the anxiously awaited changes when the Eagles transferred to the USAAF was getting American food. Because of the priorities of men and equipment, there were not enough supply ships to begin shipping food to the American troops until the end of 1942. Thus, the members of the Fourth, as well as most of the other personnel assigned to the Eighth Air Force, remained on English rations. This was not a problem to the pilots who had been in the RAF, but those who joined the squadron directly from the United States had a difficult time getting used to the Brussels sprouts, boiled potatoes and tea, not to mention the shortage of eggs, meat and sugar. It was a red-letter day when, on February 1, the Fourth Fighter Group began getting American food. For Lee, the occasion was tempered by the loss of his airplane and his friend who was flying it.

Monday, February 1, 1943 Well, well, well. We went onto American rations today here at the mess. Had pancakes for breakfast, grilled hamburgers for lunch with corn and beans, and peaches and cookies for dessert. Then we had prime roast beef, mashed potatoes and dill pickles for supper—sure damn good. We lost our first pilot on the P-47 today. Lieutenant Mitchellweis, who had been in 133 Squadron, took my plane, *Sondra Lee* the 10th, up for a height climb. I had just come down from 35,000 feet and he wanted to try it. All we know so far is that the plane buried itself and he was two miles from the ship and his parachute was two miles farther on. All he had on when found was a pair of socks and a necktie, so he must have had a terrible time. Seems he tried to get out and was going so fast when he popped his chute that he was torn out of it. So goes another good boy. He was my number two man——It makes you think.

The urgency to get the P-47 operational made all those in the checkout program eager to fly as much as possible. Gover flew once on February 1, twice on the second, three times on the third and once on the fourth. After his flight on the fourth, he went into London "to deposit my paycheck and send some money home."

Went over to the Eagle Club and who should walk in but Jack Mause. He was in and out of the hospital but it was good to see him. He had gone to Typhoon fighters, 400-mile-per-hour jobs, after OTU and then transferred to the USAAF and started in the P-51. He had a sack with him, which he said was for me. "One of my friends brought these along to London on leave and I'm giving them to you," he said. I opened the sack and in it were six bananas. Man, was I starved for a banana. I was about to eat one when Mrs. Dexter, one of the ladies who runs the Eagle Club, said, "Wait, Lee. I have a notice here that urgently requests anyone with any fresh fruit to please bring it to the hospital as there is a small child that needs fresh fruit to survive." I took one last look at the bananas and handed them over. I bet I never see another one while I'm in England, but I feel good.

Sunday, February 7, 1943 Cleared up pretty fair today, so I jumped in and flew around a while in my Thunderbolt. Barclay, an old squadron mate of mine in 66 Squadron, dropped in to see me and get a square meal. We had lunch here and then I flew my P-47 in formation with his Spitfire back to Southend, where he is stationed. He's an Australian and the best that they come. It has now fogged in and is it cold, so think I'll write a quick letter and hit the hay.

The letter read:

Dear Folks: I'm sitting here by the fire trying to get warm and so I thought of you. Everything is going along OK for me. We went on American rations February 1 and the food is now damn good. It's pretty cold, but this winter I have warm clothes, not so bad that way. Boy, I mean I'll never forget last winter in Wales though with nothing but a uniform. Doing plenty of flying also. I haven't had any mail for a long time now—guess it will all arrive together.

"During the checkout in the P-47, we were generally scheduled to fly every day from Saturday through Thursday with Friday off," Gover later wrote. "We had to stay on the base, so if the weather was bad we just waited for it to clear. Almost everyone spent Friday in London." Alternating days of fog and flying weather enabled Lee to get five more flights and boost his time in the P-47 to twenty-two hours during the week. The activity of Friday is best recounted in a letter to his parents.

Sunday, February 14, 1943 I was up over four hours today and I'm all in. I saw the sun come up from up there, which is getting to be a habit. Don't know if I told you, but I got my *Sondra Lee* the 10th the other day—only had twenty-five hours on it. I lent it to another pilot for a trip and that was the end of it. Sure glad I wasn't in it. Miley, Nee, Stephenson and I had all our hair cut off. (Well, I did so have some to cut off.) Anyway, we're now social outcasts. We were at the Crackers Club in London and after a few beers we talked ourselves into it. Boy, what a mess. We then went over to the Palladium and got some chorus gals we know and went out to the Studio Club. Really put one on. Then went on over to the Astor Club. Who should I see there but a kid I went to high school with (John Diehl). First guy I've seen that I knew back home. I know my letters must be boring as hell to you, but you know I can't tell what we are doing here. Someday we'll have ourselves a fireside chat and swap lies. But I think I'm doing my part. I was just sitting here and looking at a membership card to the "Caterpillar Club" [any crew member who bailed out of his plane became a member of this club] and guess what I was drinking—an honest-to-real Coca-Cola. I'm pooped so will close.

The German attack on Debden of January 19 had left the base seriously damaged. After morning flying on February 15, the airdrome was closed for two days for repairs. "We caught the train and came into London. Had a good time at the Crackers Club. I was so tired that I went over to the Regent Palace and to bed early."

Tuesday, February 16, 1943 Got up at about 11:00 a.m. and went to the bank and out to the PX [Post Exchange] I saw a silver locket, so I bought it to send to Juanita. Met Stephenson and we went to see *Casablanca* a good show. Met Rose at about 6:00 p.m. and came over to the Crackers Club for a couple of drinks and then out to eat. We then went out to Chiswich, the area where she lives, to a little pub. There was a fire going and it was so cozy that you could forget there was a war on. I was notified that I had been awarded the Air Medal.

The next day Lee sent a copy of *Stars and Stripes* to his sister Juanita, with a short note calling attention to page 4, column 1, which listed Lee as having been awarded the Air Medal.

Not bad for an old guy like me. I just got back from two hectic days in London, but while there I bought you a very old engraved locket from the Victorian era. It's silver and I think you'll like it. Have it polished and it will be OK.

"We went to the cinema a lot," Gover remembered.

I don't recall ever taking a girl to the show, but a bunch of the guys would go almost every time we were in London. Almost all the movies were first-run American ones, and they were shown in the big English theaters in London. When we went, there would be many times more English civilians there than us Americans. You could go to the show in the afternoon or the evening, every day. I think that a lot of the English people went just to escape from the war for a few hours. I know that's why we would go.

The reality of war was very evident in Lee's diary later in the week.

Friday, February 19, 1943 Just another day. Powell was killed today on a convoy patrol. He was a new boy and it was his first operational trip.

Saturday, February 20, 1943 Fogged in tighter than hell today—even the birds are walking. A bomber tried to get in and wiped out two of our P-47s, a gun post and finally wound up in the dispersal hut. Sure is a mess. And it had four five-hundred pound bombs all fused on it, but luckily they didn't go off.

Each of the experienced pilots in the squadron would periodically serve as duty pilot. During his twenty-four hours in this position, the duty pilot was responsible for all the flying activity that took place on the entire airdrome. Whenever Lee had this duty, he wrote some of his longest and most thoughtful letters home. On Sunday, February 21, he wrote, "I'm duty pilot today. It's still fogged in so maybe I'll get time to write some letters." The first was to his sister, Juanita.

Right now I'm in the control tower. I'm duty pilot from 8:00 a.m. this morning until 8:00 a.m. tomorrow, so another twenty-four hours with no sleep. What makes me happy is the fact that I have complete charge of all flying and the whole drome. But the visibility and ceiling are absolutely zero—a regular pea-souper—so I'm without a care in the world. Now Bill [Juanita's husband], I'll try to answer some of your questions. The U.S. Air Corps has been treating me pretty good, but as you say, I wouldn't mind being there and doing a little combat instruction. They seem to want the kids to come over here and learn the hard way. It makes good target practice for the Luftwaffe boys. You asked about the numbers of my plane. Well, I had No. 10 about three weeks ago. I let another pilot take it up on a height climb and it came straight in from 35,000 feet. So it's a little bent out of shape. So I now have a brand-new one which I am breaking in—that's No. 11. I've been slow-timing it, and I also have the cannons all working 100 percent. As I told you, I'm not on Spits now. So hope you know what this is. It trims out fine and is pretty easy on the controls. The P-38s have been doing fairly well in Africa, but it is a little too fast a company here for them.

I've named my new ship *Miss San Carlos*—Sondra Lee has held the Spit honor roll, so thought I'd change now on a new ship. Another six months of high altitude and I'll be punchy. Your fillings contract and fall out and you see spots in front of you. Dive it about twenty thousand feet and pull back and your old eyeballs roll around on your cheeks. Makes you think, boy does it make you think. The German radio came out the other day and said that they know where we Eagle boys are and that we have new ships and they will be over to pay us a visit. Does it sound interesting to you? Not to me. Squeeze Sondra Lee for me.

The citizens of San Carlos found out that Gover had named his plane *Miss San Carlos* from the local newspaper. In an early-April article, which noted that the name of the town was going through the war on land, sea and air, Gover's plane was featured. "Captain LeRoy Gover is flying a fighter plane bearing the name *Miss San Carlos* across the English Channel on regular assignments," it reported.

The problems with flying escort to the bombers were mentioned earlier, but the P-47 brought other challenges in this regard than just the gunners on the B-17.

My P-47 is being painted white on the nose and tail today, so those bastards won't shoot at us. About four of us have been shot at now by Spits, Typhoons and ground defenses because they think we look like FW-190s. I hope it works, because we have enough trouble with the Jerries without having to worry about our own guys.

Friday, February 25, 1943   Big day today. General Hunter came up to our decorations parade and gave seven of us Air Medals. Then Air Marshal Sir Leigh-Mallory, RAF, gave us a medallion for our service in the Royal Air Force. It was a very nice affair, and I finally got myself a gong. ["Gongs" were awards for individual acts or achievement rather than simply for participating in a campaign or serving for a particular length of time.]

Lee described the awards parade and his harrowing activities of the following day in greater detail to his folks.

We had our big awards parade a couple of days ago, and it was very nice. All three squadrons, pilots and ground crews, were all lined up on the parade ground. A band marched on and then the seven of us being decorated marched on (a hard thing to do for someone who doesn't know how to march). Then the big boys came into their place. And I'll be damned if I wasn't called first. So I stumbled up and General Hunter pinned it on. The old cameras were clicking and also the newsreel. So maybe you'll see me. Probably won't recognize me now, as I'm winning a pound bet by growing a mustache. Then Sir Leigh-Mallory—the RAF air marshal—gave us a nice silver medallion for our service in the RAF.

I'll tell you about a little experience I had yesterday that turned my mustache gray. I was flying at 21,000 feet when an oil plug came out of the motor, and with ninety pounds pressure out a three-quarter-inch hole, she really covered the plane and windscreen. Of course it hit the exhaust and caught fire. So there I was. I called the field and told them I was taking to the silk. The fire wasn't to the cockpit yet, so I thought I'd have a go at putting it out. So I sideslipped it a couple of thousand feet and got the fire out. (I'd cut all switches and closed the throttle and pulled the pitch back already.) So there I was again at nineteen thousand feet and with a dead stick [no motor]. I was also above cloud and didn't know exactly just where I was. I called the field and told them to give me a fix and vector and I started gliding. You can imagine how fourteen thousand pounds glides. It was hazy and at four thousand I was about to bail out when I saw a landmark. I called I was coming in then. They had the field all clear already and the fire truck and ambulance there. I stretched the glide and just made the field by a gnat's ear. When I was sure I could make it, I dumped my flaps and wheels. Not having any power, she hit pretty hard, but all that happened was that I damaged the wheel rims when I touched down. My hydraulic pressure was gone and I pumped the emergency pump like mad and got it stopped. The colonel and everyone congratulated me, so I guess it was a good show. Bye for now.

This was the first time that Gover told his folks anything about his hazardous experiences, because he knew how fearful his mother was that he would not survive the war.

A month later, Lee received a letter of commendation from the commander of VIII Fighter Command, Brigadier General Frank Hunter, which read:

1. It has come to my attention that while you were on a transition flying mission at an altitude of 20,000 feet your airplane caught fire due to a defective oil plug which sprayed oil over the plane. By sideslipping the aircraft you managed to extinguish the fire and made a dead stick landing with slight damage to the aircraft.

2. I wish to commend you upon your quick thinking and good judgment in meeting this urgent situation that meant the saving of an aircraft of great value at considerable risk to yourself.

Lee was very proud of the letter from General Hunter. To his folks he wrote:

I received a hell of a swell letter of commendation from General Hunter for getting the fire out and bringing my ship down OK a few weeks ago. It was also signed by the colonel here. I'll send it along to you later.

Like most of Lee's accomplishments, his adventure with the P-47 and the letter from General Hunter were featured copy in the San Carlos paper.

Despite the fact that all of the Fourth Fighter Group pilots picked to transition into the P-47 were combat veterans, most with both RAF and USAAF experience, there was still a requirement that each have approximately fifty hours in the Thunderbolt before going into combat. And with the need to get the aircraft in an operational status to facilitate longer-range escorts for the B-17s, there was a great deal of pressure for Gover and his fellow aviators to fly as much as possible. Another reason to get the first group checked out rapidly was the need to get all the Fourth into the P-47 so the British could have their Spitfires back and the unit would all be flying the same type of aircraft. An additional group could not be entered into the transition program, however, until the first group was operational. In the last five days of February, for example, Lee flew eleven missions. No wonder his diary entries are simply: "February 27, 1943. Lots of flying today. Show in the evening. February 28, 1943. Bags more flying. March 1, 1943. And still flying."

Evidently the Germans were not anxious to have the P-47 become operational, for on March 3 they bombed Debden again. Although there was not as much damage as in their January attack, they did hit the field. "The Huns were over this evening and bombed hell out of things. The antiaircraft fire was hot and heavy and big fires starting up," Lee wrote.

"I did some cannon tests today," Gover recorded on March 4, "but also had a little fun with one of the boys."

> I was on my second flight when I spotted a P-47 flying along straight and level about four thousand feet below me. I went into a dive and came in behind him. I flew below him but with about a 150-mile-per-hour advantage in airspeed. Then I flew right under him and pulled up not twenty feet in front of him and going straight up. He just had a split-second view of me and then hit my prop wash. It was Dick Braley and it really scared the hell out of him. He was still shaking after we landed and mad as a wet hen. We busted another P-47 all to hell today. Stanhope undershot and really washed it out. He got a bump on his old hard head for his effort.

Monday, March 8, 1943   I saw myself in a newsreel at the show yesterday. Patterson overshot the field this afternoon and washed out his P-47. He wasn't hurt and is a pretty disgusted boy this evening. He's not as mad as Bob Messinger. Bob had been playing the slot machine in the barroom for about thirty minutes and got no payoff. He put in his last shilling and still got nothing, so he just kicked the machine and went up to his room. A few minutes later he came back carrying his .45 automatic pistol. He calmly walked up in front of the slot machine and shot the damn thing, turned around and went back to his room. *C'est la guerre*.

Tuesday, March 9, 1943   I took a nice long trip out over the Channel in my P-47. Was fired on by our own coast guns on my way home. I guess the white stripes don't work very well. This evening Don Young and I went to the base theater. We were sitting just in front of Colonel Anderson, the base commander. Right after we sat down, he leaned over and said, "Good evening, Captain Gover." Don punched me in the ribs and said, "It sounds like you made captain." Colonel Anderson said orders would be coming out tomorrow.

Lee's promotion to captain was very important to him. "I always had two goals for myself in the U.S. Army Air Forces," he reminisced. "The first was to become a captain and the second was to be awarded the Distinguished Flying Cross." He would have to wait another month to achieve his second goal. He was also excited enough to write short V-mail letters to his parents and his sister. (V-mail was written on one side of a form that was then photographed. When the film arrived in the United States, or a key overseas location, it was processed, printed and the photo was mailed to the addressee. In this way, scores of letters could be transported on one roll of film. While V-mail letters generally took less time to reach their destination than regular mail, they had to be very short to fit on the form. For this reason, Gover seldom used the system.)

You'll be glad to know that I was made a captain on March 10th. I've the two things now I hoped to get. [Although Lee had not yet been awarded the Distinguished Flying Cross, he knew that it was on it's way.] I hadn't expected to get a captaincy for a long time but have worked for it.

Since the first day of transition flying the P-47, every pilot, as well as the headquarters of Eighth Fighter Command, anxiously awaited the day when the Thunderbolt would be an operational fighter. The momentous occasion came on March 10, when the first operational mission for the P-47 in the European theater was flown by members of the Fourth Fighter Group.

Well, today was the big day. We took our P-47 Thunderbolts on their first operational trip today. We went into Holland at Flushing and flew along inland and came out at Dunkirk. The flak was pretty accurate. So the drinks are all on the Republic representative here tonight. We didn't have any trouble and our colonel went along with us.

Those who flew this historic mission were Colonel Anderson (base commander), Lieutenant Colonel Peterson (Fourth Fighter Group commander), Major Coen (336 Squadron commander and Gover's roommate), Captain Gover, Captain Miley, First Lieutenants O'Regan, Carpenter and Young, and Second Lieutenants Peterson, Goodson and Nee. In his log book, Gover noted "The first time P-47s have ever been on operations."

Gover flew again on March 11, but then the weather settled in once again and flying was completely curtailed. The poor weather, combined with no scheduled combat missions and the same routine day after day, caused Lee to forgo making any entries in his diary for the next ten days. "There just wasn't anything to write about," he remembered. "All we did was go to the flight line, sit around waiting for the weather to clear, and figure out ways to spend the day. It was a boring time." His next diary entry, on March 24, says simply, "There hasn't been much of importance these last few days. Just test-hopping the new ships and doing radio tests." He used some of the time to write a longer letter home.

I dropped you folks a V-mail yesterday, but it didn't say much. I've been polishing my plane today. I'm getting every extra mile per hour that is possible out of it. As I told you, I received my captaincy on March 10th. I sure make old Young mad when I tell him to call me "sir." Out of the whole bunch from my class at Bakersfield, Young and I are the only two still going up and at them. I'll enclose a picture of me and my new medal, or rather ribbon, under my wings. I would sure enjoy a month at home about now, but my busy season is just getting started. Give forth with some news—how does Betty like her job these days—how's my cabin—anything new around town—and just what do you and the other people think about what we fellows are doing over here? How about you getting big-hearted and dropping a line, say every Sunday and every Wednesday. I think a couple of letters a week—V-mails even—would really be appreciated. Betty and Dad are going to get their necks broken if they don't write.

Gover's phrase "just what do you and the other people think about what we fellows are doing over here" is interesting. On a number of occasions, Lee asked that same question of both his parents and his sisters. "We really wanted to know what folks were saying," he remembered.

You went out every day and got shot at, saw your friends killed, and came damn close yourself. I think everyone wondered sometimes if the folks back home really understood or appreciated what you were doing.

One of the reasons for the lack of flying activity, aside from the bad weather, was the need to get the rest of the Fourth Fighter Group operational in the P-47. While the first group of pilots had achieved that status, there were not enough operational aircraft or pilots to sustain any combat effort. That would not come until the end of April, when the entire Fourth was ready to go in the Thunderbolt. In the meantime, there were a lot of diverse activities for the first group of P-47 pilots while they waited to begin checking out the rest of the Fourth. Gover's daily activities for the week beginning March 24 are illustrative.

Wednesday, March 24, 1943   I went by transport to Martlesham Heath this morning. Talked to the boys of 336 and then flew a Spitfire back to Debden. Sure seemed funny to fly one again.

Thursday, March 25, 1943 Don Young and I caught the 9:00 a.m. train out of Audley End and went into London. Checked in at the Regent—had some food and to a show. We saw *Cargo of Innocents*, and it was pretty fair. Then back over to the Jules Club, where I met "Mert" Crockett, a kid I knew at Redwood City. Then we took in a few beers and ended at the Crackers Club.

Friday, March 26, 1943 Ate breakfast at 10:00 a.m. and then went down to the Eagle Club. Took in a movie in the afternoon. Young and I then walked all around town and on out to Hyde Park, where we took pictures. Then over to Grosvenor House, where we had tea and met Crockett. About 8:00 p.m. we came on back to the Crackers Club and sat. I spent the evening talking to Mary—then went back to the Regent to bed. Don wandered off with some spook.

Saturday, March 27, 1943 Came on back to Debden on the 11:55 from Liverpool Street Station. Everything quiet here, as they are making an engine change on my plane. Peterson, Young and I went to the camp cinema this evening. Came back to the mess after and had a Coke and listened to some of the drunks sing dirty songs and so to bed at 12:00 midnight.

Sunday, March 28, 1943 Didn't get up until about 8:30. Dropped a line to the folks, hung around the hangar for a while, and then to lunch. About 2:15 a big formation of B-17 Flying Fortresses flew by on their way back from a bombing raid. Hope they all made it OK. Read my *Reader's Digest* that I received yesterday, a Xmas present from Juanita and Bill. Oh yes, I clipped my new mustache off awhile back.

Monday, March 29, 1943 Flew a radio test for an hour this morning. My *Esquire* magazine arrived today, a present from Maxine, so I fought off the guys and had a look at the pretty pictures.

Tuesday, March 30, 1943 Nothing special today. Played a game of golf this afternoon. Don Nee and I took in the show this evening.

Wednesday, March 31, 1943 Went back to 336 Squadron today and started giving the boys cockpit checks on the P-47.

Thursday, April 1, 1943   April Fool to you. The boys have started bouncing the Thunderbolts around today. Sure fun watching.
Wrote home while waiting for dinner.

In that letter, Gover makes a subtle but most profound state-
ment about what it means to him to be a fighter pilot and the
hazards that he faces every day.

April Fool and such. Just a few things for your scrapbook, Mom.
My old "Alma Mater"—the RAF—is twenty-five years old today
and I'm damn proud to have belonged to it and to think I may
have helped a little bit. I told you my camera was stolen the
other day. I bought another one, a damn neat Zeiss Ikon—German, by the way—cost me fifty bucks secondhand, but it's just
the ticket. We had a softball game last night, and boy, am I stiff
today. The little poem I'm enclosing—"Fighter Pilot"—was written by a fellow here and hits the spot. So if anything ever happens to me, just remember I had no regrets.

Fighter Pilot

> I know that it will come, but when or where?
> In rattling burst or roaring sheet of flame,
> In the green blanket sea choking for air,
> Amid the bubbles transient as my name.
>
> Sometimes a second's throw decides the game,
> Winner takes all, and there is no replay,
> Indifferent earth and sky breathe on the same,
> I settle up my score and go my way.
>
> The years I might have had I throw away,
> They only lead to winter's lingering pain;
> No tears call them from those who perchance stay,
> For spring however spent comes not again.
>
> When April brings once more the gentle rain,
> Mention my name in passing, if you must,
> As one who accepted terms, slay or be slain,
> And knew the bargain was both good and just.

The poem Lee sent his mother became personal again just two days later.

Saturday, April 3, 1943 Bad luck today. We lost two planes— one pilot dead and one in the hospital. Lieutenant Smolinski was on fire at fifteen hundred feet and couldn't make the field. He didn't jump and crashed. Was burned to death. Then this afternoon, my roommate, Major Oscar Coen, was at 24,000 feet when he caught fire. He bailed out and is in the hospital with a broken shoulder.

Sunday, April 4, 1943 I took a ship up on a weather test this morning. Pretty bad. Then this noon I took Captain Stepp up and gave him some formation. Weather got bad so this p.m. eight of us went down and played a game of golf. I was low-score man with a 53 for the nine holes. It's just now 10:00 p.m. so think I'll hit the hay. Don Young is sitting here on my bed reading my *Esquire*—or rather looking at the pictures. He wants me to play a game of snooker, but I'm pooped.

Although Gover made no mention of it in his diary, he achieved his second USAAF goal on April 5, when he received the orders awarding him his first Distinguished Flying Cross. The event was anticlimactic, because he had known the decoration was coming for some time.

On April 11, Lee wrote a long diary entry to make up for having gone a week without any notations in the book. He wrote about a number of things, but of most interest is his sobering account of the fate of each of his classmates at Bakersfield.

Nothing spectacular has happened on this front this week. Just been on short missions. The Forts made a couple of good raids and destroyed twenty-five planes. We lost thirty-three bombers over Germany the other night. Boy oh boy, I feel for those guys. I've been up doing some cloud flying today. Took in the cinema last night with Don Young and Tiger Booth. There was a big crap game last night with plenty of pounds rolling around. Saw seven Huns this morning while flying out over the Channel all by myself. I just happened to see a picture of the boys when we were in training at Bakersfield. What has been their fate? There were just fourteen of us who finally made the grade and came to England. We'll start with four of the fellows who called themselves "The Four Horsemen."

1. W. Arends (Baldy). He was shot down on a sweep over France by an FW-190 in June 1942.

2. D. E. Lambert (Micky). We were together at 133 Eagle Squadron. After we transferred his nerves went bad and he was sent to an OTU training center and so is out of the war, but alive.

3. D. Logan (Dave). He was killed in training over here and never got to see action. Had a midair collision in December 1941, less than a month after we arrived.

4. G. Middleton (George). We lost George on a sweep over Brest, France, on September 26, 1942. He wasn't killed and was taken prisoner. He is now in Stalag Luft III in Germany. I received a card from him last week. And so ended "The Four Horsemen" (two dead—one a prisoner of war—and the other out of the scrap).

5. L. Ryerson (Len). A tall, lean, good-natured kid. We lost him on the same show as George. He was knocked down over Brest by flak and is buried there.

6. R. Doyle (Ray). A tough little guy from Brooklyn. He became homesick after two weeks here and caused a lot of trouble, so was sent home. But his ship was torpedoed and he was killed at sea.

7. R. N. Beaty (Dick). Dick was on operations until September 1942. He had to bail out in the Channel one day and nearly drowned before being picked up. Then a couple of weeks later he crashed out of petrol and this shook him pretty much. He asked to be sent home and so he's now back in the States.

8. G. Quinn (George). Quinn went on to bombers and did damn well. He won the Distinguished Flying Cross and was shot down a couple of weeks later on a raid to Germany. He has been confirmed dead.

9. G. O'Hara (George). He also went on to bombers and did a fine job until he was also killed in action.

10. Bolton. He was the third one of the gang to go on bombers. He was also killed in action while flying a "Wimpy."

11. J. Reed (Jay). Jay was on operations until we transferred to the U.S. Air Corps. He then went with a squadron and was in on

the invasion of Africa. He was there about three months and then went back to the States.

12.   J. Mause (Jack). He also went to Africa and then he received a fractured skull and was brought back here to England to the hospital. He was then sent back to the States as unfit to fly.

13.   D. Young (Don). We now come to the only man left in the fight besides myself. Don has been a damn good and steady pilot, taking part in forty-five operational shows to date. He was in 121 Eagle Squadron while I was in 133 Eagle Squadron. But since the transfer in September 1942, we are now together. He is a sub–flight commander in his squadron and as good a man as you can find—proven by the fact that he's still kicking after seventeen months at it. He knows the tricks and should get home. He can't play snooker worth a damn, though.

14.   L. Gover (Lee). That's me. I've been pretty lucky and lasted along with Don Young, after forty-eight operations. Hope it lasts and Don and I see the States together. We're the only two left now so have to kinda look out for one another.

7. IT'S GETTING TOUGHER EVERY DAY

GOVER'S REFLECTIONS ON THE FATE OF HIS CLASS AT Bakersfield to some degree set the tone for the next nine months of his tour in England. It was a time of intense activity and flying. For example, from April 15 through the end of May, Lee flew thirty-eight missions in the P-47, sometimes flying as many as three times a day. This extensive flying and the day-after-day exposure to combat seemed to take its toll on everyone, and certainly Gover was no exception. The entries in his diary become shorter and less descriptive, and he sometimes makes no entry for as many as five days in a row. In contrast, his letters home become less chatty and more serious and substantive. He also spends less time "on the town" in London. Part of this change is also due to the increased responsibility that went with his being a captain and leading from four to twelve pilots on almost every mission.

"Once all the squadron got proficient on the Thunderbolt," Gover reminisced,

> we really began to pull a heavy flying load. The bombing missions were increasing as more B-17s arrived in England and the Luftwaffe seemed to be rising to challenge the bombers in greater numbers. Since our main mission was escorting the bombers, we had action on almost every mission. We also were getting more new pilots in the squadron straight from the United States. They had no combat experience and there were fewer of us experienced pilots to teach them. Most of the fellows who had

transferred from the RAF had either been assigned to other out-fits or had gone home, so those of us who were left had an even bigger load. In many ways, it was the most stressful time of the war for me.

In addition to those factors Gover cited, two others were putting increased pressure on both the Americans and the Luftwaffe. The presence of large numbers of American fighters, to augment the Spitfires of Fighter Command, made it possible to significantly increase the number of sweeps over France and the Low Countries, which the Germans had to counter for both military and morale purposes. This meant more strain on both aircraft and pilots and more losses to the already hard-pressed Luftwaffe. While the Germans were inflicting heavy losses on the British bombers engaged in night raids, the addition of American bombers in large numbers, bombing in daylight, meant that the Luftwaffe and the German antiaircraft guns had to counter almost round-the-clock air activity. The side of this situation that Gover and his squadron saw was the requirement for more flying in order to keep pressure on the Germans and decrease bomber losses.

"Another bad day," began Lee's diary entry for April 16, 1943.

Captain Anderson had trouble at 31,000 feet this morning when his motor cut out and he crash-landed his P-47. He wasn't hurt. Then this afternoon there was a sweep to St. Omer. The squadron was bounced [attacked] and Anderson and McMinn were both shot down. So go another two of the boys. Lieutenant Colonel Peterson was leading the wing and he had motor trouble and bailed out into the Channel, but was picked up this evening. Major Blakeslee, Lieutenant Boock and Lieutenant Colonel Peterson each got an FW-190.

Lee flew two combat missions over Holland and France the next day.

Pretty busy today. We went over to Walcheren Island, Holland, this morning. I led Red Section and there were over forty Huns up against us. Then this afternoon, I led the squadron and we went in at Nieuport, down around St. Omer, back over Calais and Dunkirk. The factories at Bruges were bombed by Venturas. There was some flak, but not too near. We are beginning to get the feel of the fourteen-thousand-pound P-47, and it shows in the way the fellows fly. Strange thing happened about the time we crossed into Holland. I started getting an eerie buzz in my earphones. After a bit it went away. Asked the intelligence officer about it after we landed and he told me it was German radar.

Gover later remembered:

It was a scary sound, because we knew it bore bad tidings. When we heard the sound we knew the Germans had a fix on us and we were plotted on their screen. It was just a matter of minutes and the Jerry fighters would appear. You never got used to that sound, because it meant nothing but trouble. It always made the hair on my neck stand up.

Following a mission over France on April 29, Gover wrote a very long letter to his folks, which surprisingly passed the censor.

As this is a nice dreary afternoon and the boys are all very quietly playing cards or sleeping, I thought that I would drop you a line. I thought you might be interested in just what composed a fighter squadron and how it ran. The man running the whole shebang is a major. Then the squadron is divided into two flights. Each flight has twelve pilots and is led by a captain. Then there are six first lieutenants and five second lieutenants in each flight. The ground crew consists of 250 enlisted men. They are really the key to the success of a mission, because they keep the planes flying. Each P-47 has an assigned crew chief and an assistant. They are responsible for everything about the plane from keeping the engine in perfect tune to ensuring that the canopy is clean. If they have any special problem, like something wrong with the radios, they call in a specialist. We have eighteen aircraft in the squadron but fly with twelve, six from each flight in three lines of four. I have been flying in the major's place and leading the squadron. I try to fly as smoothly as possible so everyone can stay with me and keep together. It's really a pretty damn nice feeling to know that you have worked your way to the very top. In a fighter squadron the highest rank is a major, and as a captain I think I have done OK. There is a lot of responsibility looking out for the whole damn outfit, but as a captain I get my own jeep—some fun. And as I am now leading the whole squadron, I have had the experience of every part of it, from ass-end Charlie to the lead. I'll draw you a diagram of how it works.

Right now I'm flying in the major's place and he's flying right behind me. When he takes over again, I'll jump back over to A Flight. This is a rough idea of what it is all about.

"Shortly after I sent this letter," Gover later explained,

the size of each squadron was increased to twenty-five P-47s and pilots. The normal configuration of a mission then became sixteen aircraft in four flights of four. This enabled the group, which consisted of three squadrons, to put up forty-eight aircraft per mission, which provided a more effective escort for the bomber force.

Gover ended April with thirty-seven hours and ten minutes of flying. On May 1, he celebrated the weekend and his coming birthday by going into London. "Hank Ayres, our two gals and I went for a few drinks, then out to dinner and dance to celebrate my birthday next week. Sure was great to get a break." And it was good that Lee had a break, for just three days later he had his most intense action since checking out in the Thunderbolt. "I just about bought it today" were the opening words of Gover's May 4 diary entry, but the best description of the action was in the letters he wrote home on May 5 and 9. These letters were illustrative of Lee's willingness to tell his parents more about his missions.

May 5, 1943 I had some excitement yesterday when we tangled with about thirty-five FW-190s—damn, what a shambles. I'll tell you about it next letter. Boy, I'm still shaking.

May 9, 1943 We were taking the Forts over and were coming out from the target when we were met by about thirty-five FW-190s, so things broke up and we went at it. I was having a go at a guy when I noticed three vapor trails at about 35,000 and coming down at me. They went on past me and behind and kept going. I lost track of them at about 20,000 but I knew what was cookin'. I turned sharp port [left] and spotted one, but things were going on ahead, so I had to turn again. Next thing I knew, tracers were streaming over my port wing, so I jammed right rudder and shoved the stick. The next thing tracers were on the other side. He couldn't get a bead on me and was just spraying things. So I really got down to work and at the same time told the guy ahead of me to turn into him. He did and then the Hun whipped off. I was so damn mad then that I chased him halfway to Russia and gave him a little of it. [Clark] Gable was in one of the Forts and nothing got close to him. So he thinks it's pretty easy, but he'll be shaking with the rest of us one of these days. "Pappy" Lutz, a kid I knew from Bakersfield, was shot down.

The newspaper account of the mission under the headline "Gable Makes First Raid in Assault on Antwerp" describes the action differently.

Capt. Clark Gable went on his first raid Tuesday when U.S. bombers attacked Antwerp, it was revealed today. The film star, who arrived in England a short time ago, is a gunnery officer. The B-17 was not attacked by enemy fighters. Heavy fighter cover protected the whole formation and little opposition was encountered.

May 6 was Lee's birthday, and his diary entry subtly indicates how much he was beginning to feel the fatigue of combat as well as a degree of satisfaction at reaching age twenty-nine. "I honestly didn't believe that I would live that long in the war," he said.

Happy Birthday—Well, I'm twenty-nine today. Sure am getting old and I don't mean maybe. I had a very enjoyable day. Did nothing until noon and then this afternoon I played nine holes of golf—shot a 49. Then this evening we all played hearts and then had a few beers and so to bed. Didn't even look at an airplane today, let alone fly one. Sure good to take it easy for a day. Tiger Booth and I are going to Cambridge tomorrow and take some pictures of the colleges.

One of the memorable duties that Lee had during his tour was participating in the memorial service for Lieutenant General Frank Andrews and thirteen others who were killed in an aircraft accident on May 10. "Colonel Anderson informed me that I was to be in the service since they wanted a captain who had been decorated." Gover was quite touched by the experience, and on May 11 he wrote:

The service was held in the Royal Military Chapel at Wellington Barracks. I had never been there before we practiced for the service yesterday. It is a beautiful church and the service was very nice. All the U.S. generals and the ambassador and his staff were there along with the high British officials and all. After the service I just fooled around town.

Gover returned to his base the next day and began one of his busiest and most tiring periods of the war. From May 13 through 21, he flew thirteen missions, nine of them, totaling nearly fifteen hours, in combat over France and Holland. He also saw four of his men shot down. His accounts of the missions reveal very clearly the thoughts of a pilot flying combat day after day.

The Dieppe raid in mid-1942, while he was still in the RAF, was Gover's most unforgettable combat, but his flight on May 14, 1943, was equally memorable. Dieppe had been Lee's first experience in a massive raid where he came face to face with heavy destruction and loss of life. The May mission was his most effective as a very experienced fighter pilot and would set him apart as one of the best.

We were awakened at 4:30 a.m., went to briefing, and took off for Bradwell Bay, where we landed and refueled. At 12:27 we took off and were to escort Fortresses to bomb Antwerp. Here is the report I turned in upon landing.

On 14 May 1943, at approximately 1315 hours, while escorting Forts to Antwerp, I was flying Blue Three and we had just reached the bombers and were to dive in front of them when I saw four FW-190s at about 26,000 feet and coming in at two o'clock to the bombers. I was flying at 28,000 feet. I broke off and made an attack of about 25 degrees head-on and closed to about 10 degrees head-on. I gave about a four-second burst, but as he passed under me I couldn't see the result. No claim.

I then turned sharply to port and saw another FW-190 coming in about five hundred yards ahead. He turned to port and I was then line astern [behind him]. At about three hundred yards line astern I fired a short burst, then closed a little more and gave a four-second burst. The e/a [enemy aircraft] then rolled to the starboard and pieces started coming off the ship. This was followed by increased black smoke and the e/a then went in an uncontrolled spiral. I claim one FW destroyed.

I pulled up to regain my altitude and sighted another e/a on my port and below going towards the Forts. I dived and the e/a saw me and started a spiral turn to port. I closed to about one hundred yards, allowed deflection and gave a three-to-four-second burst. I saw strikes and then had to break as I was being attacked. I claim one damaged [FW-190].

As I broke away to port I was being fired on, I started to dive and turn. The e/a stayed right on my tail so I pulled up sharply and started a climbing turn to port. The e/a stayed right on me but wasn't getting deflection (shooting angle). I saw that he was starting to mush out of the turn. I then closed my throttle and threw stick and rudder to the right, which brought me in line astern on him. I had lost speed and he pulled away to about three hundred yards. I then started to close and fired. As I fired he turned on his back and hung there for two to three seconds. My tracers that designated my last fifty rounds were now coming out and I saw these striking the e/a. I was then being attacked again so broke away and started for home. I dove to six thousand feet and to the coast before losing the e/a on my tail. I was now out of ammunition so called and reported the fact and came on back to base. I claim one damaged [FW-190].

The one FW-190 destroyed and two damaged were Lee's highest total for one day. Of even more significance, on July 9, 1943, Gover was awarded the Silver Star, the Army's second-highest award for bravery in combat, for his action in preventing the attack on the bombers. Lee was the first pilot in the Fourth Fighter Group to receive the Silver Star, which made him the most decorated pilot in the group and one of the most highly decorated in Europe. He did not mention the action to his parents, but on June 1, he wrote his sister Juanita a brief account.

The other day I got tangled up with four FW-190s and I managed to get three of them. Boy, I was never so busy in my life before. It started at 28,000 feet and ended up on the deck with me out of ammunition and 50 miles of Belgium and 120 miles of water between me and home, and other 190s taking a crack at me. I did maneuvers that Al Leary and Tex Rankin never heard of.

Gover's exploits were followed very closely by the local newspapers, because he was the first local boy to become a combat pilot. Both his sisters agreed he was a local hero and that every news item about him was front-page stuff in San Carlos. "My parents had almost weekly visits from the press all during the war," Lee remembered. Thus his parents and the entire community of San Carlos, California, were well aware of Lee's activities two months later when he was awarded the

Silver Star. On two consecutive days there were feature articles in the paper recounting his exploits of May 14 and giving a short summary of his activities in the few preceding months. Under the headline "Capt. LeRoy Gover Wins Silver Star," the entire mission was recounted.

Capt. LeRoy Gover, San Carlos air hero, has been decorated with the Silver Star for gallantry in action, an Associated Press dispatch from London reported this morning. Captain Gover's Silver Star is still another honor added to the galaxy of high awards given the American fighter pilot who has been in England flying for the allies since Nov. 3, 1941. The latest award came for the captain's courageous single-handed fight with four German fighters about to attack a formation of bombers he was escorting, the Associated Press said. . . . besides the Silver Star and the Air Medal with two Oak Leaf Clusters, the San Carlos flier also holds the Distinguished Flying Cross.

Lee's diary entry for his two combat missions on May 16 is very perceptive and tells a great deal about his character.

Busy day today. We went in at Flushing, Holland, this morning and were met by thirty-five e/a. There were a few scraps. Then this afternoon, we went in at Cayeux, France, then up past St. Omer and out at Dunkirk. It was a beautiful day and I was leading my section at 35,000 feet. Looking north, I could see the Hook of Holland and to the south, the Cherbourg Peninsula of France. I could see all of Belgium and Paris as well. The nicest view you could ever hope to see, and with England lying over to the west. The Channel looked like it was only about one mile wide from that altitude. After the two shows today we were released until noon tomorrow.

Despite his being released until noon, the seventeenth was a very trying and busy day.

Wow, what a day and am I tired. We took off here about 1:00 p.m. and flew clear down to Land's End and landed at Predannack Aerodrome to refuel—about 280 miles. At 4:47 we took off and did a fighter sweep to Brest, France. Boy, there was nothing but water under us. We returned to Predannack to refuel—about a 300-mile trip. Then on back to Debden, another 280 miles, and landed here at 9:15 p.m.—five hours' flying. Its just now 10:15 and I'm hitting the hay—completely pooped out!

On May 18, "we were met at the coast by about eighteen ME-109s and several dogfights took place. One of our P-47s went in a dive on fire. He went right on in. It was Lieutenant Boock." Gover's only comment by the twentieth was that "they're working the hell out of us this month. Another sweep to Holland today—no losses." The same would not be true of the next day, however.

We went in at Ostend at thirty thousand feet and continued on to Ghent. We were met by a group of ME-109s and FW-190s. Dogfights started and we lost Lieutenant Morgan, Lieutenant Whitlow and Lieutenant McFarlane. Damn bad show. We sorta took a beating today. Things are sure getting tougher every day.

Lee's comments about someone being shot down may, at first blush, seem rather heartless, but they actually underscore the reality of combat. Death, in fact, is never very far from the thoughts and lives of those involved in war. But, because of that, it is treated in a rather matter-of-fact way. "When one of the kids in the squadron was shot down," Gover reminisced,

it was the duty of the squadron commander to write to his parents or wife and tell them what happened and offer your sympathy. I just wasn't any good at that, because I couldn't find the words, so I had the adjutant write the letters and I would sign them. Then a friend would go through the lost pilot's belongings and screen them for anything that would make the situation worse back home before we packed them up and sent them to his family. I did that a number of times, and it was tough, too. You just couldn't help relating it to your folks and see some poor mother or wife changing the blue star in the window to a gold one. I felt so sorry for them. While we were required to go to funerals in the RAF, we were not allowed to attend after we transferred to the U.S. Army. I think that was good, because the entire RAF squadron would just drag around after attending a funeral and I know it affected some of the guys on their next few missions. I saw guys standing in ranks crying. Actually, after I got in the American forces, we didn't have very many funerals. Most of the kids that were lost were shot down over the Continent and so we didn't know their fate for several days or even weeks. They just left and we all waited to hear. If they were captured, the Red Cross would know, sometimes within a week or so, and we would find out. The same was true if they were killed, although that could take longer. When you didn't get any word for a long period of time, you hoped that they were evading capture and would make it back as several were able to do. I know that on the surface it seems like we were a pretty hard group, but lots of guys cried as a result of having their buddy killed.

Events got a great deal tougher for Lee the second week of June. After uneventful flights on June 2 and 4, he spent two days in London. Then on June 9, he had two flights—the second was one he would not forget. There is no account of this mission in Gover's diary, so he recounted the story later.

We were sent out on a high-altitude escort mission taking the B-17s pretty near the limit of our escort range. I had been suffering from a very bad cold and a stuffed-up head and knew that I really shouldn't be flying but decided that I could make it. We knew it was going to be a rough flight, with plenty of antiaircraft fire and lots of fighters up against us. We picked up the bombers at the Belgian coast, and things went well until about fifty miles inland. Then all hell broke loose. Over a hundred fighters hit us. I tore into a gaggle of FW 190s and was getting hits when I was clobbered by an FW-190 I had not seen. My number two was nowhere to be found, so I pulled all the G's I could handle and went into a hard climbing left turn. The German was good, and I couldn't shake him. I then rolled over and went into a power dive. From previous experience, we knew we could outdive both the ME-109 and the FW-190. I started my dive at 32,000 feet, and at about 15,000 feet I thought I had been hit in the head with a 20mm cannon shell. The pain was the worst I had ever felt. After a few seconds I realized that I wasn't hit but that something was really wrong in my head. I couldn't find the German fighter anywhere so assumed he had lost me and returned to the battle above. I called the base and told them that I was on my way back with unknown damage to my plane and something really wrong with my head. When I got to Debden I sort of landed, bouncing all over—really almost a controlled crash—but everything was in one piece. The FW-190 had got some hits on me but none in anything vital. But when the doctor examined me he found that I had broken an eardrum from the change in altitude and pressure from the dive. Off I went to the hospital, where I stayed for a week. I didn't write about it in my diary because I didn't have the diary in the hospital.

While Lee was in the hospital, he did a lot of thinking about the future and what he might do if he survived the war. Like so many of his comrades, all he really knew was flying, so that was a logical possibility for postwar employment. On June 13, he wrote to his parents asking about the commercial aviation situation in the United States, but did not mention that he was in the hospital.

We fellows in the squadron have been wondering what kind of a test or just what we will have to do to get a pilot's license when we get home. Take my case. All my time over here has been on combat duty. I've flown everything from 130-horsepower to 2,300-horsepower. I've flown about twenty hours of twin-engine stuff, and I even got time in a Fortress (like flying a truck). I have sixty-some hours of instrument time. I don't mean under the hood or in the Link trainer, but actually flying through fog or cloud where one mistake means your life. That time is worth a thousand hours of hood and Link time. Some of the time there were guys flying formation on me and depending on me completely to bring them in. There's nothing more nerve-racking in the world than letting down through the soup and the old altimeter comes to three hundred feet, then two hundred feet and you still can't see the ground. A bomber is pretty steady, but a damn fighter just jumps all over and you have to keep on the ball. As far as judgment and ability to force-land in different spots, I'll put in with any of them. I've flown at zero feet and at 42,000 feet. So ask Vaughn just what the dope is on that. I would sure appreciate it, and so would the guys. I'm flying my thirteenth ship now and have to get a new motor next week. The airframe is still OK. but the putt-putt is tired after eighty hours.

Gover's comment about the engine needing to be changed after eighty hours is illustrative of the tremendous wear and tear the aircraft took flying combat. The double-row, eighteen-cylinder Pratt & Whitney radial engine in the P-47C, which Gover flew, had a maximum of 2,300 horsepower. In combat or very-high-altitude flying, the engine operated near its maximum output a great deal of the time. Added stress was put on this huge engine when the throttle was suddenly closed completely, then moved immediately to maximum power, as Gover described doing in his dogfight of May 14. Further, since the P-47 was a single-engine aircraft, and since every mission began and ended with long flights over water, extreme care was taken to ensure that the engine was in top condition at all times. If there was any question about the condition of the engine, it was replaced with a new one. (By way of contrast, the author flew aircraft with the same engine as the P-47 from the late 1950s to the early 1970s. In that peacetime operation, the engine generally went from fifteen hundred to two thousand hours before a change was required.)

One of Gover's dreams since becoming part of the American Army Air Forces was to be in command. That dream was fulfilled on June 26, when he became commander of A Flight of 336 Squadron of the Fourth Fighter Group. That same day he finally told his folks that he had been in the hospital, but explained none of the circumstances involved.

I guess you have begun to wonder where my letters are. I just came back to camp after spending eleven days in the hospital for repairs and have been given six days' leave, which I am spending here in London taking in the shows. Everything is OK now and I go back on operations in two days. The Duchess of Kent was up at camp two days ago, and presented us our Eagle Squadron Plaques. Everything around here has been going along OK and don't do any worrying. This morning I ordered a special battle dress jacket—set me back $35 but it's a honey. I also had a new hat tailored for $18, then my new boots cost $45, my tunic and trousers $60, and custom-tailored shirts at $16 apiece. So I have a really first-class outfit. I was just talking to a kid this morning that has made his twenty-five trips in bombers and is going home this week. I've got seventy-four now and want to make it to at least a hundred, get in on the invasion, and then I'll feel that I've done my share.

Lee's stay in the hospital was also the subject of a story in the San Carlos newspaper a month later under the banner "S.C. Flier in Hospital for Repairs."

June 29, 1943   Back at work today. I led the flight on a sweep to Dieppe and around Bologne. Few fighters up and our squadron all returned safely. The colonel of the 74th Group at Duxford was shot down and also his number two man.

Gover's mission on July 1 set the stage for the entire month, during which he flew thirty-four times, eighteen in combat.

Another show today. I am now in charge of the flight for good. We went to Abbeville, where the drome was bombed by Typhoons. There were a lot of 109s up and Don Young was shot at three different times. I went in to attack but couldn't catch them. My motor cut out on me and my radio went dead. I got my motor started but could only get twenty inches out of her [less than half the normal power] all the way home.

July 3, 1943   Nothing doing today except a little local flying. Bob Hope and Francis Langford were up this afternoon and put on a show for the boys. It was pretty poor.

The level of action remained about the same for the entire month, and the characteristics of the mission varied little. On July 28, however, the Fourth Fighter Group was part of another historic first.

Today was the big day. We put on two-hundred-gallon belly tanks and escorted the Forts clear into Germany. [The auxiliary tanks were called "belly tanks" or "drop tanks," because they were attached under the center of the fuselage of the P-47 and when empty could be jettisoned so the aircraft would be more maneuverable when enemy fighters were contacted.] It was the first time fighters have ever been into Germany. Boy, what a trip! There were about two hundred e/a pecking at the Forts. I shot down an FW-190 in the mess. My number two man, Lieutenant Henry Ayres, was shot down and had to bail out over Belgium. He called me and said he was wounded but so long and hit the silk. Sure hope he makes it OK.

Ayres was taken prisoner by the Germans but was so badly wounded that he was repatriated to the United States on the Swedish-American ship *Gripsholm* before the end of the war.

The presence of the American fighters came as a complete surprise to the Germans, since the scene of the action had heretofore been beyond the range of the P-47. Not only did the Germans suffer significant losses, they were forced to modify their air defense system, since the bombers would now be able to fly nearly to Frankfurt with fighter escort. One German tactic was to attack the fighter escort early to try to get them to jettison their auxiliary tanks so they would not have enough fuel to escort the bombers all the way to the target.

The action of the twenty-eighth was further elaborated in Gover's letter home the following day.

I've been over to the other side twice today and I'm pooped. The altitude seems to get you. I knocked down another FW-190 yesterday. We lost one boy in my flight, Henry Ayres. He was wounded but called me and said he was bailing out. We were pretty well inland over Belgium. I hope he can escape instead of going to a PW camp, but if he is as badly wounded as he sounded, I doubt if he can make it.

Eddie Rickenbacker was up today and I had a little talk with him. He told us about his experiences and all. Sure a swell guy. He congratulated me on my Hun of yesterday. He told us that the Japs were easy meat. He said the Germans were by far the better pilots and they have all their very best pilots here on the Western Front to stop us, as if I didn't know that.

Yesterday's do was really hot, boy. We were well inland and bringing the Forts out when they were jumped by about eighty FW-190s and ME-109s. I dived right at them and gave a short burst at an FW-190 and hit him right in the cockpit and a big flash came out. I whipped by and lost him then, but Jim Goodson and Glenn Smart, flying top cover, confirmed it as destroyed. One Fort was crippled and out of formation and about ten Huns were knocking hell out of it. Before I could get a 190 off my tail and get to it, it was going down. Then a wing came off and I saw four chutes come out of it. The rest must have been killed. Then the dirty yellow bastards shot two of the chutes and they collapsed and went down. Boy, the next Hun I see in a chute sure is going to get spread about. [Gover never shot anyone in a chute and knows of no one who did. He later said that he believes the incident related in this letter was isolated and was not a common practice of the Germans.] I've got ninety-five trips over now. I've won five Air Medals, the Distinguished Flying Cross and the Silver Star.

On July 30, the Germans were again caught unprepared by American fighters with auxiliary tanks. "We put on the belly tanks again and went into Germany to bring the Forts out," Gover wrote. "There were about two hundred e/a up again. I was top cover at 32,000 feet so watched the boys get at it. We shot down twenty-five for the loss of six and Don Young got an FW-190."

While the belly tanks presented the Luftwaffe with new defense problems, they also presented the P-47 pilots with a unique flying challenge. Lee remembered:

When we first received the long range belly tanks they were made out of pressed paper and had 108-gallon capacity [about 750 pounds of gasoline]. Since they were paper, they had no baffle plates in them, and you can only imagine the terrible time we had maintaining any semblance of straight and level flight. The gas would slosh around something awful and you had a hell of a time. Going out on a mission the planes were going this way and that. We looked like a bunch of first-year ballet dancers. Going through cloud was very, very difficult because of the instability of the airplane. Later, we received two-hundred-gallon tanks and they had baffle plates. Still, two hundred gallons of gas was a lot of resistance and too much weight down below for the plane to fly well.

Another big problem with the belly tanks was the connection from the plane to the tank. A small rubber tube came out of the plane's belly and hooked onto a glass tube about four inches long. Another rubber tube from the belly tank hooked to the other end of the glass tube. We had a lot of aborts because the glass tube would break because of vibration. We were told the glass tube was there to break the connection when we dropped the tank. However, we weren't supposed to drop them, because they were scarce. The damn plane just wasn't suited to all the violent moves of combat with the tank attached, so when we engaged the Germans we didn't give a damn who said what, we dropped them.

The weather was terrible in England during the first two weeks of August, and there was little flying. This meant time off and a chance to rest, go to London, and generally regroup. Lee did some shopping, including buying a bracelet for his sister Juanita and a locket for his other sister, Betty. On August 9, after flying a sweep over France, Lee talked about the significance of the mission planned for the next day.

Tomorrow is to be our big day. We're going into Germany again and I guess the whole British Island, anyway all the planes, will be over the Continent tomorrow. Well, if it helps to get the war over, I'll certainly try my best. But these long shows can get awful rough and just one motor for us fighters to ride and sweat it out.

A mission with belly tanks was generally well over two hours long and often included a flight from Debden to a staging base near the coast to increase the fighter's range. After takeoff, the flight could go for nearly half an hour over water and then another half hour before joining up with the bombers. After rendezvous with the bombers, action with large numbers of German fighters was almost inevitable. The fifteen or twenty minutes of combat left every pilot soaked with sweat and utterly exhausted, for during that time every fighter pilot was literally fighting for his life. The flight culminated with a long ride over water again and, often, after a couple of hours on the ground, a repeat performance. Little wonder that Gover refers so often to being "pooped out."

After a two-and-a-half-hour flight on the morning of August 12, during which the Germans shot down a large number of bombers and five P-47s, Lee reflected on the war in a long letter to his parents. The letter is particularly significant since Gover was one of the first American fighting men in Europe, albeit in the RAF, and had obviously been a close observer of the action and progress he believed the Allies were making against Germany.

I was just thinking this morning about what a difference there is over here now from when I first came over in 1941. Boy, I remember that I wasn't here four days when the Huns dropped a thousand-pound land mine on our drome and sure kicked hell out of it in general. Sort of shook me to the quick. That was when I was in Wales. Then I went down to Cornwall and onto operations. The Germans used to come in about every morning and drop little eggs on us. And at night a few high-flying aircraft would scatter a few more. The old antiaircraft would be popping all around. Then the squadron moved up to Bournemouth to replace another squadron that just wasn't anymore because all the pilots had been lost. There we used to be busy as hell, and I don't mean maybe. That was when we had to be in our planes and had thirty seconds to get airborne. We chased Huns for four months there—and vice versa. Once a JU-88 came swooping down over the field and we dived in the old ditches. Another time we were down in Portsmouth for the night taking on a few of those warm beers when about six German aircraft swooped in low from the sea and really did the job. Five of us dived behind a stone wall, and, lucky for us, the bomb hit a bit on the other side, but it sure covered us with mud. We had damn little to eat then and the civilians had even less.

Then when I went to the Eagles, we went up to the east coast for a week of gunnery and we were bombed for seven nights in a row. Began to get damn monotonous, believe me, old bean. Then we started to get the edge after Dieppe and things started to go our way for a change. The United States was getting a few more men over here and the food situation began to perk up.

Then in September 1942, we fellows transferred to the U.S. forces but kept flying the Spits and mainly taking over low-level bombers and going on fighter sweeps just looking for trouble.

They still had us outnumbered, but we were beginning to do pretty fair. They began to come over here only in the early mornings then, and those that did come over were getting the hell shot out of them, so the raids became fewer and fewer.

Then in about March of this year we were operational on the Thunderbolts and then the B-17s started going over in number and we started taking them also. Now there are hardly any enemy aircraft over England at all. For ten days now there hasn't been a bomb dropped on England. The B-26 came off the secret list today and they have been pounding the airdromes in France and Belgium. We also act as high cover for those jobs. So the way things are today, we are doing the bombing—all of it. The Hun is on the defense now. The RAF is giving them hell during the night. Then in the daytime, the B-26s pound the close dromes and such and the Forts go way in and give it to them. The Forts are doing a good job. I know because I see plenty of the packages they drop and where they hit. 'Course, I've seen lots of Forts go down also, plus some of our boys trying to save them.

The Huns now have over 50 percent of their fighter strength on our front, which is plenty when you think that they have plenty on the Russian front and then in the south. But we are taking care of all these, and they are the top Jerry fighters up here against us. [Because of the increasing threat in the air on the Western Front, the Luftwaffe began transferring its most experienced pilots from the Eastern Front to the West in March. This process continued throughout 1943.] They are really putting up everything trying to stop the Forts. I think, maybe I know, that the little man in Berlin will wake up to an awful sight one of these mornings. So in two years, the tables have been completely reversed, and that looks pretty darn good to this old man. Anyway, it leads one to thought.

Between August 20 and 30, Gover flew eleven missions, including five on August 23, when "it seemed like I was in the air forever today. We flew three local missions this morning and then this afternoon went over to Bruges, Ghent and Rotterdam, which are always good for plenty of flak." On a nearly identical mission three days before, "we lost three Forts and two P-47s." Still, there was time for socializing. "Went into London the other day when we were grounded because of rain," he wrote to his folks.

A man had left an invitation at the Eagle Club for two officers to attend a party, so one of my boys and I decided to have a go at it. Well, it turned out damn good. Took in nothing but the best joints. There were three fellows and three gals, and what happens but I end up with a sweet young thing whose old man is worth a cool four million quid, about sixteen million good old American dollars. They have a manor up north and she invited me up to give it a look someday, so maybe I'll go. My friend Grace sent a clipping showing Allen Martini there at home in Frisco. He flew the *Dry Martini* Fortress. Then there was another picture of Morgan—*Memphis Belle*. Seems funny to think of those guys all home. I was here a year before they came over and now they are home and I'm still here. They all put in their twenty-five trips and got out. I don't know why I hang on. I have 108 trips in now. I thought I'd be satisfied when I got in 100 but I hate to leave now when things might really get hot. Don Young has decided he's had enough and is going home next month. That leaves me the only one left out of the whole works.

Gover later commented on the requirements to rotate back to the United States.

Bomber crews were required to fly twenty-five missions, after which they could rotate back to the United States if they so desired. It was just the opposite for fighters. We had to fly two hundred hours of combat before we could come home. We counted our missions, of course, as a matter of pride. But that's all it counted for. It took a lot of missions to get the two hundred hours of combat. When I started with 66 Squadron, most of the missions were real short, some less than an hour. Even in the P-47 they were seldom more than two hours. Later in the war, when missions were four or five hours in the Mustang, the boys got home real soon. It took me 159 missions to get 233 hours and 55 minutes of combat time. I could have come home in September or October of 1943, but I wanted to try and get 150 missions, which I did.

September began where August left off. "I was so busy and so tired during the first part of September that I just couldn't bring myself to write in my diary," Lee later said.

I just flew, then tried to relax, ate and went to bed. I was pooped. It was just like when I was in the RAF. The batman would come in to wake me up and I wanted so badly to tell him to go away. But I had a duty to perform and an obligation to the other men in the squadron, so I just got up and flew. All of us were volunteers, after all, and I felt strongly that a man's word was his bond and so I had an obligation to fly even if it meant that I might get killed. Not all the guys felt that way, and there were several who asked to be taken off combat flying because they just couldn't take the pressure anymore. After the United States entered the war, patriotism had a lot to do with keeping us going. It was our country that was fighting the Germans and it was probably easier for most of us to identify with that cause than it had been while we were in the RAF. Still, the pressure of almost daily combat got to a number of pilots and they just had to go to some other type of duty.

On September 6, Lee took time to recount the preceding few days to his parents. By then, he had stopped being concerned about his parents' worrying and was more interested in giving them a good appreciation for the war and what he was doing. One of the amazing things about all of the detailed letters, such as the one Lee wrote on the sixth, is that they passed the censors. Early in the war, a letter such as this would have been cut to shreds.

We have been pretty busy again these last few days. On August 31, we took Forts into Paris, and boy, did we have a battle on our hands. They came down on us out of the sun, and man oh man. One of my new boys got an FW-190 on his tail and he spun out and got away, but boy, is he still shaking. Then on September 2, we went into Beavis-Tille and about thirty came down on us again. I saw about ten coming down on us out of the sun and at the same time two ME-109s came in on us from dead ahead. I pulled into the ones coming head-on, gave them a blast, and damaged one. The ones behind were now shooting at my number four man and he was a new boy and got excited and pulled it back and spun out. The e/a then overshot him and by this time I was around and giving them hell. We had to pull out then and hit for cloud cover, but it sure was hot and heavy for a while. They have changed their tactics this last week. They now go after us escorting fighters instead of the Forts. I don't know why but it helps the bombers.

Then on September 3, we escorted the Forts to Provins, about fifty miles southeast of Paris. We were taking care of 180 Forts, and just as we got over Paris, we could see the FW-190s and ME-109s coming up in swarms. We had the toughest scrap you ever saw. At one time there were about thirty-plus coming in on the Forts in a head-on attack, and I took a section of four down to engage. Four of them got in before I could get down, and they took a squirt at the Forts and half rolled and went down. One e/a stayed a little too long and got blown all to hell. We broke up the other twenty-some and then I pulled up into the sun, and holy Christ, man. There was nothing but FW-190s all around me. I was in the sun to them, though, and they didn't see me at all. I circled around on them and down I came at them for a change. Those FW-190s can flick over on their backs and go down faster than you can damn well imagine. The Forts had bombed by now, and they sure blasted the joint too. I still had two of my boys with me, so I climbed to thirty thousand and started back. Seemed that we flew for a week before we got back to Paris. It sure is a beautiful city, with the river winding through it and the old tower and arch right in the middle. They all stood out just as plain as could be.

One of my boys came in just all shot to hell. An explosive cannon shell had hit his tail and there were about seventy-five holes in it. Another shell had hit his engine and knocked the rocker arm box off and cut a few oil lines and some wires. But the old motor kept on humming and he got back all the way from Paris. Another of the guys, Dale Leaf, was hit and didn't make it back. So now I have 111 missions and still going strong.

As increasing numbers of B-17s arrived in England, the escort mission requirement continued to grow. By early September, Gover's squadron was flying escort almost every day. "It was impossible to fly those missions and not just feel so bad for the bomber crews," Lee reminisced.

I don't think any of them completed their twenty-five missions until the *Memphis Belle* did sometime in 1943. It was just so hard to see those big planes get hit and ten guys were gone, just like that.

Gover's account of his escort mission to Paris on September 15 provides a vivid description of the situation and the action.

We took 120 Fortresses into Paris this evening. Saw one of the saddest sights yet. Just as we were taking them on their bombing run, five FW-190s came in at them, fired, rolled over and went down. The Forts knocked one of them out. Then the most terrific flak I've ever seen came up. One Fort was hit direct and just exploded. It went all to pieces and down in flames. Not one chute opened. Then about ten seconds later another Fort got a direct hit in the wing. It caught fire and started down. It began breaking up and all on fire. Small dark objects, must have been the crew, started down, but not one chute opened. Guess the explosion also killed them. Then about another minute and another Fort went all to pieces and no chutes. God, but I felt sorry for those poor bastards. Thirty boys gone just like that. If it had been fighters we could do something about it, but flak! Well, we just dodged to beat hell ourselves. Came back across Paris, and boy, how the guns were flashing, as it was now fairly dark. Came back and landed at a forward airdrome (Ford), all pooped out and hit the hay.

Gover's words reflected the thoughts of almost every fighter pilot and probably explained why none of them wanted to be in bombers.

The B-17, the primary American bomber used on the Western Front, was a large airplane for its day. Built by Boeing, it first flew in 1935 and was continually changed and upgraded from that time until the end of World War II. With a wingspan of 103 feet and a length of 73 feet, it was indeed formidable. Its four Wright Cyclone engines combined to produce a total of 4,800 horsepower, which enabled the craft to cruise at about 170 miles per hour between 25,000 and 28,000 feet. The bomber, called the Flying Fortress, was so named because it was thought to be capable of defending itself against fighter attack with its ten machine guns—two in the nose, two each in the belly and top turrets, one on each side and two in the tail.

It was thus thought to be the perfect aircraft to carry out the doctrine of high-altitude, daylight, unescorted, precision bombing that had been adopted by the Army Air Corps in the late 1930s. Because the highly sophisticated Norden bombsight used in the B-17 required that the aircraft be completely stable for about ten minutes on the bomb run, the automatic pilot was designed so that the aircraft was really controlled by the bombsight during that period of time. This meant that the pilot of the B-17 could not change his heading, airspeed or altitude during those critical minutes on the bombing run to evade either flak or enemy fighters. Beyond this, the large formations of heavily loaded B-17s were never able to engage in any significant evasive maneuvers during their entire mission.

The Germans developed several highly effective tactics to counter the B-17. The first was to wait, if possible, until the American escort fighters had run out of range and then attack the bombers. That was the tactic that failed for the Luftwaffe in July when the Americans first used drop tanks on the P-47. Once the escorts were gone, the German fighters had a much easier time attacking the slow-moving B-17s. A second tactic, the one Gover saw in use over Paris on September 15, was to form a "flak box." This was an area of the sky, sometimes as much as a mile square, through which the bombers would have to fly. The Germans then aimed all their antiaircraft guns into this box and set the shells to explode at different altitudes. Thus, the entire box was completely saturated with explosive shells and fragments for about two thousand feet above and below the altitude at which the bombers were flying. It was this type of flak that caused the most damage to the Forts. The sequence was timed so the bombers would have to engage almost constant fighter attack, then fly through the flak, then engage the fighters again when they left the flak box. This same situation could be repeated several times during a bombing mission.

When a B-17 was damaged and unable to keep up with the formation, it proved to be easy and short-lived prey for the Luftwaffe. Losses sometimes amounted to over 15 percent on a bombing mission, with even more so badly damaged they crashed on landing. During several periods in 1943, the first ten days of August, for example, the Eighth Air Force could not launch any bomber missions because losses were so heavy that there were insufficient planes and crews to fly them. It is no wonder that fighter pilots felt a great deal of compassion for these heroic crews who flew straight and level through enemy fighters and flak to deliver their ten-thousand-pound bomb load.

Although the primary casualties from flak were bombers, fighters were not immune to damage and loss from the huge antiaircraft guns.

September 24, 1943   Escorted the B-17s to Nantes, France. We sure got the hell shot out of us by flak over the Guernsey and Jersey Islands. We were lucky that we didn't lose anyone, although some of the guys had some damage. Unlike the bombers, we can dodge and move around and even get the hell out of there if the flak becomes too bad. The Germans always shoot the shells in fours, so you watch the first burst. If the second is in line with you, then you'd better get out of there quick, but if the second is off to one side, then the third and fourth will miss you, you hope. Then in the p.m. we took another 120 B-17s to Nantes again. Two Forts were shot down by flak which was damn accurate. Some of the bomber boys were on their first mission and thought it was rough. They ain't seen nothin' yet. Put in nearly seven hours flying today, well over 2,500 miles. I don't see how we can keep this up. We pilots, as well as our planes, are taking a real beating. Staying tonight at Exeter in an old castle. Pretty grand but also spooky. If the folks could see me now.

Between September 14 and October 3, Gover wrote three letters to his parents that are particularly interesting because they touch on many different aspects of his life and his thoughts about the war.

September 14, 1943   I've gotten in 115 trips now. Got myself another Hun the other day, an ME-109G. The little old bastard just wouldn't leave me alone so I just up and shot him. Don Young and I went into London for a forty-eight-hour pass. Took in a show or two. Also took some pictures and such. We get a big kick out of going into town now with our combat ribbons sewn on our uniforms. We really get the salutes. Don's sure a good guy, and we more or less hang out together, since we are the only two left out of the old Bakersfield gang and the only ones still flying from our OTU class as far as I know. Makes you think, don't it. Oh well, guess I'm just still too damn mean to get killed. Don will be going home in another two weeks or so now. I'm going to stick around and set myself up a record of 150 trips over. Sure hope the hell that I can make it, but I think that I will. After I have been home for about six months or so then maybe I'll take a squadron out and take a crack at the Japs. They are easy meat compared to the Hun, and I think that I could really roll up a score on those little bastards.

September 30, 1943 I was certainly surprised to hear that one of the bonds had finally arrived. There are only about four or five of the boys here that have ever saved a dime. They just throw it away on drinks. You can go out here for an evening and spend twenty pounds ($80) and not even know where it has gone. I can't see the future in doing all that drinking and partying. It catches up with you the morning after when sometimes there is an early mission. I've seen a lot of them go in that way. Just a little slow on reaction after too much the night before. I came home and they didn't. I do like to go down to some of the little pubs and have a few beers and really do enjoy myself (I even like warm beer), but that is about the extent of my drinking life unless I have a long leave in London.

Juanita has written and said that you people are doing a lot of worrying. Well, you kids just cut that out. I'm taking good care of myself and doing plenty of looking around. So please don't worry, because when you worry, damn it, then you get me worrying. Don has been taken off operations now and will be going back in the next week or so. The colonel here (Peterson) has made some of my combat hours disappear so he can keep me here longer. That is a damn good compliment. He has a lot of faith in me and wants me to stay on a little longer and lead the boys. So it's a good thing for me and it doesn't mean much longer when we are busy. Colonel Peterson is the only one of the original Eagle Squadron men left. And in our whole group there arc only five of us from all three Eagle Squadrons. It has been a long and hard row to hoe, but I have come from the bottom and am now a flight commander, which makes me pretty happy. By the way, I was awarded my second DFC last week.

In an interview with the author in 1987, retired Major General Peterson remarked that Lee Gover was one of the best leaders and combat fighter pilots he had ever commanded. Commenting in later years on his leadership style, Gover said:

One of the things I always tried to do when I was leading a flight or squadron was to think of the other pilots. That sounds pretty obvious, but I knew a few leaders who had forgotten what it was like to be tail-end Charlie. I had been there, and I swore that if I ever became the leader of any formation I would not forget how tough it was to fly tail-end Charlie. I knew that you had to fly smoothly and try to be the best, but most of all to take care of your men. When you do your best and never ask your pilots to do something you wouldn't do yourself, the guys know that you really care about them. Then leading becomes easy. I think it also helped that I was always ready to go. I flew every single mission the group flew unless I was on leave, so my pilots knew they could count on me to be there and fly the mission. I never had much use for leaders who flew in such a way that it was almost impossible for their men to stay with them and keep the formation.

On October 2, 1943, Gover wrote to his father. Although he was not told by his family until December, his father had been quite ill during mid-1943, so this letter was particularly important to his dad.

I made a one-day trip to Glasgow, Scotland, the other day and picked up a few plumes for the gals. I was just in and out so didn't have time to get you anything but this bit of heather. I don't know what you can do with it besides look and smell. Anyway, I don't want you to think I've forgotten you. You know how it is when you see little things, you just naturally think of the women folks. I'm on the lookout now for a couple of those old English beer tankards for you and me. I enjoy a beer now and then, and the tankards are really darn nice. I have one now that I've had since I have been over here. It is about 150 years old. But I will probably leave it here when I leave as they want to put it on the shelf here in the mess.

Don't spend a lot of time worrying about me and I'll take care of myself. Remember you told me to always keep my safety belt tight, and I have. It has paid off in a couple of crash-landings. I've had quite a few exciting experiences and I've always come out OK because I used my head, meaning keeping cool, not putting a hole in it. Anyway, it all dates back to when you and Mom would always make us think for ourselves. I want to thank you for being such a good egg.

I'll sign off, but let me hear from you, Dad. Say, those little things with my medals that you wear in your buttonhole. Well, members of my family, you, Mom, Juanita and Betty, can wear them. So put yourself up a medal or so in the old buttonhole. [Gover is referring to the miniature ribbons that accompanied the award of a major decoration such as the Silver Star. These miniatures were designed to be worn in a buttonhole on a coat or jacket.]

Auxiliary fuel tanks—drop tanks—had been available for the P-47 for several weeks, but there was a continual shortage, which limited the number of long missions that could be flown into Germany. The Eighth Air Force had tried to continue sending the B-17s on without an escort, but the losses were too great. By the beginning of October 1943, enough auxiliary fuel tanks were being produced to facilitate longer, escorted bombing missions. Thus, on October 2, 1943, Gover flew his longest mission yet in a fighter, three hours. "Another escort job—360 more Forts to Emden, Germany. Quite a bit of flak and about fifty e/a up on us. We got eighteen e/a and lost one P-47. It was the longest escort job of the war we've done." He elaborated further in a letter to his sister.

Went to Emden, Germany, yesterday. Took in 360 Forts and really plastered the place and shot the hell out of all the fighters that they sent up after us. We're just getting meaner than old Billy Hell. Once in a while now, when I'm in there pitching to beat hell, I stop and think about Christmas coming along and just sorta pull the throttle back, and say to myself, "Give the new boys a chance." I'm not so dumb.

"Although I didn't mention it to my sister," Lee later said, "this was a memorable mission to me for another reason."

As we were coming out of Germany, I just had to relieve myself. Since all seemed quiet, I unbuttoned my flight suit and pants and reached under the seat for the relief tube. Just then someone called in enemy aircraft at nine o'clock and coming fast. I immediately broke hard left into them. We all went round and round with them, but had to break away as we were low on fuel. In the excitement of the moment, I forgot about relieving myself and just joined up and we flew on home. When I parked the aircraft, the crew chief, as usual, jumped up on the wing to help me out of the harness and inquire about the status of the plane. He got up beside the cockpit and then stepped back. I wondered why he hadn't taken the harness straps and put them behind the seat like he usually did. I looked down to hit the quick release on my parachute and saw the problem. I had a hell of a time trying to explain what happened. That damn crew chief went around for a week with a smile on his face. He was one fine mechanic and always kept the aircraft in top condition, so I didn't mind.

Throughout the course of his stay in England, Lee made regular entries in his diary about his social life, both in the small towns around the base and in London. It is indicative of the intensity of the flying activity, the fatigue suffered by the pilots, and the seriousness of the job at hand that these entries almost completely stop in September 1943. In October, for example, Gover has only one entry for London.

October 4, 1943   Caught the train yesterday p.m. and came into London. Got a room at the Jules and went to the Crackers Club and then the Rye and Dry Club. Did some shopping this morning. Bought three yards of material to send Mother so she can make a suit and some Victorian silver earrings for Juanita. Took in a show, *Five Graves to Cairo*, and went out to Rose's until 8:30. Caught the 10:00 p.m. train out of Liverpool Street Station and came on back to camp. The air raid sirens are going at it. Raid on London last night also.

Although the pilots had neither the time nor the energy to go into London regularly, they did entertain themselves in the mess. Gover vividly remembers one evening in October.

Bert Stewart and Deacon Hively [both friends of Gover's from the Eagle Squadrons] had been feuding all week long, calling each other names and even threatening to kill one another. One evening, when the lounge at the mess was pretty full of pilots waiting for dinner, the name-calling started once again. Then each one of them pulled out a gun and started firing. You never saw a room empty out so fast. People were crawling out the windows, out the two main doors, and those that couldn't get out were hiding behind the sofas. I was the only one left, and since they were my friends I figured I had to do something. I dived on Bert Stewart and tried to grab his gun. We rolled around on the floor for a while fighting. Stewart weighed about 200 pounds and I was only 145 so it was just a matter of time until I was going to come out on the short end. As luck would have it, I got struck on the side of the head with the gun, which stunned me. Blood was running down the side of my head and face. Stewart got up and he and Hively started to laugh. I then realized it was a put-up show. The CO told me next day it was a pretty brave thing I did. I told him it was a pretty stupid thing.

The week of October 8 was one of the most critical in the entire air war. During this week the bomber losses were so great that the strategy of sending unescorted or inadequately escorted bomber formations deep into Germany had to be abandoned. Beginning with the attack on Bremen on October 8 and ending with the second large attack on Schweinfurt on October 14, the Eighth Air Force lost 148 bombers, 60 of them on the Schweinfurt raid alone. This loss represented over 20 percent of the force and clearly could not be sustained. Since the P-47 did not have enough range, even with drop tanks, to escort the bombers on very long raids, such as that to Schweinfurt, further deep-penetration missions had to await the arrival of the P-51 in large numbers. Despite the unacceptable number of bomber losses, the raids did force the Luftwaffe to come up and fight, and its losses, too, were huge.

Gover was on all of the critical raids that week in October, and although his comments are rather brief, they give an appreciation for the action.

October 8, 1943 We escorted about 240 Forts to Bremen, Germany, today. Lost two of our boys but destroyed five ME-109s. I had one all lined up but only damaged him. It was about the biggest air battle of the war. We were jumped at the Dutch coast by ME-109s and fought our way to the target and return. We lost thirty bombers and twenty-six more were damaged. There were 142 e/a destroyed total. It was a damn big show.

Sunday, October 10, 1943 We escorted 360 Forts into Münster, Germany, today. Once again, we had to fight our way to the target. The flak around the target was terrific—just a solid wall. Plenty of enemy aircraft all around, and I saw chutes coming out of three different Forts that were shot down. They just wiped a town out with their bombs, but we lost thirty more bombers— those poor bastards. I went down on four ME-109s but couldn't catch them. Our squadron all returned safely.

October 14, 1943 What do you know—I made major today. We started off on a sweep this afternoon to Manston, but it was socked in right to the deck and we were forced to return. The Forts were out already, on their way home in fact from Schweinfurt, Germany. The poor bastards got the hell clobbered out of them. Lost over sixty Forts—that's six hundred men. Bomber Command doesn't seem to care what kind of weather or odds they send those poor kids out in. I don't care about myself but those boys sure have a rough time.

This series of large-scale raids on Germany precipitated a letter of appreciation to all of the bomber and fighter crews in the Eighth Air Force from Prime Minister Winston Churchill.

I shall be obliged if you will convey to General Eaker and his Command the thanks of the British War Cabinet for the magnificent achievements of the Eighth Air Force in the Battle of Germany in recent days culminating in their remarkable successes of last week. Your bombers and the fighters which support them in these fierce engagements have inflicted serious losses on the German Air Force.

These comments were echoed by Air Marshal Charles Portal, U.S. Army Chief of Staff General George Marshall, General Ira Eaker and Army Air Forces Commander General Hap Arnold.

After the ill-fated Schweinfurt raid of October 14, however, large-scale bomber operations against targets deep into Germany ceased until February 1944. This did not mean that there were no bombing raids. It simply meant that Eighth Air Force changed its strategy and sent the B-17s only on raids that could be escorted by the P-47s, or the newly arrived P-38s, for the entire mission. This meant that most missions were over France, the Low Countries and the western part of Germany, no farther than Frankfurt.

At the same time the air action and the heavy losses were making headlines in the American press, Lee's promotion was a big item in his hometown newspaper. Beneath a picture of Gover in his dress uniform there was an article reviewing his exploits.

LeRoy Gover of San Carlos has just been promoted from captain to major by the Army Air Forces. He was presented recently the eighth oak leaf cluster to his Air Medal, which, along with his other medals, have been sent to his parents, Councilman and Mrs. Roy D. Gover of Cedar Street. They have his Silver Star and Distinguished Flying Cross awarded by the U.S. Army. Major Gover's P-47 plane, which he has flown on some of his 115 missions over enemy territory, bears the name of his home town, *Miss San Carlos*. He has been flying in England since November 1941.

In addition, his parents sent a telegram congratulating Lee on being promoted.

Because of the bombing lull, Gover's last combat mission of the month was October 20.

I led 336 Squadron today and we escorted Forts again. The target was covered by cloud and they bombed a secondary target at Antwerp. One Fort exploded in the air right over the target. It just disintegrated and left a big cloud of smoke. I was only about a quarter mile away. The P-38 went on operations today. They relieved us at the French coast and we came home. Hope I can get in enough trips so I can make it home for Christmas.

All of Lee's other flights were called back for weather except one he took to Portreath "to see my old Number 66 Squadron of the RAF." The squadron was gone on a sweep, which disappointed Gover, but "saw Doris Patterson, my WAAF gal friend I hadn't seen in eighteen months." By the end of October, Gover had 141 missions but was lamenting the bad weather, which was keeping everything on the ground and preventing him from making any progress toward enough combat hours to go home on leave. His letters also mentioned the probability that he would not make it for the holidays.

Most of the bombers lost in October were replaced by early November, and the Eighth Air Force wasted no time getting back into the air. The requirement for sufficient fighter escort limited how deep into Germany the raids would be flown, but fighter range was also being increased with the use of more effective auxiliary tanks for the P-47 and the advent of the P-38. The latter aircraft, with auxiliary tanks, had even longer range than the Thunderbolt. Thus, on November 3, 5 and 13, massive bomber raids were staged against Wilhelmshaven, Gelsenkirchen and Bremen, all with acceptable losses. As had been the case in July, the Germans were caught off guard by the American fighters escorting in heretofore unescortable areas. Gover's comments about the missions are short, in keeping with his tendency late in 1943, not to make extensive diary entries. "Events that were exciting a year earlier just didn't seem to mean as much by that time. It was all kind of routine. I guess that's why my diary has so many gaps in it and why the entries are less descriptive," he explained.

"By late in 1943, I was getting physically tired from consistent combat. Many times I had to be helped out of the plane by the crew chief," Gover remembered.

It is difficult to describe the fatigue that comes from flying a fighter in combat. As I look back on it, I can truthfully say that there is nothing I have ever done that is as all-consuming, as physically and mentally exhausting or as violent as flying combat. Everything is constantly moving and changing. You must be looking to each side, up, down, ahead, behind and at your instruments all the time. Your head is never still for more than a second. Because you had to look around so much, your neck would have been warn raw before the mission was over if we had not worn our silk scarves. There is also the constant change in the forces on your body. One second you are pulling so many G's that you are almost blacked out as you are pulled into the seat and your head is driven into your body. The next instant you are being held in the cockpit by the shoulder harness or being jammed against the right or left side of the cockpit as you violently maneuver to deal with an enemy aircraft. And all this time you are moving the stick with your right arm, the throttle with your left and the rudder pedals in coordination to fly the plane. You are trying desperately to keep track of all the aircraft in the sky, the guy you are after, the one who is after you, talking on the radio, and trying to line up for a good shot. And when you did get ready to shoot, it required complete concentration so you could watch the tracer bullets to know how to change your aim. But the biggest fatiguing factor is the tension that goes with combat. There is literally not one second to relax, and you are always reminded that every engagement is a life-or-death situation.

When a combat is completed you are completely drained mentally and physically and absolutely drenched with sweat. I have often wondered just what my heart rate was during aerial combat. I know that sometimes my heart was pounding well after the encounter was over. I often found it impossible to relax for hours after I landed. That is one reason we would go into town with no idea what we might do, try to find a movie somewhere, just have a drink or lose yourself in a letter from home. Finally, there was the stress of having one of your friends killed or shot down and knowing that tomorrow you were going to have to do it all over again.

Lee's diary continues:

November 3, 1943   We went to Halesworth and refueled. Took off and escorted over four hundred Forts to Wilhelmshaven,

Germany. We were jumped at the Dutch coast and two of our boys, Lieutenant Moon and Lieutenant Galleon, were shot down by ME-109s. There were over fifty e/a up against us, and it was a pretty rough show. Just remembered, I left home two years ago tonight. Wow, a lot has happened in that time!

November 5, 1943 Escorted 440 Forts to Gelsenkirchen, Germany, "Heart of the Ruhr." The flak was terrific and very accurate. Plenty of fighters and kept damn busy.

November 7, 1943 Escorted seventy-two B-26s to Meulan, France, near Paris. We went in at twenty thousand feet, which is the best altitude for the B-26, but I didn't like that much because that is where the Krauts' medium-range antiaircraft fire is very, very accurate. Gentile [one of Gover's good friends in the squadron who later became one of the highest-scoring aces of the war] was being shot up by three FW-190s and called for help. When I asked where he was, he said, "Down by the railroad tracks." Hell, there are hundreds of railroad tracks around Paris. He stayed with it, though, shot one down and made it home, all full of holes. Meanwhile, Don Blakeslee [probably the greatest fighter pilot of the war], who was leading the group, was being clobbered by two FW-190s. I took my section down to help him out, and Jim Goodson, my number three man [Goodson also became one of the highest-scoring aces of the war], was on the inside of the turn, arrived first, and shot down both of the fighters that had Blakeslee in a bad way. When we got back, Blakeslee chewed me out for leaving the bombers. Next time I'll wish him well and fly on by. I'm pooped and disgusted, so I'll hit the hay.

"As I have thought about that event over the years," Gover remembered, "Don was probably right, since protecting the bombers was our assignment."

Three days later, Gover was even more upset.

Took another bunch of B-26s over France today and those damn idiots went in at twelve thousand feet. Damn good thing nothing came at us. I hope they don't get the idea that they can go over Europe at any altitude they please, or they are in for a big surprise, because the Jerry gunners can hit a flying duck at twelve thousand feet.

That same day, Gover wrote his parents and gave them the first clue on what he had yet to do before coming home on leave.

Guess that I told you that I have been leading the squadron this last two months. I used to lead most of the time, but now it's all mine. Boy, you should see all of the Christmas packages that are arriving for everyone—that is, everyone except me. But that certainly doesn't bother me in the least, because I'm still hoping to get home. But in case I don't make it—well, it still doesn't make any difference. All the packages that are arriving are being opened as soon as they arrive, and so goes your Christmas. It wouldn't be any fun unless I was home with you birds anyway. I'm going to do fifteen more trips and then home it is. So you can start sweating them out with me. As you know, the weather is pretty lousy here these days and so not many trips in a month. Probably be lucky if I get in five a month now. So don't be disappointed if I don't make it by Christmas.

On November 13, Gover, in his capacity as one of the most decorated fighter pilots in England, was part of a group that opened a patriotic exhibition in Leeds.

There was a press conference and a lot of pictures taken. Then to lunch, and after lunch we came back to the exhibition and made little speeches of thanks and such and the affair was opened. The colonel introduced me, and what an introduction. Embarrassed me no end, but it sure sounded good. I would rather face a sky full of Huns than give a speech, but I did OK. We then had tea with the Lord Mayor and a couple of other big shots. There was an American gal there from the American embassy (Betty Lee Sargent), so we got together and really put on a party.

November 14, 1943 There was a staff car to bring us back to London. We rode for seven hours through snow and rain. Miss

Sargent asked me up to her apartment for dinner and so ended the evening there. A good time was had by all.

November 20, 1943 Hasn't been a damn thing doing this week. The weather is right down on the deck, so I've been in town the last two days. Took in a couple of good movies and did a lot of sleeping. Came back to camp this evening and the fog is right on the ground and visibility about twenty-five yards. Son of a bitch, if I don't get a few more trips in, it looks as though I'll never get back to the States—least of all by Christmas. Was awarded my third DFC last week, so that's not bad.

Through the first week in December, Gover got only three more operational missions. His mission on the fifth was significant because he flew as the deputy wing leader, second in command of the nearly one hundred fighters on the mission, as he did again on December 16.

Weather has been closed in all the time. We took off regardless and went up through it. It was only two thousand feet thick but was absolutely 10/10ths all over [everything covered with clouds]. Took 720 Forts and Liberators to bomb Bremen again. It was completely 10/10ths every bit of the way except an open patch over the Zuiderzee. We shot down a JU-88 just before reaching the target. Visibility was awful. The fellows landed all over the country coming back, out of gas and lost. I made it back OK.

Gover's log book for his mission on December 20 notes a flight of two hours and thirty-five minutes with one ME-109 probably destroyed. The margin describes the action. "Escorted six hundred Forts and Libs to Bremen, Germany. ME-109 shot down near target. My prop and electric system went out over Holland and I damn near didn't get back. Makes ya think." Lee later added, "Ken Carlson came back with me. He was a pilot you could always depend on."

December 22, 1943 I led the squadron on a show to Münster, Germany, today. Took in a lot of Forts and Libs and they bombed the hell out of the joint.

With this entry about his three-hour flight, Gover's World War II combat career closed.

December 24, 1943 This evening the Colonel called me into his office and said I was grounded. I started screaming "Why?" and then he told me that he was sending me home on a thirty-day leave. So it was a pretty damn nice Christmas present. Later in the evening I was at a party with General Anderson, our old group commander, and he called me to one side and told me that when I returned from leave, he was going to move me up to wing headquarters and promote me to lieutenant colonel. We even shook hands on it. Boy oh boy, isn't that something!

December 25, 1943 CHRISTMAS. Merry Christmas. Well, here I am spending my third Christmas in England. Knowing that I'm going home makes it a pretty swell one for me. The officers went down and served the enlisted men their dinner. The colonel had six of us out to his house for drinks from 2:00 to 4:00. Then we came back to camp and had our Christmas dinner. Roast turkey and all the trimmings, and I'm all grins now.

8.   GOING HOME ON LEAVE

THE EUPHORIA OF GOING HOME CARRIED GOVER THROUGH
the last week of 1943. On December 26, "Foggy weather today
but who cares. I've been checking in all my stuff today and getting ready to leave." He also wrote to his parents telling them
he would be home on leave so they should be ready to celebrate a late Christmas. "My hope was to turn in my equipment,
get my leave orders, pack a bag and be on my way before the
end of the year," Lee remarked. That, however, was not to be.
During the week, his daily checks with the adjutant produced
simply a "come back tomorrow and maybe we'll have your
orders from Eighth Air Force." There were few operational
missions being flown because of the weather, so Lee's daily
activities were about the same as always, with plenty of people
around to play cards or snooker and always someone sitting in
front of the fire ready to chat about most anything. Still, Gover
could not help but feel some apprehension about his plans

On December 31, 1943, Lee wrote, "Here we are on the last
day of 1943. The time is going fast. There's a party here at the
mess tonight. Tell you about it tomorrow."

January 1, 1944   Another year. I took in the party here at the
mess last night, but about 11:00 p.m. there were too many drunks
around, so I came on to my room and hit the hay. It's no fun celebrating a New Year unless with old friends.

What a contrast with the year before when he had been in
London at a fancy dinner with Lord Louis Mountbatten and

plenty of wine, women and song. Gover reminisced about some of the reasons.

> During the past year I had moved from being one of a squadron full of Spitfire pilots to my position as a major and the commander of an entire squadron of pilots. This was part of the reality of being in command, and it just didn't seem right to me to be going out and raising hell with a few of my troops. I was their leader and wanted to be with them all. I hadn't been able to go into London very much during the last part of 1943 and so hadn't seen most of the young ladies whom I would go out with for quite some time. Since I was going home, I thought it best to not get anything going with any of them, at least until I got back. I had also said goodbye to Rose. On top of that, almost all of my old friends from the Eagles had gone home, been taken prisoner, or been killed during the past year, so I felt less at home in the unit. Finally, even though I was going home for a month, I was coming back and would be on the wing staff. All of this just made me feel that I should go to the mess and celebrate with the pilots but didn't need to stay too late.

Since he was leaving and because he had had an uneventful New Year's Eve, Lee flew on January 1.

> This morning I went flying—the first and in fact the only one to fly this year. I flew three hours this morning and then this afternoon flew two more hours. I wanted to fly enough to get flying pay in case I leave soon. Played a game of snooker with Garrison this evening and called it a day.

These two flights raised Gover's total time in the P-47 to 327 hours. Since he had 234 hours of combat time, he could not return to operational flying until after his leave, so his only choice was to wait for his leave orders to arrive.

> **January 5, 1944**   No orders as yet, so I just sit and wait as I have for the past few days. Flew the Fairchild up to North Weald and back on squadron business. Seems funny now I'm all through with my ops [operational flying]. I watch the boys go out and

count 'em as they come in. Gentile and Messinger each got an FW-190 today and Godfrey got another damaged. A good day.

On January 8, Gover's trip to the adjutant paid off and he finally received his leave orders. "Went to my room and got things in order, packed my bag and I am ready to go."

January 9, 1944 Said goodbye and came into London. Stayed the night at the Regent. Had a few beers at the Crackers Club and then to bed.

January 10, 1944 Caught the 8:32 and came on up to Preston. Changed trains and then on to Chorley. Transport met me at the station and brought me out to Washington Hall. Checked in and had supper and hit the hay. A nice place this.

January 13, 1944 Still waiting for a boat to take me to NYC. And this is a boring place to wait. Nothing to do but hope that your name comes up to get on a ship.

January 14, 1944 I'll be a sad bastard. A teletype came in today telling me to report back to the Fourth Fighter Group immediately. I don't know what the hell's cooking.

January 15, 1944 Up at 6:00 a.m. and was taken by transport to Preston. Caught the 8:52 a.m. Foggy as hell and it took the damn train eight and a half hours to get to London. Checked my baggage at the Eagle Club and went up to the Crackers Club for a few beers to drown my sorrows. Then over to the Jules Club for something to eat. Caught the 10.00 p.m. (which didn't leave until 11:30) and came on back to camp, arriving at 2:30 a.m. Threw a guy out of my old bed and hit the hay.

January 16, 1944 No one here knew why I was brought back. Called Fighter Command and seems they screwed up the orders and now I have to sweat the whole thing out again. I'm one mad bastard, let me tell you. Sure be glad to get out of here.

The same day, Lee wrote his first letter home in several weeks.

Just a few lines to let you know why I haven't written lately. I finished up my ops the first of the year and then hung around here waiting for orders. On the 10th of January I went to a depot awaiting transportation home. Was about on my way when I was recalled back here to my squadron. Seems they had the orders screwed up. I'm off of operational flying now, so you can all stop worrying. It will be at least three weeks anyway before I leave England, so I'll keep you posted. I'll wire you when I get to NYC.

For the next week, Gover again waited for orders and did various jobs around the unit.

I was bored out of my mind. I watched the guys go out and then couldn't concentrate until they came back. After all, these were my boys, and after I got back from leave, I might be flying with them again. I mostly did staff work around the headquarters and took life easy.

The whole process got to Gover on January 25. "Boy, did I get stinko last night. Been three years since I got that drunk. About six of us tore the joint down. I woke up at noon today." Since no orders were forthcoming, Lee was put back on operations on January 28. He did not fly the rest of the month, because "Colonel Peterson didn't want me to fly unless I was really needed since I had so many combat hours." Gover made no diary entries about his activities but wrote several about the action of his unit.

January 29, 1944 "Jersey" Weyman was shot down over Holland today. The group destroyed nine e/a.

January 30, 1944 Lieutenant Mead shot down over France today. Group destroyed six e/a.

February 1, 1944 There was a decorations parade today and I received the second oak leaf cluster to my DFC. Maybe the parade was the reason they brought me back from leave before I could get on a ship.

February 2, 1944 Lieutenant Cox, a new boy that only arrived in England January 11, was shot down today. I flew four hours today in the Tiger Moth, so that takes care of my time for February.

Near the end of the three weeks needed to reprocess Lee's leave orders, fate dealt him another cruel blow. "February 9, 1944. Feel like hell today. My ear hurts and I have a bad cold." The next day he was sent to the field hospital near Debden, which was to be his home for the next week. "February 12, 1944. Well, it seems my broken right eardrum is now infected from my cold. Have a hell of a headache also." On February 16 he wrote a short V-mail letter to his folks telling them about the delay and saying that he would get home around the end of March.

Upon his departure from the hospital, Gover received the news he had been waiting for. The adjutant gave him his leave orders and a railway pass so he could get from London to the port.

Roy Evans was also going home on leave, and we were told to go to London and wait for a sailing date. It seems that there was a big backup of people at the port waiting to go to the States and so they decided to keep us in London. We checked at the embassy every morning for our departure date.

Little did Lee know that one of the most dangerous periods of his tour in England was about to begin.

February 19, 1944 About 1:30 a.m. the sirens came on and so did the Germans. Biggest raid since the big blitz on London in 1940 and '41. The ack-ack (antiaircraft) really went up and the planes screamed around the skies. Bombs were dropped about a block from here. The skies were full of flares and incendiaries. Seems every time I get to London it catches a big packet. Met Roy Evans this afternoon and we took in a show.

To commemorate the experience, Gover wrote his folks a short letter and enclosed several clippings from the *Times* that showed the destruction from the previous night's bombing raids.

But if Lee thought he was out of the woods, he was wrong. The daily check at the embassy failed to produce a sailing date, and two days later the Germans came to London again.

February 21, 1944 The Huns came over again last night. There were about sixty-plus and they got into the center of town here. Worst I've ever been in. Bombs were dropped on Pall Mall, about a block from here, and really shook the place. Big fires were going all around town. The ack-ack barrage was terrific and shell splinters were dropping all over. One Jerry plane was shot down and crashed around the corner, starting a big fire. I thought sure the Jules Club here was going to catch a packet. It lasted quite awhile, and was I ever glad when it was over and the all clear rang out. It really makes you feel for the people who went through this day after day during the blitz. I don't know how they did it. Boy, are they tough. When you are flying against the Jerries you have a chance, but it is terrible to just have to sit and there is nothing you can do about the bombs.

February 23, 1944 Damn near didn't get a chance to start this book [the ninth volume of his diary]. The Jerries were over again last night in good strength and seemingly good cheer as they really bombed the hell out of the place. That's three times that we've had it in five nights. I'm about fed up and would just as soon get the hell out of here. The gunners here really put up a barrage, and ten Huns bit the dust during the night. Seems as though they're really out to give London the works. It sure gives you a different view of the war when you are on the receiving end of the bombs. Roy Evans and I walked up to Grosvenor Square this afternoon to see about our orders. We report tomorrow at 3:00 p.m. for the word on when we start for home. Did a little shopping. It's now just 8:30 p.m. and I think I'll hit the tub and to bed and then start to sweat out the sirens. So, cheers for now.

Lee's comment on sweating out the sirens was very perceptive. The ensuing raid produced the longest entry in his diary.

February 24, 1944 God damn dirty sonsabitchin' bastardly Germans. I had just finished writing in this book last night. Went up to my room and rolled around a bit, took a bath and got in bed about 10:00 p.m. At 10:15 p.m. the sirens went. I stayed in bed and listened to the planes overhead and the heavy barrage of antiaircraft fire. At about 10:30 I heard a plane about overhead and said, "No, no, no." About then I heard the bomb coming down. It hit about fifty yards away and the most terrible crash and rumble I ever hope to hear came. About then I was blown out of bed and onto the floor. The windows were all blown out and all over me. The door landed in pieces on me, as did the plaster and other bits of stuff. I was on the fourth floor and thought the building was going to go down. All the lights were blown out, of course, and fire had started. I threw the stuff off me and had some cuts and a piece of glass in my eye. I actually thought I was dead. Scared the living hell out of me. I scrambled into what clothes I could find and groped my way down four flights of broken stairs. The dust was suffocating and I could hardly breathe. The lobby was full of people all cut up and bleeding. Someone took the glass out of my eye and I went through the rubble to Roy Evans's room on the first floor. He was still in bed and covered with rubble but OK. I then dashed across the street, which was covered from one end to the other with glass, doors, bricks and such. I stood there and cussed awhile and watched the guns going and the flares coming down. Pretty to see but not so good to be in. Pretty soon the all clear went and I made my way back up to my room. There were holes right through the walls where bricks from the other buildings had gone right through. I straightened my bed up and shook the fine glass and dirt out and crawled back in. There were no doors or windows and so it was cold as hell. I must have fallen right to sleep, because the next thing I knew was when a warden shook me and asked what I was doing there. The building had been evacuated as entirely unsafe and I was the only one in it. This shook me to the core, and I dressed, grabbed my bags and went out in the street. An American truck came by and I got a ride out here to the Princess Gardens Red Cross Club, where I was given a room, and I hit the hay once more. A very tired little boy.

Then about 8:00 this morning the sirens went again and I looked out and saw two contrails at about thirty thousand feet. A couple of Huns over trying to photograph the night's work. They passed soon and the all clear went. Evans and I had gotten together again here, and so we went back to the Jules Club to get his luggage. The building that received the direct hit was completely destroyed, and those around it were all smashed up. It was a thousand-pound bomb and really did the job. Hundreds were killed. There are 180 people in an apartment building that are still all buried underneath. All in all, it was a pretty close call.

February 25, 1944 Well, at 9:45 last night the bastards came again and dropped bombs pretty close. They were close enough to take some of the windows out. The raid lasted about forty-five minutes and was pretty heavy. They're sending over about 150 to 200 planes and about 100 get into greater London. Casualties were pretty heavy again. Roy and I went down to see about our orders. We are to leave here tomorrow night at 7:30 p.m. I will certainly be glad to get out of this place. It's just now 5:30 p.m. and I suppose that they will be over again tonight. Hope I live to get out of here tomorrow. It only takes one bomb on you to make a firm believer out of you. I know.

February 27, 1944 Fooled around London yesterday looking for trinkets to take home. After lunch I went down to the Boyce Tailors and had my ribbons sewn on. I am still amazed at how the British continue to conduct business as usual despite the destruction from German bombing raids. Then back to the Grosvenor House and sat around until 6:00, when we ate. Then we walked over to 7 Grosvenor Square and reported. About 8:00 p.m. we were taken to Euston Station and caught the 9:15 train for Glasgow, Scotland. Heavy snow on the way up, and we arrived a couple of hours late. Changed trains and came on out to Gourock. We were then put on a boat and taken out in the channel, where we boarded the liner *Île de France*. It's a big boat of 44,000 tons. [Before the war, this ship had been one of the world's great luxury liners.] Had lunch, cleaned up, and it's now 3:00 p.m. and I think I'll take a stroll on deck. It's cold as hell and snow around the surrounding country, but we're not being bombed. Cheers for now.

The next day the voyage home began—and what a far cry it was from the voyage on the *Emma Alexander* over two and a half years earlier. Gover, too, was a much different person.

Rather than the apprehensive young man embarking on the adventure of his life, he was a seasoned combat veteran intent on getting home for a month.

Monday, February 28, 1944 We upped anchor and headed out of the harbor at about 6:30 p.m. The big old ship scoots right along, and the seas are pretty calm. It's now noon and so will be heading down to lunch.

Thursday, March 2, 1944 —7:30 p.m. Still going along at a pretty good clip. The radar picked up a sub about five miles away yesterday about noon, so we really poured the oil to the old bus. Slowed down again after dark and out of danger. It's been a damn smooth trip and the old bus glides right along. Played a little cards today, but spend most of the time sleeping. That is, when I'm not eating.

Friday, March 3, 1944 Well, we've set our watches back four times now so must be over halfway there. The seas started getting rough last night and the old boat bobbed around like a rowboat all night and its getting worse now (10:00 a.m.)—people are sick all over the joint. I feel fine and hope I keep that way all the way across.

Sunday, March 5, 1944 Seventh day at sea now. The storm quieted down last night and we are running along pretty smooth. Should be getting in soon now.

Monday, March 6, 1944 We sighted land about 2:00 p.m. and soon came along past Sandy Hook, Coney Island, Fort Hamilton, Staten Island and the Statue of Liberty and on into Pier 90. Boy, did the Statue of Liberty look good. I can imagine what all the immigrants think when they see it. The *Queen Elizabeth* was in the next berth. Docked then at 5:45 p.m. and Roy Evans and I walked onto U.S. soil. It was a happy feeling, all right. We talked a Red Cross gal in a station wagon into driving us up to the Hotel New Yorker. Took a shower for about an hour and then walked out onto the street. Sure seems funny to see the bright lights again, and plenty good too, let me tell you. We went into a fine restaurant and had a shrimp cocktail, a big steak, peas and French fried potatoes, French bread and butter, then some chocolate pie and chocolate ice cream. Took a look at their subways and then to Times Square. Sent a couple of telegrams, had some more ice cream, and then Roy went up to the room and I went into the cocktail bar for a while. We're on the twelfth floor and it's a pretty sight looking out over the lighted city. Only a week ago I was bombed in London and now I'm safe in America. Two and a half years I've waited for this, and happy as a lark. So, good night.

The next day, Roy and Lee took the train out to Mitchell Field to talk to their former commander, General Hunter.

We talked about the course of the war and gave him a report on how the Fourth Fighter Group was doing. We also talked about tactics and the new aircraft that were being developed. Had dinner at General Hunter's tonight and then stayed at a very lovely estate on Long Island.

Lee did not know it at the time, but this meeting with Hunter was to change his future.

Wednesday, March 8, 1944   Up at 7:00 a.m., breakfast, and in to Mitchell Field. Flew down to La Guardia Field in a Cessna (fifteen minutes each way) and tried to get a ride home on a plane. Would have to wait a day or so, so I came back to Mitchell Field and Roy and I came on back to New York and caught the 6:00 p.m. train, the *Wolverine*, out of Penn Station for Chicago.

Thursday, March 9, 1944   We came on through New York State. Saw the Yankee Stadium, West Point and such on the way. The Hudson was full of ice and it was cold as hell outside. We had a private room and it was real nice. We went through part of Canada and arrived in Detroit at 8:30 a.m. Then on to Chicago and arrived there at 2:00 p.m. (two hours late). Here's where Roy and I split up. He took the *City of Los Angeles* and left at 6:00 p.m. (just ten minutes ago). I wait until 8:15 p.m. and take the *Overland Limited* out direct to Oakland.

Friday, March 10, 1944   At 8:15 p.m. I pulled out of Chicago on the *Overland Limited*. We were in Omaha, Nebraska, about

8:00 a.m. this morning. Everything is still all covered with snow and ice. At 2:30 we pulled into North Platte for ten minutes. I ran out and bought four candy bars to get sick on. Arrived in Cheyenne at 6:46 p.m. and on to Laramie at 8:50. Time now to hit the hay.

Saturday, March 11, 1944   Arrived in Ogden at 7:30 a.m. Called Mrs. Johnson [a friend of Lee's mother] and said hello. Called home and told Dad that if San Carlos was going to put on the parade for me that he told me about, I was just going to stay in Ogden. He said he would do what he could to stop it. Met Miss Edith Marrick as we were pulling out of Ogden, so we played cards the rest of the day. Pulled into Reno at 10:10 p.m. and it is raining to beat hell.

Sunday, March 12, 1944   Well, well, I finally arrived at Oakland at 8:35 a.m. and Mom, Dad, Betty, Juanita and Sondra Lee met me at the station. It was certainly swell to see them all. We drove on down to San Carlos and here I am. Home, Sweet Home!

EPILOGUE

"I spent the first few days in San Carlos just enjoying being home and with my family," Gover reminisced.

While my dad had got the parade called off, there were all sorts of calls to the house asking me to speak at service clubs, the VFW, American Legion and the like. I really hated speaking in public and so I would just thank them for having me and for their support of all the folks fighting the war and then I would answer their questions. One they always asked was what made a good fighter pilot. I always told them that it is hard to know who will be good until you are in combat, but there are some attributes that I think are important.

To be a really good fighter pilot you have to be able to keep calm and concentrate on the situation regardless of the circumstances. Keen eyesight is essential, because whoever sees the other guy first has a great advantage. I think that physical stamina is essential. Fighter pilots were often referred to as "muscle pilots" because they had to throw the aircraft around the sky so violently and so fast, and there was no boost on the controls on World War II fighters. Certainly you had to have courage or guts, confidence in yourself, great faith in your airplane and your wingman and quick reflexes. Probably most important was that flying had to be second nature, because you had no time to look at your instruments or think about your maneuvers. There were just too many things going on at one time. While I knew good fighter pilots who did not possess all of these qualities, if flying was not second nature you just couldn't be successful as a fighter pilot.

One neat thing that my mother did was to have an open house and invite all the kids in the neighborhood over to see me. I didn't know it when I was in England, but I had quite a fan club among the young people of the town, and so it was fun to talk to them. After a couple of weeks I guess I had talked to everyone in San Carlos, because I finally got some time to myself. Everyone in town gave me some gas coupons and I drove down to Long Beach to visit my aunt and cousins.

The newspapers were full of stories about Lee, and his picture seemed to be almost daily fare. The first week in April the *San Carlos Enquirer* announced, "Gover Headed Back to Europe Air War." The ensuing article detailed much of Gover's record and noted that "LeRoy Gover, veteran of two and a half years of air warfare over Europe, will soon be on his way back to England to climb again into the cockpit of his fighter plane." On April 14, 1944, Gover boarded an Army Air Forces transport for the first leg of his return to Europe, a stop in Washington, D.C.

Lee fully expected to follow the same routine as several of his friends, who had been on leave previously, and talk to the people concerned with fighter tactics and operations at the Pentagon for a few days and then be on a plane for England. But his fateful conversation with General Hunter at Mitchell Field, a month earlier, had changed all that. "Evidently General Hunter had decided I could be better utilized as an instructor in the States than as a combat pilot in Europe," Gover later wrote.

My old roommate, Oscar Coen, was now a colonel and in charge of fighter assignments at the Pentagon. He said I was to go to a fighter training base in the U.S. and gave me my choice. I picked Florida, since I had never been there. So on May 30, 1944, I reported to Page Field, Fort Myers, Florida, as training group commander. There were three squadrons in the group, and we were flying P-40s.

Thus ended Lee's combat career. Certainly his accomplishments were significant and he could be justly proud of his record. He had flown 233 hours and 55 minutes on his 159 combat missions. He participated in the ill-fated commando raid on Dieppe, flying three missions that day, and was on the first combat mission flown by the P-47 as well as the first escort mission of that aircraft into Germany. He destroyed four German fighters, probably destroyed three more and damaged nine others. For his achievements in combat, Lee was awarded the Silver Star, three Distinguished Flying Crosses and eight Air Medals. Gover had indeed done his part, but he still had mixed feelings about staying in the United States. "I guess that I was happy to be out of the war," Lee recalled, "but I was also disappointed that I was not going to go back to my old unit and have the chance to fly the P-51 in combat."

Over the next few months I saw a number of the pilots whom I had flown with, so I was able to keep pretty well up to date on how things were going in the Fourth Fighter Group, and I certainly was proud of the record they were compiling. But the only ones of the old Bakersfield gang I ever saw were Don Young and Mick Lambert. I never had any contact with either Jay Reed or Jack Mause, and I don't know what happened to them. Mick and I saw each other a couple of times a year and we talked a lot on the phone until he died in 1993. I see Don once a year at the Eagle Squadron reunion and we occasionally chat on the phone. He went with Delta Airlines after the war and flew for them for over thirty years. Just like in 1943, he and I are the only ones of the Bakersfield group left.

"I really enjoyed instructing at Fort Myers," Gover remarked, "but I had never had any real training in teaching instruments." So, on November 1, 1944, Lee was sent to the Instrument Pilot Instructor School at Bryan Field, Texas, where he became reacquainted with his old friend the AT-6. After completing that school in December, Lee returned to Page Field, where he remained as the training group commander until the end of March 1945.

Gover's next assignment was as commander of the P-40 squadron and Instrument School at Luke Field, Phoenix, Arizona, but in mid-July he was transferred to Kingman, Arizona, as base operations officer. "I flew both the B-25 and the B-17 a lot at Kingman," he recalled. "Flying the B-17 certainly gave me a new appreciation for what those poor bomber crews were up against in Europe. It was easy enough to fly but was so slow."

Lee was flying over the Colorado River in a B-25, returning to Kingman from Glendale, California, on August 14, 1945, when World War II ended. Gover remained at Kingman until the middle of September, helping close down the training operation. He was then given another nostalgic assignment, base operations officer at Minter Field, Bakersfield, California, where his military flying career had begun four years earlier. Interestingly, most of his flying was again in the AT-6. In December, Lee decided to leave the Army Air Forces and return to San Carlos, where he once again went into the construction business. On the way to San Carlos, he bought a "well-worn" Great Lakes biplane for $800 so he could maintain his flying proficiency.

In early 1947, Gover applied to come back into the Army Air Forces because things weren't working out as he had planned. "All I really knew was flying, and there just weren't any jobs," he remembered. On June 19, 1947, he was appointed an officer in the Regular Army; he transferred to the Air Force when that service was created. He was initially stationed at Biggs Field, El Paso, Texas, but in January 1948, he became the regular Air Force instructor for the Air National Guard unit at Morris Field, Charlotte, North Carolina. "That was a great assignment for me," Gover recalled, "because they still had the P-47, and I had always liked the 'Jug.'" Just four months after his arrival at Morris Field, Lee was detailed to take sixteen P-47s from his unit to California so they could be used in filming the Warner Brothers movie *Fighter Squadron*. "That was a very interesting experience for me," said Lee.

Since I had so much more P-47 experience than anyone else, I did all of the low-level and precision flying and led all the formations. But every time they showed a close-up of the planes, Edmond O'Brien, Robert Stack, or one of the other stars would be in the aircraft. I did convince them to let me be in one scene, but it was cut out of the final film. Still, it was great flying, I found out a lot about how a movie is made, and the stars really were a pretty good group of guys.

A few months after completing *Fighter Squadron*, Gover led the aircraft formation for President Harry Truman's inauguration.

Lee's next assignment, with the California Air National Guard at Oakland Municipal Airport, gave him the opportunity that was denied him when he was kept in the United States following his leave from England in 1944—flying the P-51. This duty was rapidly followed by a temporary assignment at the Fighter Gunnery School in Las Vegas, where he checked out in his first jet fighter, the F-80. In the summer of 1950, he moved to Kirtland Air Force Base, New Mexico, as an F-86 fighter squadron commander. He was promoted to lieutenant colonel in February 1951.

Lee's subsequent assignments took him to Tyndall Air Force Base, Florida, and McCord Air Force Base, Washington, as F-94 fighter operations officer and finally to Hamilton Air Force Base, California, as the officer in charge of Air National Guard fighter operations in the eleven western states. Gover was promoted to colonel in 1961 and retired from the Air Force in May 1962. His entire career was spent in fighter aircraft.

Following his retirement, Lee combined his love of the outdoors with his love of flying and for eighteen years did charter work, flying fishermen to Mexico in the winter and Canada in the summer. He retired from that business in 1980, but continues recreational flying. Gover's total flying time exceeds 28,000 hours. Now in his eighties, he lives in Palo Alto, California.

Lee has never returned to England. "I didn't have occasion to be in Europe in connection with my Air Force assignments, and I never really had a desire to travel back to England on my own," he explained.

I have such fond memories of England, the beautiful countryside, the quaint villages and the great city of London. But most of all I have a warm place in my heart for the people. They were all so nice to me, and I admired their spirit so much. And the young ladies whom I met were each special in their own way. All of this just made me want to remember England as I had known it during the war, and since it is impossible to go back in time, I have been content with my memories, even that of warm beer.

SUGGESTED READING

There are thousands of books about World War II and the air war. The books listed here are a few that I have found to be particularly valuable or interesting and that should be available in most libraries.

Bowyer, Chaz. *Fighter Pilots of the RAF, 1939–1945.* London: William Kimber, 1984. A number of short chapters about individual fighter pilots.

Caine, Philip D. *American Pilots in the RAF: The WWII Eagle Squadrons.* Washington: Brassey's (US), 1993. The most complete volume available on the Americans who flew for the RAF in the three Eagle Squadrons prior to U.S. entry into World War II.

Freeman, Roger. *The American Airman in Europe.* London: Arms and Armour Press, 1991. An excellent account of the experience of the Americans who flew during World War II.

Fry, Gary L., and Jeffrey L. Ethell. *Escort to Berlin.* New York: Arco, 1980. One of the most complete books about the Fourth Fighter Group.

Galland, Adolph. *The First and the Last.* London: Methuen, 1955. World War II from the perspective of the most famous Luftwaffe pilot of the war.

Goodson, James A. *Tumult in the Clouds.* New York: St. Martin's Press, 1983. Stories of life in the Fourth Fighter Group as told by one of the leading aces of World War II.

Gunston, Bill. *Aircraft of World War II.* New York: Crescent Books, 1980. Contains over six hundred superb drawings of forty different aircraft used in World War II along with a fairly comprehensive narrative about each.

Hall, Gover. *1000 Destroyed.* Dallas: Morgan Aviation Books, 1946. A comprehensive history of the Fourth Fighter Group by the man who was their public information officer during the war. (Republished in 1978 under the title *Death Squadron,* New York: Kensington, 1978.).

Kaplan, Philip, and Andy Saunders. *Little Friends: The Fighter Pilot Experience in World War II.* New York: Random House, 1991. Primarily a book of pictures from both World War II and the present focusing on the fighter pilot experience on the Western Front. There is a narrative accompanying the photos.

Kaplan, Philip, and Jack Currie. *Round the Clock*. New York: Random House, 1993. The same type of book as *Little Friends* but about bombers. The pictures in both volumes are superb.

Murray, Williamson. *Strategy for Defeat: The Luftwaffe, 1933–1945*. Maxwell AFB, Alabama: Air University Press, 1983. The most thorough analysis available of the buildup and demise of the Luftwaffe.

Perret, Geoffrey. *Winged Victory: The Army Air Forces in World War II*. New York: Random House, 1993. The story of the USAAF in all the major theaters of the war.

Robinson, Derek. *Piece of Cake*. London: Pan Books, 1983. An exciting novel about the RAF during the early days of World War II. The book gives a very accurate picture of life in the RAF at that time.

INDEX

ABOUT THE AUTHOR

BRIGADIER GENERAL PHILIP D. CAINE, USAF (RET.), holds a doctorate in history from Stanford University and has more than 4,500 hours of flying time. He served as deputy commandant of cadets at the Air Force Academy as well as acting head of the history department. General Caine was also a professor of international studies and a senior research fellow at the National Defense University and is the author of *American Pilots in the RAF*. He and his wife, Doris, live in Monument, Colorado.